A RAGGED SCHOOLING

Robert Roberts was born in a Salford slum in 1905. He left school early to take up a seven-year engineering apprentice-ship, at the end of which, like many of his generation, he was left unemployed for three years. During this period he voraciously studied languages and politics and eventually became a teacher, writing stories, plays and BBC scripts in his spare time. After sixteen years hill farming – undertaken after Roberts had contracted TB – he returned to teaching, working in prisons and with adult illiterates. He lectured on the problems of non-readers at universities, in public and on the BBC and in 1968 published *Imprisoned Tongues*, a standard work on the subject. This was followed in 1971 by *The Classic Slum*, a brilliant and intensely moving account of the lives of the Edwardian poor based around his own childhood experiences. The autobiographical *A Ragged Schooling* was written shortly before his death in 1974.

ROBERT ROBERTS

A RAGGED SCHOOLING

Growing up in the Classic Slum

FONTANA/COLLINS

First published by Manchester University Press 1976
First issued in Fontana 1978
Fourth impression March 1982

The frontispiece drawing by Harold Riley shows the
corner shop on Waterloo Street ('Zinc Street') where
the author grew up.

The photograph of Robert Roberts and other
children from his street c. 1912 is reproduced by
courtesy of Mrs Robert Roberts. The other photographs are from the Frank Mullineux collection and
were taken in and around the streets and markets of
Salford in the early 1900s by Samuel Coulthurst, using
a camera concealed on a handcart.

Made and printed in Great Britain by
William Collins Sons & Co. Ltd, Glasgow

To Ruth

CONTENTS

We know little or nothing today of the multitude of people who inhabit these islands. They produce no authors. They edit no newspapers. They find no vocal expression for their sentiments and desires. Their leaders are either drawn from another class or, from the very fact of leadership, sharply distinguished from members of their own. They are never articulate except in times of exceptional excitement; in depression when trade is bad; in exuberance when, as on 'Mafeking' nights, they suddenly appear from nowhere to take possession of the city.

C. F. K. MASTERMAN, *The Condition of England*, 1909

They [the people] could not even make a tally of their own wrongs. They did not even experience life fully enough! People of the surface, they had no powers of penetration. They had made deference and loyalty a vice and now lived at second-hand, taking their opinions and views of the world from parsons, journalists, lawyers and members of parliament—all of them men with an interest to protect which they did not declare, all of whose attitudes were governed by that interest.

A. W. THORNTON, *The Habit of Authority*

IN THEIR SMALL CORNER

EVERY decent Edwardian biography begins with the death of Victoria, and this one, though making little claim to decency, is no exception. I wasn't around for the passing of 't'owd queen', as we called her in Lancashire, but older members of the family remembered it well. They were playing *Quo Vadis?* at the Regent Theatre, Mother recalled: an odd question to be asking, she thought, in the week of Her Majesty's expiry – 'To which place goest thou?' 'Then again,' she said, 'poor Toby passed on the very same evening! Such a loss!' Toby, a gravy-coloured tomcat, had, it seemed, slipped over our backyard wall, cleared the 'entry' and was about to select still another homer from Joe Seddon's loft when he fell into a trap and died, as the fortune tellers say, 'by water'.

Father, she told us long afterwards, was far more shocked by this than by the death of an empress. Home that night, half 'kettled' as usual, he came singing through our corner shop, but on hearing the news, being fond of the departed, he scowled, removed jacket and waistcoat and announced his intention of pushing Joe Seddon's 'bloody face in!' This, my mother pointed out, would indeed be a victory, since Father stood then, well built, twenty-nine years of age and a middle-weight fighter of some local repute, whilst old Joe reached little higher than the broom he plied for Manchester Corporation. She thought, too, that Joe perhaps had other reasons for breeding pigeons than to provide our cat with poultry. At this my father subsided, sliding a meal kept waiting for him for two hours up the table; but he rumbled on, till sleep caught him, about 'bloody little sparrow-starvers' (his name for scavengers) and cruelty to poor dumb animals. Queen Victoria he forgot to mention.

A fair, handsome man, violent in drink and, when sober, eloquent after a loud-mouthed Celtic fashion, Father stood a formidable figure in our neighbourhood, a district known to history as the world's first industrial slum. For my mother, her removal there in the 'nineties of last century had meant disaster. She remembered her first home after marriage. 'A house in a lane by a river,' she said, 'and beyond, fields – almost the country. And now this!' Fifty years before, our area had horrified even Friedrich Engels, and Engels knew a slum when he saw one. Since that time, it is true, many of the vilest hovels had been swept away; but much that was unspeakable still stood. Here, if anywhere on earth, when darkness fell, lay the 'city of dreadful night'. Once in that place, young, vigorous, intelligent, Mother strove with a single thought in mind – to get out. Yet she remained there for more than thirty years, and brought seven children into the world.

Three of our uncles already kept shops about the town, small but prosperous, and Father, an envious man, ached to join the ranks of our budding Liptons. A mechanic of high skill, he was engaged at that time, a period of depression, with a firm of engineers in Derbyshire. To get there he rose each day at 4.30 a.m. and returned about eight o'clock in the evening, 'grey with exhaustion', my mother said, 'though he was a strong man'. 'Derbyshire bloody slave-drivers!' he told her. 'They like to have you staggerin' out, holdin' on to the wall as you leave! That's what they call a fair day's work! A goddam non-union shop, of course!' Business of any sort, he must have felt, might at least save him from that sort of bondage. And soon our clan claimed yet another little shop-keeper.

With forty pounds in cash, borrowed from a sister, he came home tipsy one Sunday evening, my mother said, to announce the purchase of a 'lil' gold mine!' He then began to sing 'Queen of the Earth'. In between verses she learned that the prize consisted of a 'lovely lil' dairy and "mished" business' combined – 'all ready for you to step into, my love!'

Mother went, saw the place and turned the whole thing down in contempt. But too late: he had bought it and signed on the line. She damned him for fecklessness and drunken male arrogance and gave him instruction. 'Right!' she said. 'You bought it, now you keep it!' He then turned on the blarney, but to no purpose. In a year or two, 'working together', he said, they could build the place up, then sell out at a vast profit. Meanwhile, no more drinking! That was a solemn promise! And didn't she know how good he was with his hands? He'd put in a new counter, tile the dairy, extend the shelves. And out with those bare gas jets! New incandescent mantles everywhere – a little palace! Aware he could

10

do all these things, and with fine skill, she still shook her head. 'I'm not going.' 'Then new lines,' he urged. 'We'll join in with the other three – buy in bulk – and undercut everyone around! With your head for arithmetic and accounts I'll treble the trade in three years, then out of it! We'll get a nice little house with land – on the Cheshire side.'

My mother listened, unmoved. Without his wife, he knew, the venture was hopeless. Then Father got down to the truth and said quietly, 'I don't want to live there any more than you do; but it would get us enough to eat while I'm seeking work nearer home. This other job's breaking me.'

And that defeated her. 'Two years, then,' she said. He promised. So she came with him into that dark little world with many fears and little hope and already big with her first child.

The family was of mixed Welsh, Irish and English blood. My Saxon grandmother, on Father's side, a fine, handsome woman – like a queen, they said – married a Welshman from Neath. Both reached the altar under the belief that the other had wealth to come from unsettled estates. How often, after naming the day, had they strolled on Sunday evenings in Salford's new Peel Park, dreaming of a future all aglow! When eventually Grandfather's ship came home it brought him seven pounds ten shillings and sixpence. His wife, whose own expectations had been merely of the mind, naturally took this very hard. A woman much sought after before marriage, she had determined to sell her charms only in exchange for a life of ease. This 'shocking deceit' soured her for good. 'It was a blessing your grandfather died young,' my mother used to say. 'He was spared much suffering.'

Widowed in her thirties, Grandma soon became the consoling friend of a cabinetmaker and artist craftsman in comfortable circumstances, unfree for a time to marry, true, but this suited her very well, since she didn't at all care for looking after male needs, except in bed. Regular alms, sponged from her deceased spouse's great-uncle, Clerk to a Lancashire borough council, gave her both ready cash and a feeling of superiority over all other tenants in Carter's Court. Avoiding the local mission altogether, she despatched her three handsome daughters to a chapel in a middle-class area. All became teachers in the Sunday school and, in due time, married well. Girls of kindliness and good sense, each made her home in the outer suburbs and severed connection with

Carter's Court. Gladly they paid Mama a weekly 'retainer' in advance, and by post, to keep her visitations to a minimum, for it was said that one husband, a ranking police officer at that, on hearing her voice in his kitchen would turn again and tiptoe into the night.

My father, much the youngest of his family, stayed firmly embedded in the working class. Starting a formal education at the age of eight, he completed it, at least to his mother's satisfaction, at nine, when he was taken away to help at a blacksmith's. And there, to the age of fourteen, he remained, untroubled by the new 'School Board' officers.

But 'expectations' in my mother's family, who lived in a 'good' street close to Carter's Court, were both real and agonizing. The grandmother here – and all the district knew it (though it was none of her telling) – stood to gain real wealth under the will of some relative; no less, in fact, than twelve thousand pounds. Unfortunately for us, the rich 'uncle', in the last few months of life, married again, leaving his estate in entail to a woman who, before her own decease, reduced this sum to a mere nine hundred while the family watched her at it from the sidelines. Grandmother's husband had died young. Unaided she was bringing up a large family of sons and daughters. But not once, my mother said afterwards, did she show the slightest sign of rancour towards the woman who was spending what might have been hers. Still, nine hundred pounds, when it did come, put the family on its feet. Grandmother set two children up in business and even then had plenty of cash to use generously with the others.

As a child my mother had shown such scholastic ability she was put on to 'perform' at local schools. In our day Father used to boast about it. 'But what did you *do*?' I asked. She answered, very offhand, 'Oh, long, silly sums, very quickly on the blackboard in front of the class; or add pounds, shillings and pence – all three columns at once. Meanings of words – spellings – yards of verse! A great show-off! I've often found it harder to forget than to remember,* and that's been no blessing at all!' At the age of nine, when her father

---

* She used to remark that the ability to take in facts and reproduce them, unchanged, when required, was an accomplishment much overrated in this world. People with little else but a good memory, she said, were no more than 'mental pawnshops'.

12

died, she went to work in a cotton mill where the owner showed a certain regard for the education of his employees. After an eleven-hour stint at the looms all girls had to forgather once a week to receive lessons from their master's daughter on 'economical cookery'. One lecture, she recalled, enlightened them on 'three ways of stuffing a cod's head for a penny'. She worked at weaving, until marriage to an upstanding young mechanic who knocked about with a group which her elder brother, Edward, led. Father's mother did not oppose the marriage, merely commenting, 'Eh, well! God makes 'em and the Devil pairs 'em!' But ever after she referred to her son as 'our poor Bob'.

Teddy, my mother's favourite brother – a great reader, bitten deep, as were other brothers, with Morris socialism – didn't care for his sister's choice at all. 'Bob's a fine singer,' he said, 'a trade society man and a good spouter: but it's Liberal talk. He doesn't really know what it's all about!'

'We aren't marrying to talk politics,' she told him. Father's reputation for being a 'royal boozer' was already well known enough; but he had sworn, on marriage, to 'have done with it for good and all'. She took him at his word and made the mistake of her life.

TO BUSINESS!

IN the 'thirties of last century two competing railway companies had sliced their way through the slums of central Manchester, leaving our own district, not far from the city, 'ghettoed' between two walls some two hundred yards apart, and this over a quarter of a mile in length. Soon the borough, at that time the fastest-growing town in Great Britain, added a vast gasworks, which polluted the area for the next century. Behind some decent working-class houses on the main way lay a long straggling maze of streets, courts and alleys, and in the middle of it all stood our corner shop.

Less than a week after becoming, as he liked to call himself, a 'master grocer', Father pushed his foreman's head into a vat of water usually kept for tempering hot steel, and was padding Manchester with a boxing friend, Bill Hazel, looking for other labour. From this he came home one evening, my mother remembered, pale and quite sober, his right hand wrapped in a newspaper sodden with blood. 'No job yet, love!' he said, sat down in his chair and fainted. The flesh about his knuckles was cut to the bones. After calling and being rejected at a dozen firms, walking all day, they had reached by nightfall a workshop in the Cornbrook district, knocked at an enquiry office and asked civilly for work. A clerk stared at them for a moment, then, 'Read that!' he snarled, pointing at a notice on the wall. ' "No Hands" means NO HANDS! Now get out!'

Father drove his fist to the clerk's face, only to shatter a sliding window as it fell between them. Hazel dodged into the office, grabbed the man and shook him till he vomited. Then they ran for their lives.

Twenty-nine weeks later (the time unemployed they always counted in weeks), kept alive at the latter end by gifts from Grandmother's legacy (his own mother didn't call), Father found another job. Meanwhile his wife gave him their child through a dangerous labour that kept her in bed for two months afterwards. Father tended her and the baby, his home, hearth and shop 'as good as gold', my mother said. Then he paid the bills, laboriously balanced his petty accounts and discovered that the little gold mine wasn't clearing seven shillings a week! This shook him. 'It doesn't even make my beer money!' he said.

And liquor it was that soon divided them like a wall. Here stood the enemy, she saw well enough, which, undefeated, would keep them in servitude. His sworn promise never to touch it again after coming to the shop had lasted exactly one week, then home once more so drunk it had left him crapulent for days. But he loved her, she knew, respected her, and she was going to fight. Their marriage seemed to have been based in a passion that kept them together, through all dissension, well into middle age. He, for all his good looks, physical accomplishments and his rollicking about as 'king' of the small pubs, remained so deeply attached to his wife that he never looked at another woman. Yet over a lifetime she left him somehow puzzled, exasperated, fearful even. Hectoring, he laid down the house law but yearned always

14

for her approbation. Both were articulate, swift on the pithy phrase, enjoying each other's humour. Yet her kind of intelligence separated them; he seemed at times a stranger in his own home.

The shop, like its competitors around, opened at 7 a.m. and closed an hour before midnight. 'The rest of the time,' my mother said, 'was my own'; except that in the earliest years she had two babies to tend, both in arms at the same time. In those days most working men were too important to take care of their children: and in any case Father would often have an appointment in the Live and Let Live. If the babies turned fretful on Saturday evenings, with a shopful of women in for groceries, Mother used to hand them over the counter to be 'chain-nursed' by one customer after another, 'sometimes for as long as three hours'. People came then not only to shop but to talk, the weekly purchasing of from one to five shillings' worth of goods being a high social occasion. 'And if there was any free milk going,' my mother used to say, 'the babies got it! You've taken nourishment from half the women of the neighbourhood!' One customer, a publican's wife, had a copious supply – 'mostly milk stout!' We came back over the counter then, 'looking tipsy', and 'always slept well afterwards'.

Under Mother's direction trade improved steadily. In an ordinary week at the start of the century she served some four hundred and fifty customers and took about eight pounds, mostly in pennies, halfpence and farthings. In a district where many breadwinners, if they didn't settle in a pub at Saturday dinner time, brought home eighteen shillings as a weekly wage, even farthings had their value. The smallest coin could still buy a little candle, a paper of pins, a 'Dolly blue' for washing day, a good box of matches, cloth buttons or an ounce of toffee. We had a 'farthing shelf' by the window where Mother stacked her intake away from the other coins. Every evening before we children went to bed she would remove the calico pouch from around her waist and shoot the contents on to the table, a shower of copper, and a few silver coins, and we would build up 'shilling towers' for her. 'That'll save me a job at eleven o'clock,' she'd say. We were always delighted to come across the occasional five-shilling piece – such a handsome medal of a coin it seemed, worth every penny of sixty pence. The cloth money pouch Mother washed frequently, boiling it in soapy water, but so dirty was the coinage handled that soon the inside became soot-dark again.*

There was much spurious currency in circulation. In a dresser drawer lay a whole collection of false and foreign money, some of it left, Mother said, by the previous owners of the shop as a 'warning' to us. One day my father tipped all these coins into a bag and took them off to work, where he melted them down into a mould with other odd scraps of metal and returned with a 'bronze' figure of Ali Sloper, a popular comic ornament of the day. It was an object of art his wife didn't care for at all, so he sold it to a local publican for half a sovereign. This 'reversal' of Gresham's law, a 'driving out' of bad money by good, amused Mother much more than Mr Sloper. 'Eight shillingsworth of counterfeit,' she used to say, 'fetched us ten from the Mint!'

At bedtime we used to go upstairs leaving her weary, aching for the hour when the door could be shut and the light turned out; but custom demanded that this, in our shop, and in any other of its kind, be not done one minute before the appointed time. 'Two bundles of firewood and a farthing candle,' my mother once said, 'we sold in the last hour last night!' 'Well, another time,' Father told her airily, 'you could easily take half a crown! Put shutters up and folk just start taking their money elsewhere.' Often it was around eleven o'clock that the 'night people' were walking. They brought no trade at all!

One winter evening when I was about seven, feeling queasy, hours after going to bed, I crept downstairs into our long kitchen. Mother was sitting alone, elbows on the table, face in her hands.

'Mam!' I whispered. 'I feel sick. Can I get a drink?'

She looked up at me slowly. 'I'll bring it,' she said. 'Sit by the fire, but don't make any noise.'

From the shop I heard deep moaning. Quietly, she got me

* *Pecunia non olet* didn't hold with us: money, in quantity, had a sour, greasy smell, a fact which disgusted the Victorian bourgeoisie, who, no doubt, held their noses all the way to the bank. Thackeray tells how, in old-fashioned London clubs, when a member required change for a guinea it was always brought to him in 'washed silver', 'that which passed immediately out of the hands of the vulgar being considered as "too coarse to soil a gentleman's fingers"'.

water from the scullery. 'What – What was that?' I asked.

'Don't be frightened,' she whispered. 'It's nothing, really. Your father will be home any minute now. There's – There's a man lying on the shop floor. He's been there for twenty minutes: we haven't had a customer. He just fell in. I can't move or get any sense from him.'

I got up on the sofa and peered through a tiny window that gave on to the shop: a long, thin figure lay slumped face down on the floor, head to the counter, feet flung wide towards the open door. He moaned again. The shop light began to flicker and die as I watched, then the kitchen darkened too. 'Down the cellar!' my mother said, 'and put twopence in the meter!'

'Who – Who is he?' I gasped.

'Do as I tell you!'

I hurried below, slotted the money and then – a bull roar! Father had arrived. I could hear him on the shop floor immediately above. 'Who in Christ's name is this? Gerrout of it, you drunken . . . !'

'Lift him! Lift him, man! Don't shake him.' My mother's voice. 'On this chair! There's blood on his face!'

I rushed through the kitchen and stayed at the inner shop door. Father was standing astride the man, dragging him on to a box. Mother turned and saw me.

'Go to bed at once!' I saw and heard no more.

The next day, alone with her, I wondered if I'd dreamt it. 'It was nothing,' she told me. 'He stumbled in the shop and hurt his face, that was all.'

'Was he a tramp?'

'A tramp, perhaps, yes.'

'Was he . . . ?' But I got short shrift. She didn't feel obliged to discuss social questions with small sons.

At the western end of our 'village', over a long, narrow bridge that spanned cattle sidings, stood the great lodging houses, open to rich and poor alike at twopence a night. For late stragglers moving in that direction a shop like ours shone as a beacon. Medieval writers tell of wanderers through the empty forests of ninth-century Europe who sought a light of any kind, or a small fire by which they might pass the night – anything but loneliness and the dark. Like them, a thousand years after, men walked the night jungles of a city seeking a similar glow. 'They would stay at the window a little, hesitating,' my mother said, 'then come into the shop, heartbreakingly humble. "Just a penny to put to this, missis, and see me right till morning." ' Such was the one who had fallen exhausted on our shop floor. While some among our Edwardian upper class boasted of their twenty-one-course meals other men died of hunger on the streets.

Not that it took much to keep a man alive. 'With us,' boasted one dosshouse keeper, 'a bloke gets a kip and a meal – half a saveloy on bread and marge; a penny mix – ha'p'orth o' tea with a ha'p'orth o' sugar; *and* a Woodbine! How's that, then? Bed, breakfast, and send 'im out smokin' for fourpence!' But whilst a bed cost twopence a night, one couldn't be hired for a *day*. By ten o'clock every morning all beds in a common lodging house had to be vacated and made again, ready for the evening. A municipal inspector called regularly, and any man found too ill to rise was removed at once to the workhouse. This law encouraged lodgers to be up and out on the 'early bird' principle, and since in 1902, for instance, more than 100,000 men were tramping the roads of England, besides the normal unemployed, competition was naturally keen. To dissuade seekers from asking charity *en route*, in 1901, as a warning to the rest, more than sixteen thousand 'beggars' were sent to prison. Not, of course, that all men lay in poor straits: some were managing quite well. Lord Derby, for instance, still owned seventy thousand acres; had the choice of eight establishments to live in, besides Knowsley Hall; and spent fifty thousand a year on household expenses – though not much, nasty-minded critics said, on his property in Bootle, where houses stood eighty-seven to the acre.

Bitterly conscious of the poverty around her and the reasons for it, in a way beyond her husband's understanding, my mother snatched an hour or two a week to read the books and pamphlets left by her elder brother. For the most part a taciturn woman, she made little comment about it, but went on working, scrubbing bare bedroom floors, kitchen, shop; washing, baking and caring for children in between looking after the business. Beyond our door, open sixteen hours a day, lay a grim, noisy world. From the highway fifty yards off came the roar of carts and wagons rumbling over setts. Near at hand vegetable hawkers, rag-and-bone men, organ grinders, singing beggars, tub menders, mothers screeching for their offspring all made a bedlam of their own. Children, cats and dogs swarmed everywhere. A common sight was two ill-assorted mongrels locked in coition, one dragging the other about the street, followed by a group of howling boys. Women scarlet with embarrassment would rush from their doors and fling bowls of water over the animals or beat them with brooms while urchins danced around in glee. At such a time the suppressed sexuality that always ran in undercurrent, dark and powerful, suddenly broke the surface of life. Some matrons screamed with laughter, a touch of hysteria in their merriment. They remembered, perhaps, the stories heard in adolescence about men and women in certain predicaments. They were never true, were they? Or were they? One couldn't ask.

Then a larger uproar: hundreds of cattle* *en route* for slaughter would rush down the road, harried by dogs and bawling drovers. On still days the stench of their passing had hardly faded before another herd came stampeding by. Sometimes a cow would swerve away from the mass and charge down among us in a frenzy, followed by youths beating it with sticks. It was not unheard of, when a large flock of sheep was passing our street end, for a drover and his dogs seemingly to mishandle them, so that a score or so would suddenly 'hive off' down a certain entry. There a backyard door swung conveniently open. Two fewer sheep ran out to rejoin the mainstream. For the next few days lamb sold cheap about the streets. Once, as a small boy, I saw an escaped heifer trapped in an alley, battered to the ground and dragged by net into a cart. Standing there I caught the terror in her great eyes, and went away and wept by myself, rubbing the tears off with the cuff of my jersey and damning myself as a 'softie'. Soon afterwards my eldest sister, Janie, came by on an errand.

'Hello! Been fighting again? And losing, by the look of it!'
'Piss off!' I bawled.

She was delighted. 'Right for Mother! Using filthy talk in the street!'

The local gasholders, like vast iron dugs, bulging and sagging as they fed the town, dominated our neighbourhood. We grew up in their shadow and stench, breathing in more coal gas, it seemed, than oxygen. But the borough fathers sat proud, for had not Salford led the whole of mankind in the industrial use of gas? Not a mile away from us had stood

* Salford cattle market was the largest in the country.

19

the seven-storey building erected by James Watt and Matthew Boulton, 'the largest cotton mill in existence', and this, in 1807, William Murdock, the first gas engineer, had illuminated with '633 burners and 271 gas mantles'. Travellers coming from far afield to view the spectacle stood dazzled. 'It is impossible,' said a Swiss visitor in 1814, 'to describe the magnificent appearance of a mill with 256 windows all alight as though brilliant sunshine was streaming through them.' Over the nineteenth century such mills multiplied about us, and daily each belched out its dark reek of smoke.

Some English towns, Cambridge for one, seem to have the countryside running through them: ours kept rurality at a distance. Not that we didn't try. To stimulate an interest in horticulture our parks sold pails of 'loam' at a penny a time. At home we invested in two bucketsful and spread God's earth behind a board across the scullery window. In this my sister Ellie planted a variety of flower seeds, carefully abiding by the details given in a library book called *The Garden Beautiful*. Only the geraniums came up, and these but fitfully. Soon they sicklied o'er, lay around, long but attenuated, then died. Now we knew of several tall, thin consumptives in the district who had succumbed sadly through 'overgrowing their strength', and it set Ellie wondering about her flowers: but Mother put it down to the air.

When summer time came people lived much in the streets, bringing out chairs and boxes by their doorways, peeling potatoes, breast-feeding babies, combing and de-lousing children. But my mother was seldom to be seen there. She appeared only when someone asked her to come to a sick husband or child and advise on the seriousness of an ailment. How strange it was then to catch sight of her abroad, 'in her figure', as people said of women who walked in the open without a shawl.

Her habit of answering a neighbour's plea for help my father vehemently disapproved of. She professed no medical knowledge beyond that gained from experience of the sick around us; but an anxious woman would abide by her opinion of what could be done and whether one should call in the doctor, at considerable expense. This was often an agonizing decision in a family already stricken with poverty. 'Diphtheria! Smallpox! Enteric fever! Consumption!' Father would roll them off. 'They're all in the town! Yet you go, no matter who asks, putting yourself and me and the children at terrible risk! How the hell do *you* know what they've picked up? Have you no sense?'

Mother remained silent; but she went again the next time, when called upon, and returned to the same barrage of indignation. Regularly he complained to relations. They listened, tut-tutting, taking his part, as I did, leaving my views unexpressed but feeling none the less that my own precious existence was being wantonly jeopardized. Not for the first time, Father seemed to me to be showing plain good sense in the face of his wife's eccentricities, though it disturbed us children how often events later proved him wrong; one could only put it down to Mother's good luck. But in this matter the whole clan stood behind him. Aunt Eliza 'appreciated' what Mother did, 'But after all, Jennie, you're not a doctor or a priest!' There was 'no call' to put the whole family in peril. The elders, in discussion, fully supported this.

Mother ignored their opinions, and some time later, on request, visited a house from where, a few days afterwards, a sick man was removed to hospital and died of an infectious disease. They came from the corporation and 'stoved' his home. 'Menace!' the Old Man roared. 'And it's done out of sheer bloody cussedness!' Going on as before, she never excused herself, never explained. Only, on returning from a house of sickness, she changed her pinafore and washed hands and arms, using carbolic soap. Then, secretly, so as not to hurt her feelings, *and* get a slap behind the ear, I 'disinfected' the scullery, shaking some 'Lively Polly' washing powder on the air. After all, one couldn't be too careful! Women, we used to hear in the shop, were 'grateful', which, as Father said – and rightly, I felt – 'was all bloody fine and well!' Twenty years afterwards my sister mentioned it to her, and wondered. 'Some things,' Mother told her briefly, 'come before a family!' And they let it go at that.

Though Father had his regular weekends in the pubs, his wife went out seldom, except for occasional visits to a fourth-rate theatre at the end of the street, or an odd shopping foray along the 'Barbary Coast', a near-by lane that ran to dockland. But in 1908 came that boon to all small shopkeepers and assistants, the Compulsory Half-day Closing Act. Mother found this break a 'blessed relief'. One sunny Wednesday afternoon she took me to Peel Park. We sat on a high esplanade and looked far over the countless chimneys of northern Manchester to the horizon. On the skyline, green

21

and aloof, the Pennines rose like the ramparts of paradise. 'There!' she said, pointing. 'Mountains!' I stared, lost for words.

Sometimes in the shop my mother stood apart at the counter and with a customer, shawl on shoulders, who leaned over, talking low confidences. This, we came to learn later, usually meant 'women's illnesses'. Often, heads together, they were discussing the efficacy of certain of our medicaments for removing 'obstructions'. But if the woman stood pleading, then one knew she was seeking credit – only enough, perhaps, to ward off hunger in the family until Saturday pay time. Here a difficult choice had to be made: one wanted the trade badly, but knew only too well that a little shopkeeper lax in the selection of tick customers rapidly went 'bump' (bankrupt).

Mother would stare anxiously. 'I can't say just now. Come back later, will you?'

Then she would consider the matter with her husband. How often we heard this kind of dialogue!

'Mrs Vardon's asked to be taken on. I'm in two minds. She's hard put to it.'

'Hm. Tim Vardon's only a labourer at Jackson's – eighteen bob a week. Four kids, have they?'

'Five. The eldest is at the mill, though – on two looms. She'll be earning a bit.'

'How are they with the pawnshop?'

'Just clean washing – no household stuff. That's usually a good sign.'

'Didn't they have someone die of consumption? If Tim comes off work we'd look sick for any money!'

'Lizzie Vardon's sister died of it. Still, most folk have one relative somewhere with TB. We'd hardly take anybody if we went off that.'

'All the same, I'd put a limit on,' Father would advise, 'and stop her the first time she wants to leave a "monkey".' (Only partially pay her bill.)

So Mrs Vardon joined the happy elite who could get goods on credit. At once she and her family rose several rungs up the class ladder. But customers were not expected to borrow cash. On occasion, towards the weekend, some families about us would see their gas light die out in mid-evening and not possess a copper for the meter. With perhaps all other neighbourly goodwill exhausted, they sent a child to the shop.

where, if one 'shaped', certain palate-tickling delicacies could be obtained. 'Bob used to be that fond of Handforth's chitterlings! Very tasty! That is, if you know how to cook 'em! *I* allus kept a very good table. He doesn't look at all well to me!'

'He should sup less,' my mother told her, 'then he'd eat more. But I'm not sending my children traipsing two miles to Handforth's.'

Grandma showed surprise. 'Why ever not! Isn't that what childer are for?'

'Not mine!' Mother said.

Her husband sighed.

Then to politics! Listeners, seen and unseen, were once apprised that Charlie (hiccup), Uncle Rafe's nephew, you know, had just been nominated for Trinity Ward at the November elections. Conservative, of course! Very nice! Grandma was Blue to the marrow. 'By the way, our Rafe *was* surprised to see that brother of yours – Edward is it? – in the Constitutional Club the other Saturday. Such a red rag, isn't he! Christian Socialist!'

'Drunk!' said my mother shortly. 'Dead fuddled! He fell among Tory councillors!'

'As a rule,' said Grandma sweetly, 'in the Constitutional Club they get rather a *special* sort of people. Your Edward would be *quite* out of his element!'

'He was!' my mother told her. 'He said he felt like a nun in a knocking shop!'

Father laughed. Bridling, his mother got up, finished her toddy, looked about vaguely and shot the usual barb. 'Lemme see, there isn't anything I have to thank you for, is there?' Hiccup.

Mother stroked her chin and considered. 'Not that *I* can think of.'

'Eh, well, I'll be off!'

Father used to escort her to the tram, and returned pleased as always at the honour conferred upon us. 'Still a fine figure of a woman, y'know! People stare. Sam at the Wine Lodge was telling me only this week how many folk say she puts them in mind of the Queen.'

'Victoria?' asked my mother.

'Alexandra!' said the Old Man.

'Ye-es, she's wearing well. You do if you don't work!'

'And the hat she had on! Didn't it just suit her, now? With that gauze down – dotted silk all over the face! There's style for yer, missis!'

'That's a matter of taste,' said my mother coldly. 'For a minute I thought she had eczema! And someone should tell her – Queen Alexandra, even when half slewed, doesn't drink liquor through her veil!'

'Well, at least it's her own tipple! We give her nowt – not even at New Year! And me her only son!'

'She does very well elsewhere. Will you *ever* realize,' my mother once asked him bitterly, 'what a struggle it is here?'

After such dissension he would flop into his armchair, take a pull at the quart jug, and sulk, only looking up to stare through the window and become disgusted at something. 'Humph! There's that little Mrs Kay rollin' 'ome again' (Father strongly disapproved of beer-taking women) 'drunk as a fiddler's bitch!'

At the festive seasons of the year one could count on Grandmother's absence: she went where the pickings were! Whilst as a family we thought little of Christmas, New Year shone for us the brightest time of all. Like so many people of the north, Father loved New Year's Eve and the ceremonies attached to it. After working 'down London' once he came home to tell his wife that, in the south, they didn't know what it was all about! On the last night of the year, he felt, a family ought to rejoice as one, with no outsiders present: then, when the witching moment came, all cleaving together, the age-old rites should be performed. On the Eve he himself never left home but helped, always very cheerful, about house and shop until our early closing. He drank no ale, busying himself in listing the entertainment to which each of us, except Mother, preparing a special supper, would make a contribution. Intimacy with theatre folk who frequented his favourite 'local' had taught him some tricks of the professionals. A fine baritone voice, step-dancing ability and wit led him to agree with those who 'trod the boards' that, as a mere 'mechanical', he had 'lost his way'.

The moment our shop door closed Father called down the kitchen, 'Right! Everybody ready?' He upturned a couple of soap boxes, covered them with gay cloth, stood thereon, and burst at once into the strains of 'The Fourth West Militia Men', a satirical ditty about the incompetence of amateur soldiers. This had several choruses, which allowed us to march round the kitchen guying a military band and playing the instrument of one's fancy – a glorious bedlam! Then, in turn, the Old Man acting as compère, we mounted the stage and did our 'speciality' to great applause, Ellie always reciting 'Ring out, wild bells, to the wild sky' as a finale. And through it all Father's jollity delighted us beyond measure. Why he couldn't be like this on the other 364 days of the year remained the standing mystery of our childhood. Then, at three minutes to midnight – a hush! Whatever the weather, he put on hat, scarf, overcoat, wrapped himself up as if for a long, cold journey, took a little ash from the grate – dross of the old year – and stalked through the kitchen, scullery and yard, to leave by the back gate, which Mother bolted after him. She returned to go at once into the darkened shop and stand behind our barred front door. We followed her in order of age, eldest first, making a line that trailed back to the kitchen. Silence. Then, on the stroke of midnight, the world without burst into an indescribable clamour that sent waves of excitement rolling along our little queue. Every mill, factory, dock, ship and shunting engine around was hailing the new time with jets of screaming vapour – one hooter, high in falsetto, above all others. 'That's the Westinghouse!' Mother said. And thunder in the night! Harbingers of 'good luck', out like Father a few minutes before, now pounded for entrance on every door about us. Bugles rang. Song! And clogs came dancing over flagstones. Our panels quivered under Father's fists. Mother pulled bolts and drew the shop door wide. From the light of the street lamp across we saw them embrace, softly, my father folding her to him: 'A happy New Year!' We waited, silent, embarrassed – a whispering moment between them. Only once in a year they 'loved' each other like this. Then, gaily, both came along the line to kiss and hug us in our turn. Back in the kitchen, every gas mantle glowing, we sang:

> Hail, smiling morn, smiling morn!
> It tips the hills with gold,
> It tips the hills with gold,
> In whose bright presence, darkness,
> Darkness flies away . . .
> Hail! Hail! Hail!
> The darkness flies away . . .

'Let us hope for better times this year,' Mother said. Father sang the New Year song he always saved till last – 'The Miner's Dream of Home'. And so we rang out

the want, the care, the sin,
The faithless coldness of the times,

had supper and went to bed.

With step firm, bold in resolution, eyes set on a brighter future, Father (old style) would go out to meet another year, and sometimes, his wife said, long after, he would manage as long as a whole fortnight without touching a drop of liquor.

Each of us on the first day of January got a new penny. But ours was never a gift-minded family. Mother was unenthusiastic about presents as a way of demonstrating affection: potlatch seemed to be looked upon as some sort of mutual bribery. On birthdays and at Christmas she hugged us and wished us happiness of the day. We flung our arms round her and one another: it seemed ample. Sometimes, out of the blue, on an ordinary day, we would get a small gift 'for nothing'. On Christmas Eve, cutting, carving and serving till nearly midnight, Mother returned to the kitchen unsteady with fatigue, and the next morning, the shop being closed one full day in 365, she stayed late in bed, rising to cook a turkey dinner for eight of us. We never heard her complain about the endless toil, though once she remarked, smiling, 'Bury me with my arms folded, to show I've done enough.'

They bought us no toys, we hung no stockings, yet none of us felt in the least deprived: the shop supplied playthings galore. A great Welsh dresser, half the length of the kitchen, with a sycamore top, bare and unpainted, lay *tabula rasa* for our fantasies. We built hamlets of thatched cottages, roofing gas mantle boxes with wisps of straw, sticky with albumen from the egg crate. We borrowed lumps of washing soda from a sack under the counter to make cliffs, gorges or the Rocky Mountains, using flour, sugar and salt sweepings from shelves to scatter creation with snow and ice, and peopled it with figures carved from pop bottle corks. We dampened the bottom of 'Dolly blue' packs (sold for whitening clothes), dabbed in oceans (the 'azure main', Mother called it) and fringed them with sand scraped from scouring stones. We built harbours. One said goodbye to another and emigrated, sailing the Atlantic to put up cabins in unbroken lands at the far end of the dresser, the far-away keeping in touch by string submarine cable.

My two older sisters Ellie and Ada, happy, unquarrelsome girls, once erected for me a splendid Greek temple from half-pound blocks of Sunlight soap (which we sold loose) and carton board, with rows of candles for columns – all based on a picture in *Harmsworth's Self-educator*. Inside they put a night light on a low altar – the 'eternal flame' which, according to our reading, no decent temple could be without. Then Mother, turning out the gas to 'get the full effect', came to admire. 'Really Greek!' she said. It took her back three thousand years! This delighted us, because she didn't praise overmuch.

Our eldest sister, Jane, rather scoffed at this childishness and took no part. Janie had a peculiar mind of her own. An alert, pretty girl, well before leaving school she assisted about the house and shop, doing what had to be done, efficiently but with her thoughts on other things. No stay-at-home, no 'well-content', she showed herself from childhood eager for affairs beyond the doorstep. Quite unlike her in temperament, Ellie and Ada found street life too coarse and raucous. Both played inside, reading, like my mother, all they could get their hands on. Indeed, the printed word so gripped Ellie that several calls and a shake were needed to fetch her back to reality. And often it was a book of verse that absorbed her. At such times, one could well imagine, 'With poets and gazelles' she 'shared another world than this'.

'That child's fuddled with books!' my father complained. 'She'll go funny!'

Ellie looked up, smiling nervously.

'Leave her,' Mother told him. 'I was like that once.'

'Once! You're not much better now! I've come into this kitchen,' he fumed, 'and every living soul's been reading except the damned cat!'

Mother laughed. 'We'll have to do something about that cat!'

Still, he went on buying *Harmsworth's Self-educator* in fortnightly parts, read it studiously and liked to see us with a copy. These periodicals, in fact, galvanized us into 'cultural' activity, the foreign-language section making particular appeal. Here the editor, working on a new 'comparative' system of learning guaranteed to confuse everyone, had given a page-long list of Latin words, then, in parallel columns, translated them into French, Spanish and Italian. After this he threw in their German equivalents as a sort of Gothic make-weight. Janie decided we should learn the four Romance languages to begin with, then, on account of its squiggly letters, take up the Teutonic tongue a little later. She pointed out the advantage of our being able to throw out cutting remarks in Latin or Spanish, say, just to puzzle and annoy Father, a prospect which pleased us very much. In order to increase facility of speech, Ellie thought we should have special days for speaking each language: Latin on Sundays, say; French Monday, and so on. This was approved. For ease of study the *Educator* provided little in the way of grammar, syntax and pronunciation: it was just a matter, mostly, of picking up 'vocabulary', which each of us did, peppering our talk with words from a sort of home-made Esperanto until we grew tired of it, except for Ellie, who, every fortnight when a new number arrived, went on trying to puzzle things out for herself.

Mother never joined in our activities or made suggestions unless we asked, but left us to build and fantasticate at will. And always, in things practical, my sisters took the leading role whilst I watched, or helped clumsily; but they never chided. Already the Old Man had noticed what he called my 'cackhandedness'. 'That lad,' he said once, 'can't put one thing straight on top of another! I dunno what we'll make of him!'

My mother shook her head. 'He's not very handy, it's true, but he's got my memory. One can have other qualities.'

'He's going to need 'em!'

He admitted, though, on one occasion, that 'You don't see him missin' much! We got a detective, perhaps!' he said, and laughed.

'We want no police in this family,' Mother told him, 'and no other uniforms, either!' This objection to symbols of force and authority she made several times.

Later the Old Man had reason to despair of me entirely. Having an itch for the rural, he decided to keep a few hens in our backyard, an area not much bigger than a large counterpane, and embarked upon building the cote one Saturday afternoon, using up old shutters from the shop window, I being conscripted as labourer. Far from sober, he sawed up posts for a kind of two-storeyed box to fit into the angle of the wall, and stood with the main downpost in his hand, preparing to nail the framework to it.

'Is this up straight?' he demanded blearily.

'No,' I said.

He adjusted it – way out now! 'Well?'

'No,' I repeated, and again, 'No!' as Father shifted the post about.

'Damn it all!' he snarled at last. 'How's THAT!' It was cock-eyed still.

'Y-Yes,' I said. He hammered all into position and followed it up, without another look, by boarding the sides and roof, then stepped back to survey his edifice. 'God burst old Riley!' he bellowed. 'The bloody Leaning Tower of Pisa! I'd have done better with a helper from Henshaw's! On yer way! You're no use to me!'

Retired in disgrace, I later approached my sister Janie. 'What's Henshaw's?' I asked, thinking it might have something to do with poultry.

'The Manchester blind asylum!' she said. My humiliation was complete. And so the structure stood for years, a monument to his bullying and my timidity.

Not that Father had much success in keeping fowl. He began with two Rhode Island chicks. At once these became our pets – Polly and Biddy. We overfed them until they flat-footed about the yard like aged deaconesses, suffering from something the Old Man called 'fat rop'. One of them would plump itself on to Ada's lap and nod off while she crooned to it. Mother used to laugh. 'Better not let your father see you! That bird's supposed to be scratching for a living, like us!' About once a fortnight in high season one or the other presented us with an egg. Disappointed, Father consulted Joe Seddon, our pigeon man across the entry, who also kept a couple of 'Rhodies', both, it seemed, veritable laying machines. Joe kindly revealed his secret. On fine Sunday mornings, very early, he would tuck a hen under each arm and proceed to Peel Park, where he sat smoking for an hour while his hens picked their fill of worms, grass and grit at public expense. 'It tones a bird up for the week, yer see! Free range – keeps 'em fightin' fit! Talk about lay!'

Father stood deeply impressed; but there was one snag – he never rose betimes on the sabbath. 'Let the lad go,' Mr Seddon urged. 'He could manage.'

The Old Man looked down at me and then shook his head regretfully. 'Nay!' he said. 'If I sent him he'd end up with one of 'em in the damn duck pond and the other in Albert Square!'

I breathed a sigh of relief.

Skill seemed to flow through my mother's fingers, yet she took no pride at all and little interest in doing things practical. 'When you've half an hour free,' Father used to tell her, puzzled, 'it's always a book! Reading's all right—within reason!' My sisters said she could stare a few minutes at any garment in a shop window, then come home and make a replica. Did I, or another child, catch her at ease and want a kite that flew, a castle from a sauce box, a bow that really shot arrows? She turned them out, and well, with a sort of swift indifference. I remember a cricket bat fashioned from three layers of egg crate wood, handle shaped and correctly 'strung' and the whole dyed with boot polish and gravy browning 'to look like willow'. Once, after the sixth of her children in succession had fallen off the unrailed stairs in the kitchen, she gave out an ultimatum to our rent collector— 'No more money till we get a banister!' Upon this the landlords, a railway company, sent workmen at once—a crabby joiner, and with him his mate, a tall, sad consumptive who trailed behind, pushing the handcart. This couple were known to all as Scrooge and Marley's Ghost. In quicksticks the craftsman threw up a structure and made to leave. Mother went over and shook his handiwork: it trembled under her grasp. 'The first time,' she told him, 'our lord and master comes home drunk and falls against that lot he'll have it down!' Scrooge grunted, opened his mouth, looked at her, then closed it. She stooped, took a hammer and several large nails from his satchel and, striking down from the shoulder without a mishit, drove them through the rail into lintel and newel. The joiner tried his banister: it stood firm as a lamp post. He picked up his bag. 'Well! I'll go to hell!' he said, and went, poor Marley's Ghost, as usual, floating on behind.

Practical by need, she always enjoyed stirring us into off-beat activities of the kind small children delight in; but only 'on request'. 'What can I do?' I asked one holiday morning. She thought a moment. 'Why not make hay,' she said, 'while the sun shines?' This seemed an attractive, though in the depths of Salford an unreal, suggestion. But a minute after I was hurrying with a pair of old scissors to the near-by brick

34

'field' and, snipping among the rubble, soon reaped enough tall grasses to make a sheaf. Feeling the need to reward her for such a brilliant idea, I gathered a bunch of dandelions and pushed them up my jersey, knowing, even then, that no boy could be seen in the street with a bouquet and maintain virility; grass was different! Excited, I rushed back and presented her first with the flowers. She expressed her gratification and put them in a cup of water. Then together, I standing on a box, we spread the greenery along the edge of our low scullery roof – 'tedding', my mother called it – and the next afternoon, in hot weather, we turned it. 'This is how the farmers do,' she said. The whole operation charmed me. I loved to be with her alone like this: she seemed young then, and said funny things and made me bubble with laughter. Soon the sparrows came and picked among it all, taking seeds, and the yard smelled sweet. At last we made what she called a 'haycock' and sat it on the window sill. After dinner I went into the yard to admire it again, but the harvest had gone! Sister Janie stood swinging on the back door.

'Where's my haycock?' I demanded.

'Haycock! It's in the milk horse, cock!' she said cheerfully. 'And didn't she enjoy it, cock!' Jane had fed the lot to a dispirited nag that brought our supplies from the dairy.

I was speechless with anger. Swaying on the door, she began to chant a skipping verse:

'A for horses!
B for mutton!
C for th'ighlanders . . .'

'You – You bitch!' I yelled.

Janie got down and swept past me. 'Right again! Using dirty language to ladies!' and went in, but in no time came flying out again through the yard. Mother stood at the scullery window, waving the strap. There was justice, then, in the world, I felt.

A common feature of the time was a length of leather hanging on the kitchen cupboard for the chastisement of children. 'For bad boys,' my mother told us, 'a yard of strap is worth a mile of talk!' But the Old Man never once took ours down, because, he said, he was too hot-tempered and might 'hurt someone'. As for Mother, for a woman with such co-ordination of hand and eye her efforts at punishment were pitiful. We howled just to oblige her. 'Poor dear!' my brother used to say. 'She couldn't hit a pig in a lobby!' I had cause once, however, to dissent strongly from this view. One evening, in about my tenth year, feeling particularly vicious, I stopped a stranger, son of a new neighbour, who had just left the shop. Gingerly he was bearing two jam jars, milk in one hand, vinegar in the other. On his head he wore a man's cap with a wide 'neb'.

'Where are *you* from?' I demanded, barring his passage.

'Angel Meadow!' he said, mentioning a deep slum off Rochdale Road.

I took him by the peak of his cap and pulled it to hook firmly under his nose, gyrated him, with his liquid containers, into a blind vertigo then gave him a push. 'That way for Angel Meadow!'

He staggered a step or two and walked into a wall, shattering one jar.

I wasn't acquainted with my victim, but he knew me! Going straight back to the shop, he provided my mother with a graphic account of the assault, to which a bleeding nose added colour. In return she expressed apologies, gave him a cup with more vinegar and a handful of sweets, and me a stingingly accurate dose of the strap. This attack upon a person for whom she had so many times professed love left me outraged. Regrettably, I decided, it would have to be paid for. I would bide my time! On realizing the enormity of her offence she would come, of course, with 'explanations'. These would be met by a scornful silence. Then she'd implore pardon. I would forgive her – in a few gentle words. But from then on . . . withdraw, kind of – meet all her worried questionings with a quiet 'yes' or 'no'. Then go off my food, like Father! Grow a little thin and pale – she was always anxious about that. 'Just don't feel like eatin'! Smugly, lying on my back in bed, I looked forward to it all. But she never came! A few days later at school the boy himself sought me out, this time with his hands free. Feeling, at least with him, conscience-stricken, I fought only half-heartedly and got much the worst of it. After that we became friends. But 'Angel Meadow!' I thought – a name to remember!

Each slum had its own cachet and fighting reputation. We boys from 'down the gasworks' found our label psychologically useful against the denizens of dockland, say, the Adelphi, or Hulme, but considered twice before taking on a battler from Ancoats, Islington Square, or indeed anyone living in a district closer to the Manchester city centre than our own. Generally, the nearer the heart of things the older and worse the slum, and the tougher its inhabitants. As for Salford's Hanky Park, the area made famous by Walter Greenwood's novel *Love on the Dole*, it was so small we hardly recognized it as a slum at all. Poverty is poverty, whether endemic to a district or to a single house; but it appeared worse when, as with us, half a borough lay in it. Hanky Park, fortunately, consisted of no more than a few poor streets flanked by high working-class respectability. Quite close were fields and a free-range park. Indeed, on trips through these outskirts with bread sandwiches and bottles of sugar and water we felt this West End of Salford, with its parloured houses and red-brick new schools, looked decidedly superior.

The last years of King Edward's reign seniors within the family circle remembered as a time of misery when local unemployment reached new heights. Poor folk fought harder to ward off destitution and the Union, but somehow lacked the will to protest at their conditions. Trade, of course, slumped in the shop. Mother used all her skill and energy to attract what custom there was, each week being a battle to meet wholesalers' bills. Once, seven shillings short, she went to her little cache and found it empty. This meant only one thing. She challenged her husband. Simulating gross offence to his moral feelings, he swept one or two more coins off the mantelpiece and clapped on his bowler. 'If I've got the name,' he shouted, 'like the poacher said, I'll have the bloody game!' and strode out, all injured dignity, to one of the five pubs which stood within a hundred yards of our door. Mother looked about her in despair and said, more to herself, 'I don't know how to go on!'

Most unusually he came home again in mid-evening, rolling drunk and full of affection for the world. Mother rejected him with contempt. His mood blackened at once. Then she did an unheard-of thing – she went and closed the shop and, turning out the light there, came, took a book and sat down. By now the Old Man was rampaging about the kitchen. At sight of him we children had scattered into refuge, under the table, between piano and wall, behind the cellar door. Father slumped into his chair and began to sing, in between excerpts from his usual soliloquy. 'The finest woman in the world once. And what now! Begrudges a man a few shillings after a week's slavery! A few measly bloody shillings, after all *I* give! Proud, stuck-up, superior! Heartless! Nine hundred pounds they got, her family! Bloody aristocrats!' This reminded him of royalty, who at some point in such proceedings always got a going over. It usually started around Queen Anne (that fat bitch!) and ended with the reigning monarch and his progeny. ' "House of Windsor" indeed! The bloody impudence! They're Germans! Edward VII! His name's Wettin! Teddy Wettin! Georgie Wettin!' This fact appeared to give him much satisfaction. He repeated it several times; then, a snatch of song and back to the 'House of Jones', his wife's family, raving on, banging the table with his fists and becoming more violent each minute. My mother continued reading. Her indifference seemed to send him almost insane. From under the table I saw him rise to his feet, tear off jacket and waistcoat, then rip the front of his shirt open to below the navel, showing an expanse of naked torso. He came and stood over her. 'God damn you!' he screamed. 'God bleedin' damn you!' He then swerved, lumbering into the shop, running back with the great bacon knife poised above his heart, and stopped before her. I turned sick with terror; beside me, on her knees, I could hear Ada sobbing.

'Now!'

For the first time my mother looked up from her book. 'Don't do it here,' she said coldly, 'all over the new rug. The yard's the place for that.'

He danced with passion. 'Christ Almighty! Can't a man do hisself in now in his own bleedin' kitchen?' With all his force he then drove the carver down into a chair back. It sank deep, quivering in the gaslight. His frenzy changed now into a bawling indignation; full of self-pity, he staggered off upstairs, maundering on about the rights of an Englishman, a householder, a ratepayer, in his own home and castle. The kitchen fell quiet.

We came out, one by one, edging to get closest to where she sat, quite tearless. 'Don't be afraid,' she said quietly. 'I know him. He won't hurt either you or me – now, or at any time. So slip off to bed, will you – like mice!'

We kissed her good night; her lip trembled a little, and we crept upstairs. Last in line, I paused a moment to look through the peepholes. She sat now as I had seen her once before, elbows on the table, face in her hands, and my heart ached. For a long time I lay staring into the dark, heard my sister, now and then, catch her breath in sleep, and felt a sorrow I could find no words for.

After a few days they made it up again, Father all contrition; but each time he found her a little harder, a shade more withdrawn from him and the life about us. She was a woman of clear, firm features, with a voice seldom hesitant, who spoke briefly, sometimes with harsh effect. People on acquaintance thought her stern. Seemingly unaware, at times, of her smaller fry, she passed, busy, through the kitchen, doing two jobs at once, then, 'What do you want?' she would say shortly. 'Bun? Banana? Either, neither, both?' We'd consider the matter and wait till she came by again. 'Both!' And they would appear at once. Self-composed and certain in company, alone with one of us, in our later childhood, she seemed diffident, almost shy.

As small children, my sister Ada and I both suffered from occasional bouts of neuralgia. I used to lie on the sofa, moaning loud and making the most of it. Father, though he usually 'ignored' us, grew quickly distressed at the sight of our tears. He would call to his wife, active in the shop, 'I've given that lad the powder, but it's no use! You'll have to do something, Jennie!' Soon she came into the kitchen, taking an apron off and the money pouch round her waist. 'See to things!' This to Father, then into the scullery to wash her hands, calling peremptorily, 'Upstairs, you, boy!' I undressed and got, weeping, into bed. She followed, only pushing off her shoes and opening the top buttons of her blouse to lay my cheek against the bulge of her breast. 'Now!' she'd whisper, placing a hand softly along the jerking nerves of my other cheek and splaying fingers over. 'You go to sleep, pet! Leave this to me! I'm *not* having this!' Within seconds the pain ebbed and, transferring all care, I drifted away on bulbous bliss and the scent of Pear's soap, to wake an hour later, loving a bolster in place of my mother, but quite cured. She worked the same white magic when need be for my sister too. And there she was, busy again downstairs: brusque, cool, aloof, it seemed; but we knew different!

Nevertheless, growing a little older, for all my love of her I inclined to believe, with Father, that she often lacked a certain sensitivity of feeling. In this our friend and neighbour, Mr Murphy, regretfully concurred. One holiday evening he had brought in a piece of sheet music to play and sing to a small adult group gathered about our piano. The title page showed a curly-headed child in velvet suit and slippers holding up pennies to the clerk at a railway station booking office. Together Ellie and I read the 'lyric' attached. It seemed pathos itself. At once fancy had me in that velvet rig-out, becurled and clutching coppers! Then Murphy sang:

'Give me a ticket to heaven.
That's where Dad's gone, they say.
He'll be so lonely without me,
Travelling all that way.
Mother died when I was born, sir,
And left Dad and me all alone,
So give me a ticket to heaven, please,
Before the last train is gone!'

This, and much more.

At the end Ellie wept openly. Aunt Eliza dabbed an eye. I too sat on the edge of tears. 'A grand song, Aloysius!' Father called. 'Very touching, and a real story to it!'

Mr Murphy smiled. 'It brings a lump to the throat, to be sure!'

And everybody agreed, except Mother. 'It seemed to me,' she said deliberately, 'a lot of maudlin trash!'

The Old Man threw up his hands. There were times, one felt sadly, when Mother really wanted heart. But in this, as in many other things, dissenting from the common view, she stirred my first doubts.

JANIE

ADA'S neuralgia unhappily gave notice of graver nervous troubles. Father's drunken rages, dangerous or not, made her quake in agonies of fear, and soon she developed chorea and a thyroid illness which left her for her short life a semi-invalid. Yet she was the only child who offered him overt affection. Sister Janie showed herself of tougher fibre. A passionate attachment to my mother, whose every mood she watched, seemed to leave her with love rather measured for the rest of mankind. Serving in the shop from childhood, she was 'first assistant' in everything. 'Jane will do a job,' my mother used to say, 'and well, while the rest are wondering how to start.' Controlled, accurate in the shop with change, coolly she 'weighed up' all comers. When relatives arrived, often shopkeepers themselves, trade and customers usually formed the staple of the evening's talk. Unobtrusively Janie sat in among it, listening intently and learning while still a child about the ways of the world – how people dealt, most honestly, others by lie and subterfuge, and how, on this side of the counter, one had at times to lie and dissemble too in order to keep and gain trade. In even the smallest corner shop, business, in that meanest of maxims, was business. Janie took all in and later, a pitiless mimic, with detailed recall, she dazzled us with studies of tipsy uncles and long-winded aunts. Altogether Janie puzzled Father. 'That child's got her head screwed on right,' he used to admit, 'but she's an old woman before she's a young 'un!' And very soon she had him 'weighed up' too. There was no chance of his eldest daughter's suffering nervous collapse. At times her effrontery staggered me.

Father usually came home full of bounce to partake of an excellent meal which, if his wife was busy, Janie served while we children sat about waiting for him to finish before dining ourselves. Striding past us, he planted himself sideways on to the table, hiding all above his waist behind the *Daily News*. From time to time he lowered the sheets to make a raid upon the hot 'relishes' on his plate. Choosing the right moment, Janie would rise, cross the rug, take a piece of dry bread from her pinafore, rub it about his gravy, select a new potato and pop a little sandwich into her mouth. She would even snatch the very titbit he had cut off and left for his next assault. Sitting petrified, we occasionally saw him droop his paper and look, vaguely puzzled. He stared at Janie, then at the cat: innocently both stared back. Never once did he catch her.

'You'll get murdered,' I told her, after one outrageous picking round his plate.

'Pooh!' she said. 'He's all shout.'

And strangely enough, for all his bombast, when sober, which he frequently was, he never cowed us, or even wished to. Unlike children in many homes about, we learned self-value early, and everyone developed a gift of the gab. 'If you've anything to say,' Mother told us, 'and you think it's

41

worthwhile, say it, no matter who's here.' And both of them listened and considered. In all things, large or small, one was accepted as a person, with opinions, likes and dislikes. 'That child,' Father would remark, surprised, 'doesn't care for the cheese we've got in this week. I thought myself it was rather nice quality.' They would agree or disagree with one, he loudly, but on level terms. It made us feel we mattered.

A fair-skinned, powerful man, every night Father observed the ritual of scrubbing himself thoroughly, using carbolic soap and gallons of hot water. Highly reactive to smell, he used to damn the odours endemic to our neighbourhood. 'You chose it!' Mother told him. 'Don't complain to me!' He specially objected to having to pass a certain fish and chip frier's. Such places in the early years of the century were indulging an eating habit still fairly new. Many tradesmen's families would on no account patronize these 'low class' establishments. My father's *bête noire*, a shop close by, used a cheap cottonseed oil which, when hot, gave off a sickening effluvium. He always passed it by on the other side of the street. Two girls who lived behind the fish frier's you could smell at school, Janie said, at a distance of six feet. This fact of life revolted Father. But he was soon to meet cottonseed oil at a much closer range!

Jane, who ran constantly into trouble, as I did, for late home-coming, arrived one evening from a Band of Hope concert well after ten o'clock. Angrily my father banned her from going to the next four meetings. She took this prohibition badly: the Band of Hope was the high spot of her leisure time. She appealed to my mother, but with no success. One Friday evening soon afterwards Janie had arranged the Old Man's tea – boiled ham and salad. He settled in his corner by the table and suddenly sniffed. 'Fish and chips!' he roared. 'A stench! What's this? Jennie!' Mother popped her head enquiringly round the shop door. 'Jennie! Who the devil's brought fish and chips in here? There's a terrific pong!'

'Nonsense!' my mother said. 'I wouldn't have such stuff in the house. You know that. Get on with your tea!' She disappeared.

He turned to Janie. 'You smell it?'

'Not a thing! Must be your imagination,' she told him airily.

'Damn and blast it all!' he bellowed. 'You impudent little

faggot! My imagination!' He turned to me. 'Robert!'

'There's a smell of *something*,' I said. 'Awful sort of bad fat!'

'There!' he shouted. 'And it's going worse! Jennie!'

Impatiently my mother came to the table, and her nose wrinkled at once. 'Whatever in the world . . . !'

The Old Man stood triumphant, grabbed at me and sniffed.

'Don't you smell *my* children!' Mother said indignantly. 'They're clean enough!'

'Damn it all! Where is it, then?' They pulled out his armchair, examined it, cleared the table, changed the cloth, smelled up and down the curtains. Janie crawled under the table and searched minutely.

'Nothing at all here!' she called, ' – quite sweet!'

Father even smelled the cat. 'Well, it's a devil!' he said. At last Mother sent Ellie for some liquid disinfectant and they dabbed it all over the place. Grumbling, Father settled down to his tea, swearing he could still catch a strong whiff.

'Me, too!' Mother admitted, looking very perplexed. 'I don't understand it at all!'

He finished his meal in record time, washed, changed his clothes entirely and called, going off to the trades club, 'I hope to God it's gone before I get back. It's fair turned my stomach!'

He had hardly left the house when Mother made her pronouncement. 'I'm going now to do the shop window out,' she said grimly. 'It'll take me about half an hour. If that smell's still here when I come back, someone in this house is in trouble!'

The family dined and quickly drifted away, leaving Janie and me alone. She washed up, came and sat in Father's chair and looked at me on the sofa. 'Want something?'

'Yes,' I said.

'What?'

'I wanna watch!'

'You're a nasty little pig!'

I grunted joyfully. Janie, in fact, was a dangerous enemy, carrying far too many guns for me. In several family skirmishes I had been badly worsted. But now! She went on staring at me for a minute, then: 'I know something *you* do,' she said, in a low, sinister voice, 'that's very very bad, and I could tell Mother about it!'

'W-What?' I gasped.

'Breathe one word about me,' she whispered, 'and I'll go straight to her!' I crumpled. 'Now, off into that scullery and get me a wet cloth, washing powder and carbolic soap!'

When I returned she was under the table, and from in between the two loose leaves of its extension she drew a mass of greasy, odoriferous papers. 'Got these,' she said, 'from that chip shop girl!' She cast them into the fire, then, ducking under the table again, quickly washed the boards. The smell faded at last. 'And that,' she said, 'was for stopping my Band of Hope!' I looked at her in awe: Jane was too much for me!

In early years I had that instilled respect for all adults which was common among all small children of the time. They seemed larger than life, striding the earth, possessors of total power. Janie from infancy paid no such homage. Some grown-ups felt her gaze disconcerting. 'She looks brassy at you,' complained one, 'but you just can't put your finger on it!' People either found her a 'deep one' or 'very forward!' 'One thing Janie *is*,' my mother used to say, 'and that's resourceful!'

As a small boy I often went with my sister on errands for the shop, in preparation for the day when this chore would be delegated to me. Once, as we returned through the Adelphi slums laden with packets from a wholesaler, a lad of about thirteen blocked our way. He tweaked my nose, pushed me around, grinning, and pulled Janie's hair. She went up to him, stared with big dark eyes and managed, burdened as she was, to put one finger against his chest. 'I've a sharpened knitting needle up my sleeve!' she said. 'Touch us again and I'll shove it through your heart!' Alarmed, the lad backed away at once and we passed on.

I was aghast: her awful threat had really scared me. 'Y-You wouldn't have pushed it into him, would you?'

'I've not got it with me just now,' she said.

'Well, it was a big whopper, then!'

'Oh, yes,' she told me carelessly. 'They've a big black book in heaven full of my lies!'

Walking home, Janie told me I'd no need to be all that overwhelmed. Slaughter by knitting needle was by no means uncommon, particularly among gypsies. She could quote local instances. 'If they're short of meat, now,' she said, 'at night, a gyp will sneak out of his caravan – in them fields by the racecourse – creep up to a sheep and stick a needle right

44

through the wool into its heart! The poor thing doesn't feel any pain, and there's no blood, but next morning the farmer finds it stone dead! "Hello!" he says, "it's pegged out! Christians won't eat this one!" So the gypsy comes along then, pretending, see? "Any sheep that's died, mister?" And the farmer sells it to him cheap!'

This story made a great impact, and Janie, who seemed to have consorted much with Romanies, said she could tell me plenty more. I was often given to understand that girls of initiative like her were able to draw, if need be, on various methods of self-defence – one involving hatpins, a common weapon of the time – but that she herself would never use them unless attacked by footpads or similar evil characters when going, say, for Father's stiff collars on Saturday nights. I used to applaud, but hoped that no robber would have the misfortune to waylay her.

Like Chaucer's pilgrims, to ease the tedium of travel Jane told and repeated many stories, all of them 'true' – 'Finger wet, finger dry, Cut my throat if I tell a lie!' – and mostly about gypsies. She knew personally of a 'little boy' (a standard character called Laurence) whom one band had snatched, then dressed in rags and sent out selling racing tips and stealing off clothes lines. Laurence had been rich and very beautiful, but he never went home. His mother died of a broken heart. 'He's a Romany now.' I expressed personal fears. '*You!*' she said scornfully. 'Why should anyone want to steal *you*?' This hurt a little, but it left me a thought more content with my plainness and poverty.

One whole chapter of Jane's celestial bad book must have been devoted to her sagas about certain of our ancestors. Until her researches the family as a whole seemed rather short on forebears. I could only recall Mother's mentioning a Great-great-uncle Thomas, who, she said, died 'through drink', being knocked down by a brewer's dray. But never once had she alluded to his glorious martial career! 'When you're older, though,' my sister assured me, 'she'll tell you about him all right, just as she did me, and Great-uncle George too! But don't mention it to her now.' Meantime Janie produced their medals. This was a hazardous business even for her: it meant prying into the only drawer, locked and private, that the house possessed. Mother being at the shop door buying fruit from a handcart, Janie snatched a key from behind the clock, flew upstairs and returned with two small leather cases. Each contained a medallion glowing on plumped velvet. 'Won,' she gasped, 'for bravery in battle!' I hardly caught a glimpse. Then she was up and down again, with the key replaced. On our errands for weeks after, Uncle Tom and his brother George chased the gypsies out of Jane's imagination. Both of our predecessors, I learned, had been of near-noble rank: the family's social nosedive into Salford she left unexplained. As we followed the streets Janie fed me with their exploits, deeds of such valour, from Waterloo to Balaclava, that even Queen Victoria, she said, had been wont to clap hands and cry, 'Oh, the brave, brave boys!' I listened entranced, her earnestness stilling any doubts. 'They won handfuls of medals, of course, but gave them all away. Only those two,' said Janie, 'have come down through the family. Don't tell anyone I showed them to you!'

Unfortunately one night Father came home rather early and, stuttering drunk, cast two more decorations on the table and began to sing.

'Once a drunk,' his wife remarked bitterly, 'always a drunk!'

The import of this observation defeated me, but I soon discovered that Father was 'Grand Primo' in the Royal and Ancient Antediluvian Order of the Buffaloes – 'Once a "Buff", always a "Buff" ' – a sort of working man's Masons. His Lodge members met fortnightly in great public secrecy at a local pub, calling each other 'brother'. The shining awards Janie had showed me had been won by Father soldiering in their service. One of my sisters made so bold as to ask my mother once the purpose of this organization, only to be told uncharitably that, as far as one could gather, it was an order dedicated to beer and to assisting those 'brothers' who fell ill through supping it!

Once more I charged Janie with prevarication. She looked at me coolly. 'Pooh! I didn't make those stories up for you!' she said. 'I made them for myself.' After imagination she had impudence.

En route together one day to a paper merchant's for parchment and sugar bags Jane stopped and surveyed the window of a fancy shoe store on the high road. She pointed to a pair of natty brown button-on bootees. 'Ooooh! I'd love to see you in them! Just your size! Let's go in.'

'Oh, n-n-no! Janie, please!'

'Come along this minute!'

Nerves taut, I followed her through a glass door to a great bay of blue lino dotted with chairs on carpet islands. Immediately an assistant came up, staring bleakly through pince-nez. 'No string! No empty boxes!' He pointed. 'Out!'

Jane stared up in dignity. 'My mother sent me. She's across the road in the draper's. Robert needs a pair of new brown bootees. She'll be over in a minute!'

'Ah, now then! Come along, six-foot!' He led me to one of the 'atolls' and I got on a chair. In no time we had the bootees out of the window and half a dozen other boxes of footwear open besides. Janie was hard to please. In the friendliest way they discussed style, quality, fit, price, while I sat stiff with apprehension. She chose the 'button-ups' after all, and I walked up and down in them. 'Thank you very much!' Janie said. 'We'll go and fetch Mother now. She's very busy. I'm sure she'll choose these right away. Those lovely bootees *were* nice and comfortable, weren't they?' I nodded dumbly. She turned to the assistant. 'And you haven't an empty shoe box, have you?' Smiling, he found her one and we left.

'They just suited you!' she said. 'I thought they would.'

'You're a great big liar!' I told her, and got the usual answer:

'It's all in the black book!'

After this and similar episodes I rebelled. Her stories fascinated, but she made my nerves ache. 'I'm not coming with you again!' I complained at last.

'You're lucky!' she told me. 'Lots and lots of boys would be glad of the chance!' And this was so. At school she attracted the young male in embarrassing numbers. 'What's that damn lad hanging about the shop for?' Father would ask, puzzled.

'That's a new one again!' Amused, Janie treated all these beaux with a sort of contempt. It was the start for her of a complex romantic career.

A FEARFUL JOY

LOVE, it must be said, smote me even sooner than Jane, two ladies at once dividing my passion. In Edwardian days women with hair long enough for them to sit upon possessed peculiar feminine appeal. Mrs Mallin, my mother's friend, had tresses in this required length, and of rippling gold! A goddess, full-bosomed in a whalebone corset, she kept a drapery along the 'Barbary Coast', a road which ran to the docks. Leonie, her niece, equally endowed, gleamed metallic too. 'The old one hennas it up!' my eldest sister used to tell us. 'She drinks gin and her husband beats her.'

Ellie protested every time. 'I think she's beautiful; Leonie too. You shouldn't say such things!' Janie laughed. 'But don't let on to Mum I told you!' There were times when I didn't like Jane at all. For me, both these gorgeous creatures, gliding back and forth behind the counters of the cavernous store, seemed loveliness come alive. From early childhood I had been taken to the shop in the slack of mid-afternoons. Mother and her friend stood at the back in shadow, heads together – dark and gold, strangely intimate, laughing sometimes, withdrawn. I sat alongside the counter, still as a stone, on a bentwood chair, in thrall to Leonie. Shimmering through sunlight, she treadled a machine by the window, getting up from time to time to sell elastic or reels of thread, with a smile or a cluck in my direction. At last the two older women would come down the shop, Mother carrying some small purchase, and always, it seems to me now, the same ritual followed. Mrs Mallin cupped my chin in her plump hand. 'Such a patient little chap he is, now! Never a murmur! May *we* have him, Jennie? You've so many children already! Just let us keep this one!'

Mother smiled. 'Would you like to be Mrs Mallin's little boy and live with her and Leonie?'

Neither of them knew it, but this was Freudian dynamite! 'Yes,' I whispered, desire springing wild already, ' – if you come too.'

My answer seemed to give them both much pleasure. 'Just the four of us, then?' said the blonde Juno. 'Now wouldn't that be lovely!' It appeared to please Leonie too, who smiled, all golden, down.

'Oh yes! And he'll be *our* little boy!'

Of course, we had need to dispose of the husband. Mr Mallin, a thin-faced man in a Norfolk jacket, materialized only when the shop became busy. There was no laughing then, but nods, half-sentences and an occasional sharp word in the background. My mother stood waiting attention, always with a shoulder turned to whichever counter he happened to be serving at. Now and then I saw him behind a high clothes rack in the rear, staring through at us like an animal. On the way home from these *tête-à-têtes* with her friend Mother seemed distrait and walked at times, I thought, with a sort of elation. As for me, the visits stirred such proto-sexual fantasy, life burst into new radiance.

But first, off with the old love! A postcard in the local newsagent's showed Marie Studholme, darling of the theatre world, and but late my heart's queen. She bulged through roses out of a thatched cot window, all in a garden with blue love birds. For weeks, on every errand that could lead me past the shop, I had stopped and gazed and dreamed. Had ever woman been so fair before? And so embowered! At a moment's notice I now evicted Marie, lock, stock and bosom, and installed my mother with the two plump drapers, and we lived there in bliss, often to the strains of faint barrel-organ music. Once or twice fancy brought the wife-beater up our garden path in his Norfolk jacket. I imported my father to fill the doorway. Mr Mallin turned tail at once. Father chased him and conveniently disappeared. And duly, with the lamp-lit dusk, the ladies disrobed me in that bed-room under the thatch, my mother absent. But I knew she was there, snug below in our love nest, lost in a good book. Throughout the proceedings I stood tumescent, which characteristic both gentlewomen appeared to observe with set, wall-eyed smiles. Leonie would put a nightshirt on me, then, with her auntie, each now turning diaphanous, we'd float like cherubim to a bosomy white bed and slide between sheets into a sort of shuddering ecstasy. Young love had bloomed early, for at school I was still marching in with the 'mixed' infants.

This free entertainment recurred at intervals until, round

the age of ten, I saw 'Little Red Riding Hood' at the Prince of Wales Theatre up the street. There a becloaked young woman with three twinkling gold teeth turned my goddesses to dross. Of breath-taking beauty, she sat in a glade and trilled the hit of the day to a comical wolf.

> I wouldn't leave my little wooden hut for you-oo,
> I've got one hubby and I don't want two-oo.
> If he comes back there'll be no knowing
> What he will do, so you'd better be going . . .

Now we boys in the street had already enjoyed a 'revised' version of this lyric:

> I wouldn't leave my missis in the house with you-oo,
> I've got one baby and I don't want two-oo . . .

'Hubby' then went on to threaten intruders with emasculatory action: a rendering which could have added Oedipean undertones to my new dreams. Then Red Riding Hood came on again – tap-dancing! – and sang.

> I'm a pretty little girl from nowhere,
> Nowhere at all,
> In a house very small,
> It's ten miles from a railway station! . . .

That did it! I had the haberdashers out of 'Rose Cot' in no time, to make way for joys fresher and a shade more explicit, while Mother, happy as ever, went on reading among the greenery.

Mr Murphy, who had seen the pantomime, came in and praised it to Father. 'A smart Little Red Riding Hood,' he said. 'Local girl, too! Mother keeps a beerhouse down Knott Mill way.' Knott Mill!

Dream, and reality! Love, and longing for what? Some spring mornings one leapt like a lamb for the wild joy of living itself. 'Hey! nonny! nonny!' we carolled in school: a lover and his lass! Songs of innocence. And on the streets – those earthy parodies of the music hall ditty, true and only folk songs of the industrial mass. Naïvety and knowingness mixed, I muddled on with the rest: artless we were, yet each one of us guilt-stained with the secrets of early puberty. The community, Christian and authoritarian, went on keeping us that way. Parents worried in secret about the 'purity' of their children. Masturbation discovered (often by lifetime masturbators) was met with horror, sometimes with severe chastisement. What did a child know? Who was he mixing with? How much 'filth' had he picked up? Constantly our elders feared, yet they blocked every rational source of information. 'Children learn,' they told one another, 'soon enough!' So millions went into marriage either ignorant or with ideas utterly distorted. 'The facts of life!' parents whispered: and even that became a soiled phrase, good for a giggle among us. And how we bluffed one another!

'I see,' said Eddie Franklin one day to a few of us, as we mooched about the school yard, 'that there girl on the front row – Cissie Craven – has started her periods. That's another one!'

''S right!' I lied carelessly. 'She told me. Have *you* begun yet?'

He looked startled. 'Me? N-No! Not yet.' Eddie whistled through his teeth as he wandered around, then he couldn't contain himself. 'What's "periods"?'

'If you don't know,' I told him calmly, as ignorant as he was, 'don't come pretendin' to us that you *do* – see?'

The other two lads looked at him, disgusted. They didn't know either.

Soon afterwards Eddie tried to impress us by announcing, without gloss, that a fourteen-year-old girl in the sewing shop where his sister worked had 'got herself up the spout just through having a bath after the lodger!' His words conveyed nothing to us beyond a feeling of their fraughtness with sex. We looked at one another. Then I chanced my arm. 'That often happens,' I said, ' – with lodgers.'

THE FOOD OF LOVE

BOTH Father and Mother were actively interested in the politics of the day. From hotel lobbies, through Al Murphy, we received stale copies of *The Times*, *Manchester Guardian* and the *Irish Press*, with certain paragraphs marked by him in red for special perusal. Of Radical faith, Father and his pot companion seemed to go on endlessly about Mister Gladstone, Asquith, Parnell, Mrs O'Shea, Redmond and especially Lloyd George, whom they loved. 'You don't need a Labour Party,' Father used to say, 'when you've got Lloyd George!' But of Winston Churchill both men thought little. Unlike their hero, the orator supreme, they considered him a shifty and mediocre speaker with a poor delivery. 'It's the cleft palate!' Mr Murphy would say. 'Congenital!'

'And you know the reason for *that*!' Father told him darkly. They would then look at each other. Exchanges like these, hinting at secrets in the lives of public figures, were repeated *ad nauseam*. Years afterwards I recall Mother's complaining at such reiteration. Not only within the family, she said, but in shops, pubs and factories, life was so limited that people recounted the same stories, incidents and witticisms time and again until one became 'word-perfect and weary'. 'Some folk,' she said irritably, 'were like drunken parrots!' Then came the cinema and the upheaval of world war to break through the stifling parochialism of it all. Among the unskilled working class, tradesmen like my father and his friend, through an interest in national politics alone, stood out as 'intellectuals'.

So they ranted on together, supping their ale and, from a newspaper, picking crabs' legs, shrimps, whelks or winkles which Murphy had filched. Out of his coat-tail pocket he would often take a beer bottle and hand it to my mother. 'Oxtail soup, Jennie. It was "on" today. For the children. Very nourishing!' Mother would thank him; but later I used to see her pouring it down the lavatory. 'You never know where it's been!' she would say, remembering, no doubt, Murphy's tales of hotel kitchens in twilight, 'crawling with cockroaches!'

These domestic boozing sessions were often augmented by Mother's brothers and their friends, who arrived with bottled beer and a concertina, and the evening ended in harmony. Uncle Edward's appearance, however, always tended to sour proceedings. A demagogue of no small power, he would have none of what he called the 'old Irish nonsense!' After argument, long and bitter, in which Mother supported him, he scattered the opposition. 'There's one problem and one alone,' Uncle insisted passionately, catching his breath and stooping forward (he was soon to die of consumption); 'a problem for English and Irish alike – it's how to get the rich off the backs of the poor!' Then a spasm of coughing. The others looked on, embarrassed. 'All right!' my father would shout, half-seas-over by now. 'Let's drop it, lads! – "Oh, believe me, if all those endearing young charms" . . . Come on, Aloysius!' And Mr Murphy, a good tenor, would swing into one of his 'specials', Uncle Sam's concertina catching him up in mid-melody. As our kitchen filled with song a little group of neighbours gathered outside the window to listen. At last Mother would ask, 'Is nobody going to work tomorrow? I've a shop to see to in the morning!'

Irregularly over the years Father visited his eldest sister to pay a small instalment off the original sum he had borrowed to buy the shop. The last two pounds she returned to him. 'Get a present for the children,' she said. With Mother's consent he bought something we all yearned for – a piano. But in pre-1914 days, as we were to discover, two pounds' worth of piano didn't amount to much. A man in love with music, Father always gave a copper to all street performers, with the exception of the Salvation Army, which he detested. Whenever Beecham or D'Oyly Carte opera came to Manchester he went: the only occasion, Mother said, on which one could be certain of his sober return. A 'muzzy' head, he told her, not only spoiled the performance for him but also the memory of it afterwards. Such was the pleasure, he came home walking on air and talked of it for days. 'If every night were opera night!' his wife said.

Aloysius shared his enthusiasm and an even greater passion for the bottle. A failed, or spoiled priest – I never knew which – drink, it was said, had ruined his career. Like his 'Pater', who lived with him in squalor, he had worked as head waiter in good-class hotels, but drunkenness had driven him to poor commis jobs and kitchen work. In sobriety a jovial man of education and wit, he always found a welcome with us. During his spells out of work Mother, for whom Al expressed the highest regard, did much to keep him and his father from the workhouse. But finally, alcoholics beyond reclaim, they both ended their days there. In youth Aloysius had been taught to play the piano well, and it was him we called upon when our instrument arrived.

Three men brought it on a handcart, heaved and struggled over the counter and dropped it in the kitchen. The next scene passed into our archives! Father, still panting after giving assistance, went and ripped off the sack-and-straw covering. 'There!' he announced at last. 'The Collison's "Sweetone"! Parlour Model!' A wreck of an 'upright' leaned against the wall.

We gathered in an arc and stared, shocked with disappointment. No one spoke. 'It's a Collison's "Sweetone"!' he said again, as if we hadn't heard the first time, '– all rosewood throughout!' and he turned back the keyboard lid. The instrument suddenly grinned at us like an old mare. He struck a note; nothing happened; and another. We heard a distinct thud. Bits of straw now began to detach themselves from the carcass. A green baize underbelly gaped open, and again more litter. And the talk, as we remembered, went something like this.

'Has someone been keeping hens in it?' my mother asked.

'It's been in storage,' the Old Man explained. 'Customers in the Boilermakers' ill used the woodwork. A damn shame! Look at them pint-pot rings on the top! Harry's had it packed away in the stable a while.'

Mother sniffed. 'It smells of beer!'

'What wouldn't, after thirty years in an alehouse! But a bloke that really knows pianos says – old she is, but sound enough in wind and limb! Once done up and tuned – I've a man coming – we'll get a lifetime's pleasure out of it.'

We children went on gazing. Mother stepped forward and felt above the music stand at an object which protruded like a horizontal udder. 'What's this?'

'Ornament!' the Old Man said. 'There've been two others – one at each end, see – but they've fallen off.' He turned to Janie. 'Run and tell Mr Murphy!'

Aloysius came in and, catching sight of the instrument, 'Holy Jesus!' he said, not quite sober, and went over and fondled its wooden bub. 'Sure, an' it's the one-titted wonder you've got! If I can't play it, I'll milk it!' Then he shot back his cuffs and without even a preliminary scale ran into a version of the 'Fairyland Waltz'. The strains which issued reached us etherialized, not, it seemed, from the piano we saw, but rather from a second, ghostlier instrument deep within. Aloysius stopped. Father waited judgement. 'A mellow tone, to be sure. "Refined", I would say.'

'What's wrong with the bass end?' my mother asked. 'You could have got nearly as much sound out of the dresser!'

The lower registers, Mr Murphy agreed, were unresponsive.

Certain keys, once down, stayed down, whilst others . . . he hit several with his thumb. They resisted, rock-like.

'Could it be the damp?' my father asked.

'It *could* be the damp,' said Aloysius. He then 'loosened her up' with practice runs, opened the top flap and launched into a powerful rendition of the 'Blue Danube'. Half-way through, a faint cloud began to form about the lid and along the baize chest, like smoke. Aloysius started to sneeze. 'Bigod, an' she's on fire now!' But it was only dust rising.

Father looked inside. 'All this instrument wants is a real good goin' over, inside and out.'

And that's what it got. Grandma's boyfriend, the cabinet-maker, 'came to scoff', Mother said, 'and remained to scoff', but he put a rich polish on it, leaving not a beer ring behind. Father re-covered the chest and belly, washed the keys with lemon juice and refurbished the 'gold' candlesticks beautifully – that being in his line. Then a repairer came and worked, head down, for hours, giving it finally as his professional opinion that the instrument was 'buggered really', but one could 'knock a tune out of it now', and it was 'all right for children to learn on'. He played 'The Bluebells of Scotland' and left. Mother thought it still sounded 'refined', but her husband was happy with the result, so happy, in fact, that soon after he made an awful error of judgement.

Mr Murphy brought us the news first, knowing, as he did, what was what in the hotel world. 'Val Colleano and Partner! – on at the Prince of Wales!' Val was married, as Aloysius had been told several times, to Father's niece. He and Cousin Frances played two evenings a week in the Italian restaurant at the Great Northern, where Murphy used to wait on. He came hurrying into the kitchen one evening, Mother remembered. 'Your Val and his missis! – appearing with all the London stars at the "Wales"! Mayor's Charity Show! How's that!' Father swelled with pride. For long he had looked upon his relatives as one of the finest duos in the north and had indeed bragged of them in many a Salford pub. Genius, he felt, was to be recognized at last! London stars! The greatest charity show of the year! And all in a theatre not one hundred yards from his own doorstep!

For the mayor's annual effort prices, except in the gallery, rose steeply to keep out our local *hoi polloi*. This angered Father, who refused to attend on conscientious grounds; the cost of his usual seat in the pit he considered far too high and the company on the 'top shelf' much too low. Cabs and even motor cars outside the theatre on the great night made it clear that all the cream of Salford was bestowing its patronage. After all the boasting Father seemed a little abashed when his wife found it difficult to find the Colleanos' name on a bill which Janie brought in; but it was there, all right – next to the bottom. The 'London stars' turned out something of a disappointment too: 'top of the bill' was an artiste who had not headed any other for many a long year, and the rest were run-of-the-mill performers of no more than regional note. Still, Mr Murphy, pianist himself, stood by and praised the Old Man's relations with loyal enthusiasm. He considered Val 'after the style of the great Paderewski' and thought more would be heard of him.

Father returned home one evening from a visit to his eldest sister (mother to Frances) looking immensely pleased with himself, and, hardly waiting to take off his coat, 'Val and his wife will be calling after the show!' he announced. Mother got up, shocked. 'However could you! Look at the state of us! Holes in the lino, no decent rugs, couch split, wallpaper peeling – years old! And you invite middle-class folk in and put *us* on show!'

'They must take us as they find us,' he said. 'Frances told me – and quite right too – "Uncle," she said, "we wouldn't come to the end of the street and not drop in for a minute!"'

For the next fortnight, when visitors called, Father bragged insufferably. 'He's got letters, you know! "Val Colleano, A.L.C.M.!" Cap 'n' gown! He's reckoned one of the finest players in the city!'

'Classical, of course,' said Uncle Sam.

'Every time! None o' this beerhouse ragtime stuff! Mozart and Verdi and Wagner and that lot! He has a studio in town, you know – gives lessons – "Val Colleano! A.L.C.M.! Piano and organ – four shillings an hour!"'

'Four shillings! Phooh!'

'Brumby's his real name,' Mother said, '– Freddie Brumby!'

'Is he related to that family,' asked Uncle Sam, 'that kept the cookshop off Greengate?'

'*He* was the grandfather, I understand,' Mother told him.

'Brumby or not,' the Old Man snorted, pointing at the piano, 'when he comes he'll make that talk!'

'Lord help us!' said my mother. 'You're not going to ask

him to play, are you?'

'What's the use of inviting 'em if they don't give us a duet!'

'But the piano!'

'It's in good fettle now,' he told her, and in fact he had just had it tuned again.

On the great day Father, out of work at the time, strolled about the shop whistling snatches of this and that and trying to decide just what items he would choose to hear in their brief recital. The whole house was agog. Mother scrubbed the kitchen floor and brought down the only bedroom carpet to cover larger holes in the oilcloth. Janie helped after school, cleaning, dusting and polishing. But not the piano! Father saw to that and noticed to his dismay that several keys in the lower octaves had started to stick again. That would never do. Opening the base, he inserted a lighted candle and a holder somewhere in its bowels and closed it again. I watched it all, fascinated. 'Just a little warm air!'

Then Father decreed, as we feared he might, that all children except Janie should go to bed before the 'stars' arrived. I can feel the shock of disappointment yet. Ada, all hopes dashed, began to weep quietly. 'I did so want to see them play!'

Mother looked round at us. 'That's all very well – "everybody in bed!"; but look at that sofa! I've got to have somebody on there to cover up that great tear in the leather. Ellie and Ada, you must both settle on it before they arrive, and stay settled. Understand?' They wriggled with pleasure. 'The rest of you, as Father says, are too young to be up so late.' That left me, as senior, free for the peepholes on the stairs. And all was ready at last. This was to be the night of our young lives, and indeed none of us forgot it.

The visitors were late in coming, and I must have dozed at my post, a shirt wrapped round cold legs. Voices raised in welcome stirred me. They had arrived – the Colleanos! I glued my eyes to the spy holes and followed the scene with an interest almost hypnotic. Val! He stood in the middle of the kitchen, deep in his overcoat, with an astrakhan collar buttoned up to the face, fat and unsmiling. Shortish he was, about up to the mantelpiece. A disappointment, this; I had imagined him towering even over Father. He possessed the 'lion's mane' just as Mr Murphy had told us, flowing over his collar, but an upturned nose gave him the air of a peevish pug dog. And our honoured guest looked clearly unhappy. He nodded round, put his wife's fiddle case on the sofa, where the girls sat stiff as idols, unbuttoned his collar and accepted a glass of beer from Father. Cousin Frances, whom I had never seen before, was plump and pink, and all the time she talked, breathless, gabbling things like 'Ever so nice, really! Place packed to the doors! Yes, Mother said we should call. Of course! Only too glad, I said. Go to the top of the street and not drop in! I said to Freddie – Val! I said, didn't I? I said *that* wouldn't do at all!'

Flushed and beaming, Father asked her how the show had gone. It seemed to have passed off very well; but they appeared second on the programme, and it *did* take time for an audience to warm up! 'One encore. Quite nice.' Mr Murphy came in, spruced and sober, and Val lifted fingers in recognition. The conversation then took a direction too intellectual for me; but Janie remembered it years afterwards. Val's solo, it turned out, the Moonlight Sonata, had, unfortunately, not been full-bodied enough for some of his audience. This had caused a disturbance on the 'top shelf' and cries of 'Play up, lad!' Father and Mr Murphy looked disgusted; but my mother remarked she'd heard before how poor that gallery was for sound, whereupon Cousin Frances told her, lips pursed, 'When Beethoven says *pianissimo*, Auntie, it has to be *pianissimo*, no matter what they hear up in the gallery!'

About this time a low but imperative tapping made itself heard on the kitchen window. Father's boasting had had its effect; a little knot of music-loving neighbours had gathered outside and were growing impatient for the free performance. He rose angrily. The impudence of it! But Mr Murphy got up before him. 'It's for me!' he lied diplomatically, and went out, to return in a couple of minutes. 'All right now!'

There was some talk then about which of the children was going to learn the piano, and Cousin Frances asked what about the very pretty one, and Janie said she would be taking lessons as soon as Mother could afford the ninepence. Mr Colleano enquired who in the world taught piano for ninepence, and Father explained it was a lady in a row of houses on the main street, near the gasworks, who had the same letters behind her name as Val. Soon after, they got up, the gentleman making a splendid display of looking at the watch on his wrist, a gesture new to me. (The wrist watch for males,

just then on its way in, was damned by many as 'effeminate'.)
Father rose at the same time. This was it! He went over to
the piano and patted it like a horse. Val stepped forward a
pace or two and peered at the keyboard. Father pulled out
the stool invitingly; our visitor ignored it, but leant forward
and struck somewhere in the middle. Vibrant the 'Sweetone'
rang out. Val recoiled as if stung. There was a clatter inside.
'Something's – fallen off it!' he said.

'It's only a candlestick!' Father was desperate now. 'Come
on, Val! Give us a tune. Frances! Just one duet before you
go!'

My mother sat silent, but Aloysius rowed in, wheedling.
'Just one, now, for the children!'

Our cousin hesitated, but not Mr Colleano! 'Oh dear, no!
No!' he said. 'No, it's too late – far too late! Another time,
perhaps. Come along, Frannie, let's be off!'

Father didn't see his guests out, but went and sat again,
his face like thunder. Mother escorted them through the
shop, Mr Murphy leaving at the same time. I heard the front
door bang, and they were gone. The three girls still sat bolt
upright along the sofa. Father went over and crashed down
the piano lid. A faint chord trembled protest across the
kitchen. He strutted back to his chair and buried his face
deep in a quart jug, then he looked over the rim and saw
the girls. 'You still here? To bed! To bed!' I flew upstairs
just before them.

The day after, Aloysius slipped in at the back door. 'An'
is the master at home, now?'

'I haven't one' (Mother told him this regularly), 'but my
husband's out.'

Mr Murphy settled himself at the piano stool. 'So he
wouldn't play – ould high-an'-mighty! Come around, boys
and girls, I'll give ye a tune!'

Some time afterwards, perhaps in compensation, Father
and his friend came home with a gentleman who, they said,
would really make our piano 'talk'. He too turned out to be
a 'professional', long-haired and having, as Mother noted
with all her husband's acquaintances, a great capacity for
putting away beer. Mr Higham also, we heard, had played
piano in hotels, and opulent picture palaces now opened in
the city, but 'bad luck' had reduced him latterly to perform-
ing at our local fleapit. There, we learned, in the course of
the evening, he was plagued by a problem of hygiene un-

known in bourgeois entertainment circles – our 'Kinema' floor had, he complained, to be swilled out and disinfected every morning. And no wonder! Owner-managers of slum cinemas,* out for every penny they could get, crushed their youngest patrons so tightly along the cheap benches that no child dared even get up for fear of losing his seat. In our establishment, even before the lights went out, retaining position could be difficult. Theoretically, no standing was allowed. The chucker-out would bring a small paying customer to an already packed bench, push his posterior against the end occupant and make room for the newcomer; but this sent pressure running along the row, and another child slid off the other end. Once in the dark, no one dreamed of going to the lavatory. Through need or mischief children relieved themselves where they sat, and often the lower reaches ran awash. Down slope, before the silver screen, Mr Higham, we understood, battled on at his music, feet upon the pedals, powerless, despite threats, as King Canute. But already he seemed to have grown tolerant, looking upon the phenomenon as a mere occupational hazard. Indeed, at a later date he referred to it airily as the 'Falls of Lodore', which shows one can get used to almost anything. Mr Higham took to popping in occasionally late Sunday evenings, and entertained us much. So long as a glass, constantly replenished, stood within sight, he would play till morning – a sort of 'mechanical piano', Mother thought, 'but you slip beer into the slot instead of coppers!' It was through his kindness and expertise, though, that we eventually acquired a much better instrument to replace Father's two-pound bargain.

Before our old 'Sweetone' finally left us, however, it got me into trouble in a peculiar way. Unsatisfied with the effect of lemon juice for blanching its keys, Father bought some expensive 'Everwear' enamel and painted the whole keyboard white. The result, however, dismayed him. 'It looks like it's got false teeth now!' he said. We were at that time in the spring of the year and had music in the streets: little girls with maypoles passed in dance and song from door to door,

* Strangers to the town were puzzled when invited to patronize a local picture house referred to by all as the 'By Joe' – our native rendering of 'Bijou', a name chosen for high inappropriateness on every count.

collecting coppers for a tea party. Nearly every street of any length had its own gay totem, the event being organized almost invariably by the daughters of labourers, artisans' children being forbidden by parents to go 'begging'. These girls had their own maypole in a backyard; but compared with the public emblem it was a pretty dead affair. The maypole itself had always had to be carried by a small boy – an unconscious admission, perhaps, of its early phallic significance. Any child wishing to take part in the 'professional' event needed to invest a halfpenny or a penny in something called a 'hail-hail'. This consisted of a thin tube of cardboard about a foot long with coloured paper ribbons pasted on one end; penny ones had double the number of streamers. During late April at the shop we sold these in quantity. One lucky team of girls near us was allowed to make its preparations in a barber's saloon on early-closing day. He lent them the paste and scissors needful to decorate their pole and hoop with ribbons and blowsy paper roses. Then, the next Wednesday after May Day, Figaro again kindly permitted the use of his premises for the banquet. This, the rest of us felt enviously, was really doing it in style! The doggerel children sang around their maypole (lines varied from district to district) seems to have been 'home-made' and owed little to the more literary verses learned in school. One thing all these joyous greeters of the spring possessed was a money box, kept usually in the grip of the largest girl. If the 'treasurer', however, was seen indulging in sweets or tiger nuts before the great 'carve-up' we had no lack of suspicious types who muttered about sticky table knives pushed through the cash-box aperture!

With a small 'queen' decked out in old lace curtain, the maypole set off along the home street, stopping at most doors but skipping those where, the big girl knew, ill temper, meanness or the poverty of tenants made performance nugatory. They trailed, rather than burst, into chorus:

> We come to greet you here today,
> And we hope you will not turn us away,
> For we dance and sing in a merry ring
> On a Maypole Day.
> For we are, for we are gay as the roses,
> Bright as the sun,
> Happy as birds that fly in the air,

61

Happy as fishes that swim in the sea,
For we are, for we are
As happy as happy can be!
Last year we had a maypole,
It was a pretty sight.
We danced around the maypole,
And cheered it with delight.
With hearts and voices singing,
We merrily claimed the day,
For gentle Lizzie Smithson
Was crowned the Queen of May.
Hail! Hail! Hail! Hail!
Hail to Her Majesty, Queen!
Hail! Hail! Hail! Hail!
Hail to Her Majesty, Queen!

Dance
Round and round the maypole,
Merrily we go,
Skipping, skipping lightly,
Passing to and fro.
Such a happy pastime,
On the village green,
Dancing in the sunshine,
Hurrah! for our queen!
Fah, lah, lah, lah! . . ;

Joyousness! Which was all very well in its way; but, as they
now pointed out, Her Majesty was also in business:

She is our May Queen, our May Day Queen.
Her voice is sweeter than any queen.
You can fetch your money, honey,
You can fetch your money, honey.
For our May Queen, our May Day Queen!

After this blatant appeal to the purse there followed a
moment of silent expectancy which only too often died in
disappointment. Then the small May Queen, still gawping
before the closed door, was given a nudge and her retinue
shuffled off to the next house. A maypole usually went out
each night for a week, with a final going over the locality on
May Day itself. The kitty, whether 'knifed' or not, commonly
yielded between one and three shillings, out of which, by
good budgeting, it was often possible to throw a party and

give a little something to each ribbon-holder in hard cash*
besides.

Hating to be deprived of all the spring pickings by dancers
round the maypole, groups of boys went forth in competition
tricked out as 'nigger troupes'. As the impresario of one such
band, a dazzling idea occurred to me. Swiping what remained
of Father's piano enamel, a white sediment at the bottom of
the tin, I decorated my sooty performers with eye and mouth
rings. The effect was so taking that I added superb moustaches all round. House audiences expressed great amusement
at their appearance. 'Real minstrels, these!' they said. On
May Day, I remember, we took three shillings and eight-
pence, a colossal sum to divide among six of us. But con-
sternation! 'Everwear Supergloss', drying thick in the pores,
proved impervious to soap and water: no one had paint
remover. Soon parents come to the shop in turn, each with a
blanched offspring, loud in complaint at my artistry. Father,
apoplectic, called me in and sent me off to bed at once. 'That
blasted lad,' he swore, 'loses us pounds a week in trade!'
Already I had an ill name for taking others into trouble:
even my mother, who required cast-iron proof of any of my

* With the summer season approaching, many small girls felt
the urge to divert themselves in a tradition which was already old
before the pyramids were built: they used their maypole pay-off
to get a set of 'bobber and kibs' (called elsewhere 'alley and jack-
stones'), a game played in the caves of prehistoric man and illus-
trated on ancient Greek vases. One penny bought a white opaque
marble about three-quarters of an inch in diameter and four half-
inch earthenware cubes, often in different colours (our ancestors
used the ankle bones of sheep and goats). These cubes were placed
on the pavement at the four corners of an imaginary one-foot
square. A girl (never a boy) knelt on the kerbstone before them.
She bounced the bobber lightly, chanting, 'Pick a cherry!' Then,
before her marble could bob twice, she snatched up both kib and
falling alley. Bounce again! 'Eat a cherry!' Back to the pavement
with this cube, and so on, catching the marble each time. If she
failed to do this she was 'out'. Finally, in weird combination, the
winner scooped up the whole four kibs together with a flick of
the hand like that of an anteater's tongue polishing off a square
meal in circular motion. Two girls would meet for competition,
one usually holding the baby while the first had her 'cale' (turn),
then, on a 'breakdown' – failing to catch the bobber – the other
took up position on the kerb. To watch two experts contesting
was to marvel at the prehensility of small female fingers.

misdemeanours, had to admit that things did seem to 'occur' when I was around. 'He'll be getting birched next!' roared the Old Man. For days after the last episode, odd white-eyed spooks with handlebar moustaches used to pass the shop, gazing across reproachfully. Until the 'hue' faded from the streets I found it politic to make my way home via back entries.

About twice a year a travelling fair settled on a vacant lot near the school. It brought us tattered gaiety and a music at times so plaintive that, heard in the dark approaching lanes, it filled one with a sort of infinite regret, a sentiment echoed by Ellie, who always cried when it came in 'on the wind'. Under bursts of naphtha light the 'croft' ran alive with Lowry-like figures; but I never felt easy or happy there. Perhaps the gypsies around, and Janie's early tales about them, had undermined confidence. 'Don't let me hear of your doing odd jobs on that Cow Lane fair!' Mother used to warn in one of her few snobbish moments. 'We're not so poor as that!' But some lads jumped at the chance. Jim Bellis, I remember, was hired at the shooting gallery by a Romany woman, and business turned out brisk indeed. After an eight-hour stint the owner took her assistant into a caravan, gave him a good meal, then – 'Right! Empty your pockets!' He did so, to reveal nothing that wasn't his own. 'You're an honest boy,' the gypsy said, and handed him 2s 6d. 'Come again tomorrow.' Outside on the street Jim removed two shillings in small silver from his left clog and 1s 6d from the right: a profitable day's labour. The next evening after work he stood again in the caravan. 'Take your clogs off!' ordered his employer. She collected the pilferings, slapped his face and hurled the footwear far into the night. Jimmy soon found the first clog, but it took him twenty minutes, he complained later, to trace the other, searching painfully over cinders.

Soon after our second piano arrived Father decided his eldest son should take lessons, despite the fact that, though loving music, I showed no practical aptitude at all. After the first ninepennyworth of tuition, however, his plan collapsed. Up to the age of ten (an ideal time, he thought, to start learning the piano and keeping me inside) I'd had a passion for scaling any local obstacle that seemed climbable. This led one day to impalement. In a morning of 'Teachers' Rest', idling along outside a railed strip of garden at the mission

64

church, I spotted no fewer than four 'American' butterflies upon some Michaelmas daisies. Unaware of the perennial lure these flowers hold for the red admiral, I considered this event unique in nature. And what a prize! Four rare butterflies at one and the same time down Salford! A wild lust took me to have this lot prisoned in matchboxes to the dazzlement of my peers. I climbed up the spear-like barrier, slipped, and slid to the ground, lifting my arm off a spike to feel a hot gush of blood coursing past the left wrist. I pulled back my sleeve: a wound gaped below the elbow, and in it sinews like fiddle strings moved with my fingers; all of which sent me home howling alarm.

My mother was ill in bed. Mrs Tabley, a neighbour, wrapped the gash in a Turkish towel and we rushed off on foot to the hospital half a mile away. They put fourteen stitches in the arm while I sat dumb with fear, not through my injury, but petrified by the bevy of white vestments around. 'You're a brave boy!' said the head stitcher at the end. 'You ought to be at the Front!' and, turning to Mrs Tabley, 'We can't take your son in, I'm afraid, we've military casualties even lying on the floors.' The lady said she 'understood'. A tall, heavy woman, she took me home slowly in the rain, my head under her shawl, face against the wall of her corsets. Sick and light-headed through loss of blood, I walked half-fainting. And in an effort to soothe, perhaps, all the way she sang softly to herself, the same tune, over and over again; a new ditty to me:

> Sons of the sea, all British born,
> Sailing every ocean, laughing foes to scorn,
> They may build their ships, my lads,
> And think they know the game,
> But they can't beat the boys of the bulldog breed,
> Who made old England's name!

I drifted along, eyes closed, in and out of awareness, left arm burning in its sling, while the chant droned on above. Soon her words tangled in my brain, irritating. That second line – 'laughing foes to scorn'. Why *should* foes 'laugh', I wondered feverishly, and our men 'scorn' them? Weary, I didn't want to think about it, but heated fancy insisted on sending a British man-o'-war stiff with sailors, noses in the air, to slide past German battleships whose crews stood pointing and rolling about with merriment. Surely war wasn't like that! Didn't they attack each other on sight? Didn't they . . . Suddenly I pushed my head into the rain. 'I wanna be sick!'

'Here's a grid, love,' said Mrs Tabley, all real concern. Then on again under the shawl – 'Sons of the seeeeeea! . . .'

Some days afterwards three white-coats stood in their dispensary arguing whether or not to amputate the limb, which, my escort told me, had 'taken bad ways'. 'Mortification,' the doctors said to one another. They didn't think I knew. But wounded soldiers were dying of 'mortification' on battlefields: the newspapers at home said so. Two doctors were for the deed; one, the tall one, much against. 'We'll have him in twice a day,' he said, persuading the others, 'and see how we go on.'

For a fortnight they treated me, morning and afternoon, rubbing something called bluestone round the wound, then, after the crisis had passed, once every day until well into the winter. A hundred or more casualties sat each morning along forms in a great barn of a hall. When it grew too chilly the younger of us sneaked off to warm ourselves by the wall pipes, watching out for a surly hall porter-in-charge, who rushed in from time to time calling, 'Siddown! Keep yer place! Everybody siddown!' One day a young man entered stiff-legged with a stick and, not attempting to take a seat, leaned himself, shoulders rigid, against a wall, a foot or so from a deep door recess. The porter came in and went over. 'Get sat on the form!' he ordered. 'I can't sit down, mister,' the patient said. At once the porter pushed him hard. 'Siddown, I said!' The man's shoulders slid in an arc along the painted wall and he fell with a scream of pain into the door recess, staggering white-faced to his feet to hit the official full on the jaw. He buckled at the knees and collapsed in his turn. We got up from the benches, the place in uproar. Nurses, men in white coats appeared and, soon, attendants with a stretcher to take away the patient, fallen again. Then a dozen explanations from all sides to the staff. Next morning we heard with great satisfaction that the hall porter had been sacked on the spot. Furthermore 'patients may stand by the wall pipes whenever they so wish'.

By the time my arm got better, months after, the Old Man had ceased to see me as a virtuoso of the pianoforte. My mother had saved half a sovereign towards a violin for one of the girls; but she gave it to Mrs Tabley. 'It's as little as we can do,' she said. This annoyed Father, who dreamed of seeing at least one of his children mount the concert platform, preferably in the Free Trade Hall. To that end he had hardened himself for any sacrifice his wife might care to make. 'That damned nuisance!' he grumbled several times. 'If it's not one thing with him, it's another.'

'True!' my mother snapped at last. 'I'm sure he stuck his arm in that spike on purpose! Look!' She slipped off my jacket, rolled up the left shirtsleeve and showed him for the first time the great livid scar that sliced across my forearm. Father gazed at it, startled, then joked feebly. 'Well! Well! If he ever gets lost we'll be able to tell him by that, all right.'

FIRE AND FOOD

ONE of our tick customers, Maggie Carey, had six children, a mother and a husband, Mick, who earned eighteen shillings a week labouring in a local iron foundry. Out of this sum he required two and sixpence for his beer and tobacco. On what remained Maggie fed, clothed and housed nine people. In winter, however, income was supplemented by the efforts of an eleven-year-old son, Sydney, who worked part-time at a coal yard. This brought in two shillings and half a hundredweight of fuel each week.

A woman of worth, an intelligent illiterate, Mrs Carey looked upon the credit connection with our shop as a very lifeline. Saturday nights Mother reckoned up her tick book. Maggie paid from a little cloth purse, usually handing over every penny it held. She left the shop 'skint' but happy, with enough basic foodstuffs in an apron (not owning a shopping bag) to see them through the following week. On Monday morning clothes would be pawned to get money for the gas, coal and burial club. 'A full belly and a warm backside,' Mrs Carey would announce, 'that's all our lot want! I got a sheep's head boiling on the hob and a hundredweight o' nuts in the backyard. What more could folks wish for in winter?'

Food and warmth! After bread, fuel was the greatest worry

in our world. No wonder a piece of coal found in the street
was looked upon as a sure sign of good luck. Until the first
world war brought a sort of prosperity to the shop we, like
most others in the neighbourhood, got our fuel by hand-
drawn wagon from local 'yards', or rather, gloomy sheds,
where hills of coal ranged in grades from 'slack' to 'cobs'. A
cabin stood in one corner, candle-lit. Usually the owner sat
there before a stove dull red with heat and took the money,
while some boy did the work, shovelling coal into the 'scope'
of a great balance, then tipping it into your wagon, loaned
by the establishment.

I got up one morning in a winter just before the first world
war to find we had no coal in the house at all. And the miners
were on strike. Mother, I remember, stood before the grate,
burning showcards from out of the shop. 'When you've had
breakfast,' she said, 'just go round the yards, will you, and
see if you can get anything at all to burn.'

Though she never ordered but always asked one, the
request irked me: I had other plans for the morning. 'There
are more people than me in this house, aren't there?' I asked.

'There are,' she agreed, 'and one of them has a strap!'

'I don't see why we can't get coal in bags like other folk.'

'We'll get coal in bags,' she told me, 'when we get cash in
bags. I'm not the bookie's wife!' The shop bell rang. 'See to
that, will you,' she said to Janie.

Sulkily I stared through the kitchen doorway into the shop.
My sister leaned over the counter, took a jam jar from a
small boy and slid a penny out of it. ('Always tip a jar,' my
mother had instructed us. 'It's a nuisance when you put milk
or jam or mustard pickles in one, then the money's at the
bottom.') Janie filled his receptacle with milk from a large
yellow mug, stirring the contents beforehand to distribute an
overnight layer of cream and dust so that everyone would
get a fair share. The customer served, Jane indulged a habit
that none of us other children ever imitated. 'Of course, we
don't take things from the shop,' Mother had told us. 'If we
all did that I'd just be working for nothing.' Janie popped a
jujube into her mouth, chased it down with a crumble of
cheese, stabbed her index finger into a seven-pound pot of
jam, licked it, drove and licked again, then returned, all
innocence, to the kitchen.

Breakfast we took seated, Mother scorning the idea common
at the time that children should stand at the table for meals

as an exercise in discipline. 'They were fighting at the gas-works for coke yesterday!' said Ellie. 'Police there, and everything. Real fighting.'

'Folk are very short of fuel,' Mother said, 'and it's perishing weather. There'll be trouble yet.'

'Trouble? I could borrow a wagon,' I said eagerly, 'and go and fetch some coke!' Ada kindly decided to come with me to help in the pulling.

Syd Carey, a friend though frowned upon by my father as 'low class', lounged by the coal-yard gate. Inside, the proprietor sat by his stove, making toast. 'We got nothing,' Sydney told me, 'and no yards around, neither. There's only coke.' He chose for us a free-running wagon from the rank, I handed him twopence and we made at once for the gas-works. About two hundred others had arrived already, early though it was, with pushcarts, converted soap boxes, bassinets – anything on wheels. In a bitter morning, ice frozen in the gutters, we queued along a wall, enveloped from time to time by a stinking vapour that curled over from the other side. Well ahead, I could see several of our professional coke fetchers – Mrs Temple, an old woman with her own vehicle, a high-sided wagon, in which she would bring anyone two hundredweight of coke for a fee of threepence. And Sally Johns, or 'Suckegg!', as we children called her, a raw-boned, sullen girl in her late teens, 'too daft', they said, to send out to work. She spent her winter days dragging fuel like an animal. Often street lads baited her. Sometimes, to their joy, Sally stopped and hurtled coke and obscenities at them, but usually she passed on, straining between shafts, head down, muttering. 'Class', of course, entered into domestic heating as into everything else: coke, though cheap, was hard to ignite and often unsatisfactory in the grate – a fuel of poverty. Many people boasted of never using it. But now they were glad of anything burnable.

The day before our visit supplies at the gasworks had run out early, causing a small riot among those who had waited hours in vain. But now, over the bridge and round the corner, loomed authority – a massive sergeant with two constables. Slow, majestic, followed by his men, he came along the line. 'Get back to that wall!' he ordered, 'an' just let one of yer step out today, an' I'll 'ave 'im! Just one, that's all!'

We cowered close, submissive, silent; women and boys for the most part. Stout and well wrapped, his mightiness sailed on; but only a few yards, then: 'Officer! Officer!' Mrs Rayburn, a scraggy little woman half lost in a shawl, was calling him urgently. He turned and proceeded back. 'What is it, woman? And "Sergeant" to you!'

'Oh, Sergeant,' she said wistfully, 'I'd love to put my cold feet on your big warm belly!'

We shouted with laughter while the 'law', turning puce, wheeled about and marched off, not to reappear. After a wait of two hours each of us got our four pennyworth of coke, enough to keep home fires burning for a few more winter days.

For all Mrs Carey's pride in the warmth of her family, one member of it remained unsatisfied. Sitting in his 'oil-heated detached' half a century later, Sydney looked back and grumbled. Syd was eloquent on the 'good old days'. 'In winter,' he said, 'I couldn't get near the damned grate! There were the old folk crouching over a fire about as big as a pudding basin and, squeezed in between, all Mother Carey's chickens! "How about me havin' a sniff?" I'd ask. "Any road, who brought that coal home? I'm cold!"'

' "Any more lip," the Old Man would tell me, "and you'll be warm enough!"'

'Then they'd edge me in at the back. I was getting more heat from Mars! And that mutton on the hob our old lady used to swank about! Have *you* ever had one ninth part of a sheep's head after Father's eaten the tongue? We did better for protein when she cooked twopenn'orth of "lips and lugs"!' Then, eggs, Sydney remembered! 'I'd be sent to your shop to get four. Of these Father Bear ate two – fried! Mother and the "old queen" [grandmother] had one between them, and the fourth, very lightly boiled, was broken on a saucer and "painted" on to *six* "shives" of bread. It was like eating a yellow shadow with salt on!'

Syd's father, in keeping with tradition, reigned supreme over his household. Total male dominance occurred perhaps more often in ultra-conservative lower-working-class families than in any other reach of Edwardian society. Of course, friendly fathers abounded there, too: they loved their children and had affection returned. But love within the strictly conforming families always went with subservience. The 'man of the house' compelled fear and respect, first as father, the great provider, then as dealer-out of punishment. Such men were standard figures in our community as elsewhere.

Generally the wife and mother, as secondary power, played a very subordinate role. She called her husband 'my boss' or 'my master' and sought to satisfy his every whim. While the top male – father, husband or eldest son – lorded it over a household, a shift in economic power weakened status seriously. Mrs Darby, a widow who used to wash for us, had a son, a good-natured, stupid lad, who through his teens couldn't keep any job for long. Until maturity it was his mother's slaving as a laundress that saved him from the workhouse. Though assertive enough with others, at twenty-one Albert still responded to her in everything as obediently as a biddable small child. Eventually finding regular work on the railway, he married a barmaid who brought her illegitimate daughter into his mother's home. The child, of course, undermined his wife's position from the start. Mrs Darby, still in charge, continued to do some washing professionally, but from the marriage day until her death thirty years later she remained head of the house and, after a drink or two, would make the fact publicly known. 'Is the Missis in?' a friend of her daughter-in-law's once asked at the doorway.

'I'm t'Missis, 'ere!' the old lady screeched, 'and t' bloody Master, an' all!'

This primacy, founded on a few sticks of furniture, a name in the rent book and earlier economic power, both husband and wife meekly accepted for a lifetime. Often the very poor would openly expose certain social relationships in this way while richer families no more than hinted, or revealed them only in dispute.

After excessive drinking, food was the greatest source of local friction. A boozed-up husband coming in hours late would frequently complain about a meal kept warm for him, or would push it away untouched. This habit women in the shop constantly bemoaned. 'What can you do? Jack's that funny with his food. You can't please him.' If a dinner was rejected most wives prepared an alternative dish, in an effort to suit the great one's palate. Others wept as he stamped off to bed, the children dodging out of his path.

To restore Mick Carey's good humour at all costs his wife used to come hurrying, anxious, to the shop. 'A nice bit o' lean boiled ham, love, for my master's tea, a new loaf and a penn'orth o' mustard pickles. He came in kettled – wouldn't have his dinner again!' Not every woman, though, accepted the almighty male with subservience and tears. Bolder wives boasted at the counter of presenting the drunken latecomer with a burnt offering. One lady, as soon as her 'boss' turned down his meal, called a hungry dog in from next door to polish it off on the spot. This infuriated and cured him. Mrs Huntley, who stood six feet and weighed fifteen stone, merely inverted a plate of hash over her spouse's head. I don't recall any of these husbands getting ham and pickles afterwards.

Certainly a husband ate both the best and the largest share of whatever food came in, on the grounds that his work demanded a maintenance of strength, and it is true that many men worked daily close to the limits of physical endurance. Nevertheless a few women refused to deprive their children in order to feed a male well. Through many married years an aunt of ours (my mother's sister) battled with her husband for equity in food. 'When we're lucky,' she told him, 'and it's meat, we *all* have meat. But when it's only cabbage we *all* have cabbage!' This heresy scandalized the housewives around. They pitied 'poor Alf', who dined *en famille* with the air of a Christian martyr; but unlike Syd Carey, all his children looked the better for it.

Some 'sluts', and better-off women with children earning, avoided cookery by getting 'master' a fourpenny dinner in a basin from the cookshop. In good times Mrs Layton's, on the main way, did thriving trade, though on one notable occasion she shocked even our neighbourhood, delighted us youth and suffered a setback in business all at the same time. Her Monday's menu usually consisted of two dishes: boiled pork ribs and cabbage, and the roast beef of old Argentine with trimmings. Late Saturdays she always had the baker make a massive Yorkshire pudding more than two feet square. To whet the appetite of passing natives over the weekend, this she put on show in the middle of her shop window, delicately drawing curtains behind.

It sat in single state, a soft yellow cushion. Then one Sunday morning, catastrophe! A small Catholic group coming from early Mass passed the window, stopped, gazed at her confection and gasped in horror. The shop cat was busily engaged in having kittens upon it! Some carping neighbours later offered criticism of our restauratrice on the score of hygiene, but this Mrs Layton rejected. It was, she said indignantly, an 'act of God', a thing that could have happened 'in any cookshop'!

LOW CLASS AND NO CLASS

IN youth I knew Sydney Carey as a squat, emaciated lad, a 'bad lot' in adult eyes, who had tangled with the law several times before leaving school. Syd was a boy who seemed to crave warmth of any sort. Whenever of an evening we climbed together into the abandoned brickfield that ran the length of our gasworks, he had one thought in mind – to make, as we called it, a 'jeremiah'. From various pockets he would take tram tickets, cigarette packets, slivers of wood and coal bits from the yard, thumbnail-large. I supplied the match. Soon flames curled up before us. Sydney would crouch as if at an altar, delicately adding scraps of fuel. Then, eyes shining, he spread his hands before the heat. Many years afterwards, teaching in prison, I chatted with inmates gaoled for what appeared to be purposeless arson, and each spoke of this same enthralment with fire during childhood. Not that Sydney turned into a pyromaniac; a single event in early youth seemed to have cured him for good. By error one January night he gave the village its greatest blaze.

At that time I was in business on my own account, a sort of 'middleman' to the metal trade. A scrap merchant had taken to storing old iron in a yard close by. To keep stocks mobile I used to scale the 'boards' at dusk, select a few portable pieces, and sell them next day for a copper to his competitor. On one occasion I re-acquired a corner bracket from the party of the second part and offered it again to the original owner, who snapped it up because, he said, he'd 'just the match for it somewhere!' This transaction gave me pleasure above the penny received: I had visions of selling it back to them indefinitely until each felt he had a plethora of corner brackets; but caution told me once was enough. The work itself was hard and profits small, but gratifying – until my mother found out!

Peeping over the scrap-yard fence one evening to see how the land lay, I spotted Syd alone, across an empty alley lined by stables and a large hay and straw store. In a recess made by great double doors and a wall he stood pushing a pyre of chaff together with his feet. He squatted, struck a match and, as usual, began to feed the flames from the contents of his pockets, adding oblations of coal. I was about to call when a piece of paper, big as a rabbit, came lolloping towards him on a snatch of air. Sydney whipped round, grabbed, missed, then caught it and pressed his capture quickly into a ball. He turned and I saw him stand, astonished, looking at the ground; his little fire had completely disappeared! Then he understood – the same wind bearing the litter had whipped his blaze under the storehouse doors. He lay flat and peered beneath, got up, dusted chaff from his jersey, scratched himself and moved slowly away. Twenty yards on Sydney stopped, turned, came back and lay prone again, gazing once more. What he saw made him shoot straight into the air and scutter for his life. Dropping my wares, I too fled over the boards and away. Half an hour later the alley was an inferno.

This was far too big a thing to rest on my mind. That night after going upstairs I sat swinging my legs on the bed, reluctant to get in. 'Come along, then,' my mother said. 'What is it? A trouble shared is a trouble doubled!' Then, hearing my whispers out, 'Don't mention it to anyone,' she told me. 'Poor Mrs Carey has enough on her plate.'

Sydney and his Anglo-Irish sept stood very low in our social league, where families like ours sunned themselves in the premier ranks. But happily for him he had someone to look down on: Ignatius Welby didn't figure in the register at all. Son of a drab, he lived over the iron bridge, in two rooms behind some lodging houses. Once when 'Ig' didn't appear in school, a frequent event, the headmaster sent me to fetch him. The poverty of his home shook even me. On a bare flagstone floor I saw three soap boxes, a packing-case table and no other furniture at all. By the grate Ignatius was sitting looking very sulky indeed. An almost naked child in urgent need of attention crawled about him. Out of the inner room a gaunt woman appeared, up to the elbows in suds.

'Tell Teacher,' she screeched, 'he can't come till he's cleaned that lot up!' She pointed to three cones of baby faeces on the flags.

Ignatius, sunk in his men's clothes, sat dignified and turned to me. 'It's not my job, see! It just isn't my job!'

This was no scene to report back to the squeamish middle classes! 'Welby had to go to the dispensary, sir!' I told the Head.

At times, on summer nights, Ig slept in a corrugated iron 'tent' we had put up in the brick-hills. Occasionally he climbed back over the wall and made sorties into our area, seeking human contact. The shortest way to a belting in any Christian home was to be noted in his company. At sight of him in the street you crossed over. He would come rushing to the corner as if on some errand of vital importance, then pull up dead and stand looking this way and that. After a while, the world ignoring his existence, he sauntered off. 'Let me see you with that one,' my father would say, eyeing his passage along the shop window, 'and won't you get what for!'

But Ig, unfortunately for the Old Man, had qualities which his son found attractive – a wistful fancy, for one, and an interest, besides, that was near obsessional in small living things. Of similar bent myself, I would, at times, seek him out, but advised caution. Once, having caught an outsize 'cabbage white', he came and hung about our shop corner until Mrs Carey, passing on an errand, took him by the ear and abused him roughly. From our kitchen window I saw Ignatius jerk away and disappear. She came indignant into the shop.

'I've been wantin' a word with that!' she said. 'It's him what put our Sydney up to pinchin' fruit from the sidings. Four strokes of the birch for four bananas!'

'That Welby should be put away permanent,' my father said. 'The lowest of the low. Them lads o' mine daren't go near him. They know a thing worth two of it!'

'My word! And so does our Sydney now!'

Soon after, Syd and I sat in the iron tent. 'You could have got me into trouble,' I told Ig. 'Don't, for cripes' sake, keep hanging round the shop. The Old Man sees you and it's yap, yap, yap!'

Ignatius then expressed the view, as he often did, that people 'only looked down' because his father kept going to Strangeways.

'And what about your ma?' Sydney would ask reprovingly. Our friend always looked hurt at this.

Once I complained to him about school. 'When you *do* come,' I said, 'don't edge round and sit near me *every* time!'

'Is it because I stink?' he asked.

His 'off-put', in fact, didn't trouble me at all; but one of my sisters, seeing us together, would always tell-tale it back home. 'Watch what you're about,' Mother used to say. 'We don't want the police round.' 'He's a poor soul,' she remarked once, ' – knocked about from pillar to post. But with Father you'd never hear the last of it!'

Ignatius, like Sydney, kept small receptacles about him, but for more positive reasons. He'd shuffle up to one, smiling, and, opening a matchbox, reveal an insect, his latest capture, clawing feebly on its back. 'A bumble bee!' he'd say reverently. 'Never seen one that close before, have you? And that's only one!' Then, from another pocket, a Beecham's Pill case. He'd screw off the cap and show a dragonfly, battered and dead. 'I had to slap it one.' He didn't like to kill things and always released live prisoners after display. 'Nat, Nat, the naturalist!' we chanted at him, 'All the way from Botany Bay!' and he gave us a watery smile of pleasure.

Once in a hot summer Ignatius stayed off school for nearly six weeks until, dropping over the brickfield wall one day, he fell into the arms of a School Board man and was hauled back, filthy and odorous, to the class. Big Hales, who ran Standard VI, drew a chalk circle round him and, as he knelt cowering in his men's wear, beat him with a cane until he grew vague in a cloud of dust. Iggy went on crouching there, two small boxes from his person now lying in the ring. Half an hour later, with the teacher's head turned, he stuck out his scraggy neck and gave us all a smile. Some of us smiled back.

One day, collecting books after class, I listened in on the headmaster, with Mr Hales, giving Ig's character a going over. 'We get the lowest class as it is, mostly,' he said, 'but a boy from a home of that kind!'

'One like him,' said Hales, 'could ruin the whole school!'

This puzzled me a lot. Iggy, we recognized, appeared 'scruffy' and often stank, but he was, we all felt, a nice enough lad. How he could 'ruin' anyone I couldn't imagine. 'Sin', one knew, had direct connection with sex, or with what older boys referred to darkly as 'that there!' And sin abounded, even in school itself. Already, to discourage some 250 lads from using our half-dozen privies, where it seemed especially to flourish, authority had dispensed with both doors and paper; toilet rolls were, of course, unknown either at home or at school. After one discussion with Hales the Head called me over.

'You monitors still keeping good watch on those "offices" at playtime, are you?'

'Oh, yessir,' I said. 'We're allus watchin'.'

'Tell them to report to me any boy who stays in a closet more than two or three minutes. Understand? Have those peeing competitions in the urinal stopped?' he asked, looking stern.

'Oh, yessir!' I lied. 'All that's finished now.'

Had he known that in this sport the school outcast stood all-comers' champion, having hit a brick with a stream of effluent eight feet above ground level, his fears about Ig would have found ample substance.

The Head's social 'fixing' of his pupils had much intrigued me. 'Old Rowley reckons,' I said one day at home, 'that we get the lowest class at our school.' The remark annoyed Father. 'I suppose,' he said, 'his family came over with the bloody Normans! You tell him from me, we're not all Welbys!'

Once, in a narrow entry that ran behind the street, Iggy wandered up to me with a black, snake-like object that jerked stiffly on his hands, then lay still, staring. I stepped back, afraid.

'It's a kitten,' he said. 'Some rotten pig's rolled it in hot pitch off the road! Now it's gone hard.'

'What – What can we do?' I asked.

'Your old lady,' he said, 'she's the one.' (Ignatius, for some reason, held my mother in awe and always assumed I feared her too.) He came with me to the entry end and I took it in at the back door. Face set, Mother examined the dreadful offering. 'Put it down,' she ordered at last. Then, going into the shop, she scooped up a lump of lard and dropped it into the frying pan. Soon we were kneading warm oil into the kitten's fur, after which she washed it with soap and water.

'How's the moggie?' Ignatius asked later.

'Like a lump of wool now!' I told him. 'We're going to keep it,' which seemed to please him.

One rainy afternoon when Father was working away I daringly invited our local Huck Finn* into the backyard,

* Several of us had enjoyed Mark Twain's masterpieces immensely, especially *Huckleberry Finn*. But Tom Sawyer, as a

and we squatted inside the hen-cote playing 'picture and blank' with cigarette cards. Hearing voices and laughter, Mother came from the scullery, spotted us both and frowned. 'Inside, you!' she said. Then, to my alarm, looking at Ig, 'And you too!' With surprising promptness he followed me. 'I don't know,' she said, 'which of you looks the dirtier!' By the scullery slopstone I stripped off jersey and shirt. 'Now have a good wash,' she told me, 'or I'll scrub you myself.' Then, turning to Iggy, 'You come with me, sonny, will you?' Chin down, he disappeared through our kitchen and upstairs into the bathroom, from where we heard nothing for half an hour. Then he bounced down happily, preceding my mother, cleansed almost to non-recognition. In one of my shirts and half a blanket he sat like a member of the family while she trimmed his hair, finger- and toenails. 'There!' she said at last. 'Put these trousers on. You're a fine new boy now!' Suddenly I realized that, after 'ordeal by water', Iggy, for all his low class, showed himself physically a far more attractive-looking lad than I could ever hope to be. And there he perched, shining up, while my mother titivated his 'monkey fringe' as if she owned him! A wave of jealousy poured in on me. 'Now I've asked Ignatius if he'll stay to tea with us,' she said. 'Look after him. He's our guest, you know.'

Ig gazed about in wonder, rocked by his *entrée* into the world of affluence – not a soap box in sight! And sitting there he projected such wide-eyed humility that my jealousy ebbed and gave place to a feeling of pride in possession. Class-consciousness had arrived! I watched him as he stared, and no lordling in his ancestral home could have felt smugger. First Iggy goggled at our overmantel, a late-Victorian baroque structure in mahogany, bracketed and loaded almost to the ceiling with porcelain splendour.

'What's all them?' he whispered.

'Mixed ornaments,' I said carelessly. 'Boats, dogs, fruit bowls, statuettes. Worth hundreds o' pounds!'

Janie lit three gas mantles hanging from one of the two

person, I found vaguely unsatisfactory. Like another hero, Harry Wharton, he seemed singularly free from all those inner pressures which disturbed us, and, while our 'morals' wanted it that way, these paragons left us feeling that little more guilt-ridden. Nineteenth-century *mores* had in fact compelled Twain to omit entirely any reference to the vital part of a boy's make-up.

candelabra in mid-ceiling, and the towering faience sparkled white and gold. Mother called this little lot the 'pot stall'; but her husband loved our display. It gave the room, he felt, a distinction unmatched even in any of the pub kitchens around. Folk came in just to admire. Unfortunately some months before, in a drunken fury, he had taken a swipe with a beer bottle at its lower pomp. Carnage had been great. Even a prized cast of William Ewart Gladstone had gone up in an eruption of glazed china which my brother likened to an explosion in a public convenience. Later, full of regret, Father had filled in the gaps, and Iggy gaped now, speechless before such grandeur. Next I pointed out to him our array of brass-handled fire-irons and the copper kettle gleaming on its 'toadstool' in the hearth. Then I demonstrated the uniqueness of our spring window blind – a mere flick and it soared out of sight: no hand rolling, as in commoner houses. As the girls set table for tea on a white cloth, Ig's eye examined our picture-lined walls, the mirrors, the sewing machine, and landed finally on the piano, with its rich gilt candlesticks. No obeisance to ownership could have been more sincere. Mother was toasting crumpets at the fire. 'Play a tune, Jane, will you,' she asked, 'for Ignatius?' Janie obliged, singing too, and Ellie joined in harmony:

> There was a youth, a well-beloved youth,
> And he was a squire's son . . .

And Tibby came and jumped on to the sofa where Ignatius sat. Mother remarked on it, smiling, all the time trying to make him feel at home – really one of us. Far too chatty, I felt. After all, it was only Ig Welby! Why this fuss? Pangs of jealousy struck again, mingling with mean satisfaction: whatever he might be dreaming, she *wasn't* his mother and Ig *didn't* live here; he belonged to the woman with the soap suds on her elbows. Then we had tea – egg and bacon, crumpets, watercress and jam. Ig detailed them long after. And he'd never used a knife and fork before. Quickly Mother removed them, cut up his bacon, mine too, and pushed us each a dessert spoon: Ig was here to stuff himself, not to learn table manners. I opened my mouth in protest. Couldn't I eat properly? She shook her head at me, and I took the spoon. And now Janie turned stand-offish, not caring, she said afterwards, for 'scruff', but Ellie and Ada talked all the while and said how nice it was of Iggy about the kitten.

After tea I taught him how to play ludo and snakes and ladders, on the dresser. Splendid entertainment he thought them. Then we took down a small Columbian zither Father had bought from a pawnshop, but none of us could play it, and Iggy plucked out 'God save the King'. Confidentially he began to whisper about the bath. An amazing discovery! Two taps – 'hot' and 'cold' – a moving bridge across it, with a brush and soap and sponge; a round stopper and chain. You could lie in it easily! His gormlessness exasperated me. Didn't I know, I said – our own bath! 'She never has me out of it!' But ours was the first Ig had ever seen. By now it was nine o'clock. We ate arrowroot wafers and had a glass of milk apiece. Time for my bed, Mother told us.

A lifetime afterwards we talked of that evening again, Ignatius in prison, with me his tutor. He remembered it all. 'Standing in the dark after,' he said, 'it was like being turned out of heaven!' What *I* recalled after his leaving us was that Mother had found him, as she told me quietly, 'not very clean'. 'Don't make a show of it, but you should try not to touch the poor lad. It's no fault of his.' All our school life she fought to avoid the disgrace of getting an official 'green card' which would indicate that a child of hers had been designated 'verminous'. One of her minor triumphs was that such notification never arrived, despite the fact that we all sat regularly through classes where three-quarters of the pupils, at least, had lice-ridden hair. She had taken preventive action early.

When Janie first went to school Mother had summoned a doctor, paying cash, and got a powerful recipe against the evil. Over the years all of us, in our time, went once a fortnight to a chemist's near Salford town hall and requisitioned a 'penn'orth o' powder – Red Precipitate' (how it tripped off the tongue!), ' – a ha'p'orth o' white wax, and twopenn'orth o' rose water in this bottle', the last item being a mere placebo. Janie remembered fancying a change once and asking for 'otto of roses'. The chemist, a most courteous old man, smiled down on her. 'Tell your mother, my dear, that "attar" runs out at one guinea an ounce. For twopence I couldn't let you smell the cork!' Every weekend Mother mixed these ingredients into a paste and immediately after bath-hour rubbed the stuff so vigorously into our scalps that tears brimmed on eyelids. 'You'll get no green card with Red

Precipitate,' she used to assure us. 'It's strong enough to kill tigers!' The mixture, well applied, would have performed sterling service in many of the homes around.

In judging the 'class' of a house one had to assess the particular aura that emanated from it, and children developed this sense mainly through evaluating the remarks of adults. Whatever its class rating, we knew, without being told, that a household comprising parents and from two to ten or more children was accepted as our social norm. Any 'cousins' or step-siblings included therein would need, at some time, to be accounted for to the neighbours, who would judge among themselves whether such 'explanations' seemed likely to be true. The presence in a house of anyone other than parents and fully acknowledged 'legitimates' always pushed a family off centre; even a grandparent within a group could cause certain imbalance. The childless married couple we young-sters recognized as 'strange'. Lack of family, with higher economic standing (the wife usually went out to work), separated them from the social mainstream. A certain mystery hung about their homes, so often locked and silent. When a pair went out together, to the envy of local wives, we looked up for a moment from our games and wondered a little. Why no children? Didn't they *want* a baby? Or they couldn't have one, perhaps – or didn't know how! Did they pass by a little shamefaced? You saw housewives smile at each other. There was something peculiar about them, for sure!

We had those houses, too, where one or more 'old maids' lived together without a man. They usually kept their windows, doors, step and pavement scrupulously clean and invariably became the butts of some local housewives who sneered about 'old faggots' with nothing better to do. Spinsters deprived of male protection suffered constantly from the tricks of children trading on parental indulgence, and their lives could be made a misery. Many single women, middle-aged and elderly, through the mere fact of being single had much to put up with from the taunts of youth and the amused contempt of some married neighbours – a sort of cruelty that would not be tolerated today.

Then our district, like all others of the same kind, featured one or two of those families, often large, in which the mother had become a cypher. Worn out, perhaps, by too much child bearing, or broken by chronic disease, she had lost all authority, her powers, privileges and duties (*all* duties?) being taken over by an eldest daughter. The husband might still remain in the full vigour of life. Neighbours noted these father-daughter relationships closely, watching for the mutual smiles, gestures, intimacies, indeed any little sign which might indicate a regard that passed beyond the paternal or filial. Some women were experts at this sort of detection. Usually, of course, the interrelationship passed muster – everything stood above board. Now and then, however, suspicion would grow into certainty and a family's status begin to crumble swiftly, a fall which youngsters would eventually feel without at all knowing the reasons for it.

Those retired domestic servants who lived among us after long years serving the 'quality' had homes which, like shows at the local theatre, were almost invariably 'very poor but very clean'. Few servants anywhere received retirement pensions from grateful masters; statisticians, in fact, had expressed surprise at the number of superannuated domestics ending their days in English workhouses. Some were glad to get a house in an area even as poor as ours. Generally sprucer and tidier in habit than those about them, they possessed certain skills in cooking, sewing, knitting and even in simple medicine which they passed on to grateful families near by. For the most part royalist, ultra-Conservative politically and deeply class-conscious, they looked down with despisal on the masses – a contempt returned, by skilled workers, with interest. Nevertheless retired servants were many and their total influence as opinion-formers within the lower working class may well have been considerable. Such people were, by and large, the apologists and expositors of the whole class system of the time.

All those houses which harboured 'paying guests' we duly marked. The very word 'lodger' stood, so to speak, pregnant with meaning. In plain fact, of course, many single men spent all their mature lives in other people's homes in a relationship which, despite close quarters, always remained platonic. But circumstances offered scope for scandal, and malicious tongues made the most of it. 'Three evils,' one learned judge had said, 'most commonly break up marriages; they are selfishness, greed and lodgers.' Our moralists couldn't have agreed more. Always when Mrs Slaney, a neighbour, let it be known in the shop that she had taken in 'another gentleman' silence fell upon her listeners like a shutter – a clear interval, during which several minds together held but a single thought. Elderly ladies with anything up to fifty years between them and their boarders would escape calumny, but few others. Childless married couples who gave house room to another man got the standard surveillance. Did the husband ever leave his missis alone with the lodger? If so, at what time and for how long? Did the lady walk out with him? Had they been spotted together anywhere – in the pictures, the park, or a pub? All these facts our matriarchs (and their husbands) required to know if the integrity of our area was to be fully safeguarded. In other *ménages à trois, à quatre*, or even more, where class standing was depressed and promiscuity confidently suspected, a good street row might have to blow up before the community could gauge precisely who was sleeping with whom. Then one's worst hopes were often confirmed. It was on such occasions that one beheld a woman striking a blow for true morality. She would rush out of the house bearing her 'marriage lines' aloft like a banner and so confound those of her opponents living 'tally'. Even to the lowest levels, in matters sexual, people strove to maintain a façade, for known nonconformity in sex could do more than anything else to damage one's prestige. Nobody, for instance, had any time at all socially for a lady who gaily buzzed it about that she had '*half* a bed to let!'

One husband, Erby Sloan, a 'low' type, in the 'Saturday-night soldiers' (Territorial Army), once shocked the district by giving notice of his intention to resolve publicly a marital set-up notorious even among us boys for its flouting of morals. At this prospect his wife, Abigail, a large, halting woman who sat hours on her doorstep, merely smiled. Abby, far gone in pregnancy at the time, had already presented her husband with four offspring, two raven-haired and two ginger. The latter complexion the infants shared with Harry, the Sloans' lodger, a sixteen-stone paviour of uncertain temper, though Mrs Sloan claimed that, 'out of drink', a nicer man never wore shoe leather. Now a fifth babe was imminent. People, winking at each other in pubs, sympathized with Herbert, pointing out delicately that should the newcomer turn out 'wrong' this time Big Harry would have an overall majority in the house and Erby might as well resign. Mr Sloan then laid it down that if he (all seven stone of him) returned from the TA annual camp and saw 'red' again, the kitchen would not hold both him and the lodger – a sentiment greeted warmly in the Vault of the Flagwall Inn. For the showdown, since Herbert only came up to his rival's armpits, he had called upon Cousin Jed, a known bruiser from Ancoats, who, Mr Sloan assured everyone, would knock cobblestones out of the lodger.

Well before her husband's return from a happy holiday at Aldershot, Abby was blessed again with, as the neighbours put it, 'another "ginger-bred"'. Looking round curtains and edging through doorways, they watched the warrior's stern arrival – up two steps and down the lobby – and watched, too, a minute later as he came hurtling back again into the open, with the shadow of the lodger hovering a moment under the lintel. When the coast was clear once more Mr Sloan came to stand guard in the street over hearth and home. Soon his cousin, a much larger man, appeared. Jed threw him his jacket, rolled sleeves and sailed up the lobby. Almost at once he too came scudding back, pursued by the paviour, grabbed his coat and vanished down an entry. After Harry's return his landlord went again and stood by, calling faint abuse up the passage. No crowd gathered about him. Even we boys kept clear, for here, everyone realized, was an affair quite private and personal. And so Herbert remained until his mother-in-law, an eirenic lady, arrived. Quickly she arranged both parley and reconciliation, and later in the evening all parties concerned got gloriously drunk.

A short time after this affair I overheard two women in the shop giving Abigail a going over. 'She's had the flamin' impudence,' said one, 'to go and get herself churched!'

The other gasped. 'She wants churchin', that one!'

I sought out sister Janie at once. 'What's churchin'?'

'Ask no questions,' she said, ' – get told no lies!'

In a later year one more, dark-haired, baby arrived, to leave the match all square.

Wives who sat overlong at their thresholds enjoying the passing show contravened established rule and were roundly condemned: 'Why don't the idle bitches go inside and get summat done!' Mrs Sloan came under special attack. Abby was not only lazy and immoral but a spendthrift; *and* she did the weekly wash on, of all days, Saturday! Most women could quote our version of the old rhyme:

Them as wash on Monday have all week to dry,

Them as wash on Tuesday do little that's awry,
Them as wash on Wednesday are not so much to blame,
Them as wash on Thursday are folk that wash for shame,
Them as wash on Friday most likely wash in need,

(They have no clean change, so take the clothes from their
backs.)

But them as wash on Saturday – they are sluts indeed!

And there were people who felt it their moral duty to
reprimand such trollops. One Saturday morning a plumber
went on a job down Mrs Sloan's entry. He caught sight of
Abby hanging out a few things on her backyard line. 'Are yer
late for this week, missis,' he jibed, 'or early for next?'

'Mind your own bloody business!' she told him.

'Ho! Ho! Yer late for this!'

Then again this lady had offended those about through her
weakness for buying 'lilies' in preference to 'bread'. Getting a
check in a weekly club at the local general store, she once
purchased two Marley horses (while her family were crying
out for clothing) and set them proudly on the chiffonier.
'Bloody bronze horses!' fumed her next-door neighbour, 'and
there's her eldest "selling calico"' (shirt lap hanging through
his trouser seat) 'and bloomers hanging in the backyard wi'
bloody big holes in 'em!' This was *too* much – a 'mixed'
marriage, feckless spending *and* washing at weekend! The
whole family hit social rock-bottom.

SINS OF THE FLESH

AMONG all us boys Ignatius was the one who lacked common
loyalties. In fact, except for spasmodic sessions with me, he
made no friends, joined no gang about us, and disappeared
altogether well before I left school. A haunter of cattle
markets, summer time saw him 'up in Craven', from where
he helped drovers to fetch livestock in, travelling by railway
truck. You almost forgot his existence, then one day he

would be noticed around again. His mother hardly caring where he went or what he did, Ig was a law unto himself. We, in our own group, modelled our fighting code generally on that of Harry Wharton and the Famous Five of the *Magnet* weekly, using, more or less, the honest fist alone. Not that fisticuffs occurred all that much: one sensed the pecking order, based mostly on age, and on the whole kept to it. In battle, where he wasn't much good, Iggy got a lad down simply to give him a kicking. What was the point otherwise? Most boys thought Ignatius too scruffy altogether and avoided him. One afternoon he offered to play goal for us in an *ad hoc* soccer match on the brickcroft. Now street clannishness was very strong: in any group activity boys from elsewhere were seldom admitted. But Iggy, for once, we accepted. Three times, however, in the course of play he left our goal unguarded to slip over the wall hard by. Though I rushed back in goal, as substitute, we lost disastrously. The team later fell to abuse and our captain, Bill Eccles, bawled him out.

Ig excused himself. 'I just went quick after a butterfly.'

'And the second time?'

'I wanted to pee bad, that's all – only away a minute.'

'And the third – away for good!'

Our goalie stood irresolute.

'You went,' said Bill distinctly, 'bashin' your bishop!'

Ignatius admitted the soft impeachment. This, we felt, wasn't the team spirit at all. When Ig turned up for a game again I suggested the forward line, to keep his mind more fully occupied; but they sent him to Coventry for putting pleasure before duty.

Many legends existed among us about masturbation, all aiming to warn against its dire effects, physical and mental. It was, we understood, the root cause in children of blindness, baldness and galloping consumption. Older lads told us of the fate of a boy 'down Ardwick' (details always remained vague), who, through over-activity, had fallen into a state of permanent turgescence. 'After six months' his mother (suspecting by now, presumably, that something was amiss) took him to the Royal Infirmary, where he had to undergo a 'big operation'. None of us seemed to enquire as to the outcome of this, nor about the patient's subsequent fate. Perhaps we felt that, after all, there were worse complaints.

Ignatius was the first boy I heard who spoke boldly and

without shame of his 'addiction', and though this pushed him even further beyond the social pale a few of us felt utter relief: Ig had performed a public service. Till then each had feared that he suffered from some sort of 'disease', secret and peculiar to himself alone.

Syd Carey, short on status as it was, seemed to find Iggy's 'lowness' much more irksome than I did, and often turned critical. 'He stinks real bad at times, and in them clothes, no wonder they get at you at home! Dead common, he is. You couldn't go nowhere with him!' I didn't understand this sudden urge for respectability until Sydney revealed it himself. A great reader, as I was, though forbidden by his father to join a public library, he acquired odd books through the 'open access' system made available by barrows at Shudehill market. Among volumes filched appeared a battered copy of *Scouting for Boys*. After reading it we both felt an overwhelming urge to assist Baden Powell in an organization where, we believed, our own brickhills experience would prove invaluable. We discussed the matter by our corrugated wigwam, Ignatius standing about respectfully.

'How about me joinin', then?' he asked.

Sydney showed his contempt. 'You! There's a uniform, for a start – fifteen shillings. Where'd you get that?'

Where *we* would get it Syd didn't mention. Not a single troop existed in our area; one had to make do with the Church of England Lads' Brigade, a much less glamorous affair. As easily the most respectable of the trio I went to offer our services at St John's, a troop in a lower-middle-class district beyond the tramlines, and duly reported back.

'Stuck up!' I said. 'I was the only one with clogs on!'

'But they didn't tell you to piss off?' asked Syd hopefully.

'You got to go to their church regular,' I told them, 'and buy a uniform inside a month.' This killed all hope; but, following the book, we formed three phantom patrols of our own and, overlooked by the giant gasholders, we spent days of joy undiluted among the dun heaps of earth which lay for us paradise enough.

That autumn Sydney, still hankering after the real thing, brought news of an obscure troop on the Manchester boundary in an area little better than our own. There, he gathered, uniform was not compulsory. Omitting to tell Ignatius, who would have dogged us and hung about the premises, we went and presented ourselves. The scoutmaster,

Mr Alloway, a virile, open-air type, welcomed us with surprising warmth. Dress, he said, didn't matter; that could come later. What counted in scouting was the spirit. 'Learn the Law!' he told us. 'Learn the knots!' They put us in the Eagle Patrol with boys much like ourselves, or rather, like me, for Sydney, just then at the end of his wardrobe, was looking poor by any but Ignatius standards. We came home, a rather long trek across Salford, cock-a-hoop at our acceptance. At once Sydney informed our common friend, and added, before he could open his mouth, 'They're full up with us!'

On a later visit Mr Alloway took Syd into his little sanctum and he returned, his split clogs replaced by a pair of bluchers. Another evening he came back done up in new corduroys and looking, I noted, rather thoughtful. Then came the test for our Tenderfoot badge. Each recruit had been coached separately.

'A scout is what?' asked Mr Alloway.

'A scout, sir,' we said, 'is pure!'

'Pure in what?'

'Pure, sir, in thought, word and deed.'

'Very good. But what does that mean *exactly*,' he asked, looking one straight in the eye, 'pure in *deed*?'

'Well, er . . .'

Then he told us. 'Health chats', he called them – 'health and mind!' But later in rough-and-tumble games our leader relaxed, handling us with a freedom which sometimes startled – a real romper!

Both Sydney and I remembered one such session with clarity. Threading our way home through narrow streets afterwards, our suspicions surfaced together. Conversation went something this wise.

'What's a tumbler?' Sydney asked me.

'A glass,' I told him. 'A beer glass.'

'Why can't he call it a beer glass, then!'

We walked a little dark lane together and turned the corner. Then, with sudden violence:

'I'm not puttin' nothink into a glass of ice-cold water!'

'Health an' mind?' I asked.

He nodded. We trudged on . . .

'There's a boy,' I said, 'what bent down to fasten his clog and both his hip bones snapped – through weakness!'

'In a wheelchair since,' said Syd, taking it up. 'He wasn't a scout, though.'

'Mr Alloway tell you?'

Syd nodded again. 'He told me plenty!'

'There's another lad what has to lie flat on his back. It's drained all the strength from his spine.'

Syd thought he had seen him. 'They shove him about in a sort o' wickerwork coffin on wheels – very pale. His face twitches.'

'Never walk no more, Mr Alloway says. *He* wasn't a scout . . . Since joinin' this lot,' I added, 'I been pretty pure myself – on and off.'

Sydney looked miserable. 'Not me. And it keeps you that thin!'

'Mr Alloway says we gotter fight and fight to master it. "I am the captain of my soul!" He said that two or three times.'

We walked through the dark and drizzle, each with his own thoughts.

'All the same,' said Sydney, 'I'm not pushin' nothink into no glasses of icy cold water! All flushed like that, then a shot o' cold right up the back – you could get pewmonia! . . .'

'. . . Some boys *do* go blind,' I told him. 'Some go right raving loony!' This prospect troubled me most of all. 'S-Syd,' I asked, 'does it come on you, do you think, all at once, this – going barmy?'

He twisted his features into a mad grin, snatched round in the air, whirled on a lamp post and ran at me, gibbering. I pretended to laugh, but he had scared me. Then he remembered Iggy's nerve-chilling tale about a lad, 'down London way', who had gone to bed one night quite sane, only to waken up 'screamin' batty. They had to put him in chains!'

'Perhaps his blood dried up,' I said. 'It does dry up the blood.' Sydney also recalled that it gave one pimples; but he went on insisting that the cold water application was 'cruel'. I reminded him that our scoutmaster had also recommended exercise with it. 'Say the Scout Law,' I told him, 'and go running and skipping and jumping like mad!'

'Gettin' sweatin' can't do you no good at all!' protested Syd.

'It cured Mr Alloway!'

'Mr Alloway isn't cured!' he said darkly. 'Health chats!

He's one o' the boys what make no noise, he is. You ask Iggy about 'em – he knows!' Then Sydney broadened my education. We decided finally that, in spite of all, we were still 'prepared', but not for everything! Carefully missing camp, Syd and I returned to the troop after summer break, only to find our leader had disappeared. A curate gathered us about him and explained that Mr Alloway had been compelled to resign for business reasons.

'He's gone away for a year,' I explained to Ignatius.

'He's gone for twelve months!' he said.

For all Iggy's knowledge of aberrant sexual practice, we felt his information on the normal, despite Mrs Welby's calling, was more picturesque than factual, especially his description of the role of the navel in parturition. 'They allus start on that to get the baby out, see?' As for the sex instruction to be had on the hearthstone, home stood a bulwark against the very thought of it. Of the feminine attractiveness and characteristics of my mother and sisters I remained totally unaware. In our family a prelapsarian state of innocence seemed to reign. On masturbation, menstruation, copulation or childbirth one never heard a single word. Yet I learned long after that both parents were considered 'rather forthright on sex' in adult company. With us children present, Father might refer to somebody as an old 'fornicator', but this, in the parlance of the times, had no sexual significance at all; it meant no more than a mealy-mouthed old swindler. Until I reached manhood my parents allowed themselves two 'sexual' references. Once, as a seven-year-old, I had just made water and was returning from the lavatory. My mother looked down at me and in icy tones said, 'When you do that you should pull the loose skin back.' The remark, in what seemed to me its utter pointlessness, left me mystified. Long after I had started work my father retailed a 'dirty' joke. In his own workshop, I knew, he indulged, like most other men, in all sorts of ribaldry, but now, looking round the kitchen to make sure no one else was in earshot, he told me, smiling, that his labourer, an illiterate old chap, always referred seriously to the Royal Technical College as the 'Testical' School. He then blushed down to his neck. We learned as children, and a good thing, too, in the world outside, especially from older boys in the street group. But even so, sexual facts stayed unauthenticated for us until Barney turned up.

Eighteen years of age, already married, Barney lived with his wife's large family in an alley behind the shop. A fortnight after their wedding day he lost his job as a labourer and could find no other. Undersized, ill dressed, hardly adolescent in mind, he was soon deprived in adult circles of what little status marriage had given him and fell, at night, into mixing with us senior boys on the street corner. When familiarity had loosened his tongue Barney whispered to one or two of us of sex, and specifically of his own intimacies. The 'first night', we were given to understand, had been a considerable ordeal. 'Neither of us knowed nothink, really!' They had occupied a single bed in a room which held, besides, the wife's parents, a grandmother and two younger brothers.

'Now Lucy didn't want it, see, 'cos it hurt; but she kep' on whisperin', "Go on! It's me duty now! Never mind me cryin', make me have it!" It's their duty, see?' Barney explained. 'But I had to put my hand over her mouth to stop her cryin' out, else we'd 've got a real showin' up!'

'How many times?' asked Eddie, breathless.

'Three times. All in the dark, o' course – very quiet!'

'And was it all right?' I enquired, my mind much disturbed.

'No,' said Barney, 'it wasn't. But it gets better later on.'

'And will you have a baby now?'

'She's four months gone already and her Old Pot-and-pan's dead mad, with me bein' out of collar. But what can yer do? It's natural, see?' And for us this was 'natural' history as we wanted it – straight from the 'bedrock'. Shortly after the child was born Barney got work again, pushing a handcart for a warehouse in town, and soon ceased even to acknowledge us in the street; but somehow we understood, and felt in no way affronted; Barney had become a man again. Only on one occasion afterwards did he speak to Sydney and me, and that for the strangest reason.

We both stood one winter's night at the top of Zinc Street, pressing our buttocks against bricks in a gable-end wall heated by a house fire within. A stout woman unknown to us passed, pushing a bassinet with two children in it, and disappeared round the corner. Soon afterwards Barney came from the same direction.

'You seen Mrs Danby – that missis with the two kids?'

'Just now,' I said, 'we seen her.'

He approached close in and grew secretive at once. 'She works packin' at our place, see? Her husband's in Mrs Jay's!* He reckons he's been workin' overtime, but his missis has found out what's on. She's come to get him!'

Barney had called upon us now, however, not merely to inform but with a request for our services. We went with him down the empty street. The bassinet stood on one pavement, Mrs Danby on the other, opposite our house of ill fame. Its window was darkened by a blind, but above the door gleamed a small semi-circular fanlight.

'These lads will give me a leg up,' whispered Barney. Stealthily we crept forward. He put his face to the wall and we hoisted him until, reaching transom level, he could see the kitchen revealed. And there he stayed, a full two minutes! Our arms began to ache. Something had certainly riveted him! At last I pinched his leg, and we slowly lowered our peeper to the ground. He stepped over to Mrs Danby. 'Is he,' he asked, 'a little bloke – dark, with a moustache and longish nose?'

'That's him!' she said grimly.

'He's there, all right!' Barney whispered, 'and so is Mrs Jay, and *she's* stark starin' naykt!'

Mrs Danby's next move gave me one of the shocks of my life. Wrapping a shawl about her, she hurled herself with a shriek at the window and with such force that the whole lower frame collapsed in a shatter of panes. The blind bellied. At once a light within was extinguished. 'Come out from that dirty ooer!' she screamed. 'Come out!'

Doors opened about us, neighbours began to gather fast. Barney vanished. We mingled with the growing group. Already I had enough sense, if the police came, not to be on the scene as a 'witness'. A male dressed in shirt and trousers, pushing a brace over his shoulder, appeared in Mrs Jay's doorway, clearly scared, but blustering.

'What the hell's all this?'

---

* This lady was the boldest and most attractive of the three or four professional women who dwelt among us and, years later we learned, the one whom our matriarchs frowned on most. It was bad enough for females to sin for money, but Mrs Jay performed for pleasure; and to get enjoyment out of it all was, as Jehovah once pointed out to Ezekiel, both 'whoresome and an abomination'. In this the Lord and the neighbours stood as one.

The woman rushed at him, stopped and gasped, then, swinging round, hurried across to her pram, shot up Zinc Street, and away round the corner. Whoever the gentleman might have been, it wasn't Mr Danby!

We discussed the matter afterwards, and I remember suggesting that 'There must be lots of little fellers with long noses', which brought us to 'Yids'. But Sydney discounted the possibility of our visitor having been Jewish on the grounds that not even Mrs Jay would sink to intimacy at that level; an amorous sheeny, he pointed out, would have been as bad, almost, as a nigger. On consideration, I agreed.

CHRISTIANS

Down Zinc Street, whatever one's social or economic position, everybody was 'Christian'; therefore none of us liked the Jews. Not that we knew any: we detested them on principle. Syd's father, in his teens, had been a well-known 'scuttler', one of the hooligans who, in the 'nineties, infested northern slums. He belonged, in fact, to the notorious mob down Cope Street, a lane in which our school stood, behind the shop. For a time the activities of this gang gained even national repute. Mr Carey, once a leader there, now looked upon himself as a model citizen. But in his cups at the street corner, drivelling over 'happy days', he would tell of how 'we stopped them bloody Yids'. A Jewish dealer, we heard, had opened a second-hand clothes shop in the district, only to see his goods pulled out on to the pavement and burned openly by scuttlers, while a policeman stood by to see fair play. 'That kep' 'em out! We got no more o' the buggers!' He felt he had performed a social service. 'Once them "noses" get into a neighbourhood, they take it over. Then the place is no class at all!'

In our village about one fifth of the inhabitants were Roman Catholic and the rest Protestants of some sort, shopkeepers and artisans, of course, tending to support Dissenting chapels. The great majority of Protestants, however, did not 'practise' themselves, but saw to it, perhaps as a conscience salver, that their children went regularly to Sunday school. In our home, though, it was a matter of indifference whether we attended or not. But I enjoyed going; discipline was slack, instruction vapid but short, and opportunity for minor mischief frequent. We often had speakers from other chapels who gave us little lectures on each of the virtues, pointed with parables out of their experience, but only one homilist, unfortunately, ever stirred me positively. His theme for the day was 'Perseverance'. Whenever we sinned, he told us, we must ask the Lord's forgiveness, then get up off our knees and go on fighting to follow God's will – never ever giving up trying to do good every day, no matter how small the deed. That was Perseverance! Now, however irreproachable the sentiment, we had heard it all before, and I, for one, was drifting into reverie, when the speaker offered such a signal example from life itself of the rewards of resolution that I jerked to attention at once. 'Matchsticks!' he said dramatically. In the year 1880 a friend of his had begun to collect used matchsticks from all over Manchester, persuading others to help him. Then, slowly, steadily, *persevering all the time*, he started to build with them, and after twelve years' work the gentleman had completed his erection – a perfect model, three feet high, of Manchester cathedral! And underneath it was a little notice in golden letters which read:

PERSEVERANCE, STICKS AND GLUE – 1892

The tale much impressed us. Here was a man, we felt, who had really put his time to valuable use, and in a way that any determined boy could copy. I ran home, alight with enthusiasm, to tell them all about it. And more, I *too*, I announced, would build to the greater glory of the Lord – to wit, one Congregationalist chapel in matchsticks which, on completion, would be presented to Mr Waters, the minister, before a large audience! At home Ellie and Ada, who had heard the story, quite thrilled to my idea and offered their assistance; but the whole thing, for some reason, made Jane giggle. 'Imbecility, sticks and glue,' she chanted, '1892!' Then for the next few days she kept rushing up from all parts of the house and presenting me with a spent match. In face of this my perseverance petered out.

A few weeks before Whitsuntide, Sunday schools had a temporary influx of small recruits, all sent by mothers who wanted to see their children walk in new clothes with the religious processions. In one family we knew of, the desire to testify openly for the Lord was so strong that an elder son sneaked out at night and 'did a job' to provide the wherewithal for his sisters' white dresses.

Protestants 'witnessed' publicly on Monday, the Roman Catholics Friday, in acrid competition with each other. 'God knows his own!' some Christians would say smugly if it rained on their rivals but stayed fine for the 'one true faith'. In our immediate district, however, several sects walked – separately, of course – on Whit Sunday, a practice which led once to a certain acrimony at home and embittered the Old Man on one religion at least.

A pawnbroker's stood a few yards from us, and at weekends our shop functioned as an extension of its services. Many women on Saturday evenings, waiting for husbands to come home with wages, hadn't the money to redeem their pledges before 'Uncle's' closed. To overcome this difficulty Tom Arnott, the broker, paid my mother a fee, and every weekend I transferred from his premises to ours a consignment of up to twenty bundles of clothes. These were now available for redemption until 11 p.m. and also on Sunday. Best clothes taken out at the last minute could then be worn on the holy day and social status maintained. Bundles would, of course, be hocked again early on Monday morning. When our service first began, a few tick customers saw it as an excellent means of retrieving their apparel without spot cash, but Mother disagreed. 'We're agents,' she said, 'and hold the stuff on trust. No money, no clothes!' Each bundle in pawn had a small white ticket pinned on it denoting the owner. This gave rise to a pretty euphemism. 'Where's that nice brown suit?' one might ask a friend not looking his sartorial best at the Saturday hop. 'It's still got a "butterfly" on!' he would say sadly.

Among the load I collected from the pawnshop there was occasionally a bundle my father called a 'dead 'un'. It could, at times, be very much alive, a sort of social 'bomb' that duly exploded. Some woman would arrange to do a neighbour's weekly wash on condition that she be allowed, afterwards, to pawn the clean clothes until weekend. All would go well, perhaps, for a month or so, then one Saturday night the 'contractor' might find herself without money to redeem her pledge. Afraid to face the music, she would come quietly and slip the pawn ticket on to our counter and vanish. I then had the job of going to tell the owner that a 'butterfly' had landed. If money was available she would follow me back to the shop and, raging, bail out her own clothes. Later high words might be heard in the street, or even the sound of breaking glass. 'Pushin' her windows in' was a frequent form of reprisal in public dispute. Any bundles unredeemed over the weekend I returned on Monday morning. These sometimes acted as pointers to those of our credit customers who had begun to fall on hard times. My mother, thinking anxiously of her own solvency, might then start to limit the extent of their tick 'shots'.

One Saturday night before Whitsuntide Father, in a merry mood, let Kate Sweeney, a good Irish customer, borrow a pledge containing 'our little Patrick's sailor suit – just so he can walk proud, God bless him, with St Joseph's tomorrer!' She swore on the grave of several relatives and the Holy Mother of God to return it the minute the procession was over. Father fell for her blarney. But the news got around and set up a chain reaction. Others made Christian appeal for their children's clothes and, wanting to be fair to all faiths, he allowed bundles to go out without payment to two Primitive Methodists, a Congregationalist and a couple of Church of Englanders. Mother disapproved of it all. 'Nothin' to worry about,' he told her. 'Special occasion. Wouldn't do it regular, of course. And they've got to bring 'em back, else how could they use the pop shop again?' And that seemed sound sense. So their children walked the parish and looked in 'borrowed' finery as beautiful as any others. Later in the day all duly turned up with their bundles, save one – Mrs Sweeney. On Monday night after work Father went round to get the clothes, cash, or 'knock hell out of their Mick!' But the Sweeney ménage had migrated! Deeply in debt to shops around, the family had done a 'moonlight' to somewhere, neighbours said, 'up Harpurhey'. This shook Father on Catholics. He never had a good word for the Pope after.

Surprisingly for those times, when 'atheist' was still a sinister word, neither of my parents accepted Christianity. Perhaps they felt that the Church of England especially had little to offer shorn lambs beyond preaching acceptance of the wind. This was an era in which the Archbishop of Canterbury could organize a luncheon party 'exclusively for dowager duchesses'. Every morning at school we got the

Salford Children

Street Scenes in Old Salford

usual long and, to me, tedious doses of 'scripture'. Fifty years after, looking in the school log book, I was astonished to read that the 'Bishop's Examiners' had singled out my knowledge for special praise. They didn't know that at the time I was avid to absorb anything, even the 'begatting' of Old Testament genealogy. But belief was something else again. My mother, an open sceptic, had issued an admonition to us all. 'In religion,' she used to say, 'they often tell you they *know* things when in fact they only *believe* them. Just bear that in mind!'

The parish church, 'incumbered' in our time by a large and arrogant Rector, ran three day schools and a religious outpost. This last, a corrugated iron structure, stood in darkest Salford about a hundred yards from the shop. On summer evenings a band of missionaries, backed by two curates and a harmonium, made sallies to our street corners, where with hymn and sermonette they tried to evangelize the natives. Friendly people, whenever one of them came into the shop Mother always bought his offering. Once, however, clearly showing them how to do it, came our Rector in person. Bland and booming, he went among the lowly, spreading the Good News himself, and arrived, all condescension, at our counter.

'Now, young woman, the Magazine!'

'No, thank you,' said my mother civilly.

'It's the church periodical!' he reproved her.

'No, thank you,' she repeated.

'Humph!' he said, turning to go. 'It's easy to see *you* don't attend church!'

'And it's easy,' she told him, 'to see why!' The Rector didn't call again.

One of the women who used to wash for us, Agnes Bowlin, a Methodist of the Primitive persuasion, was prey to every superstition. Horrified, she saw my mother spill salt, cross knives, open umbrellas in the kitchen, put shoes on the table, careless of the frightful consequences. 'You'll pay for that!' she said. Two of the greatest portents of evil, Mrs Bowlin believed, were cross-eyed females and androgynous poultry. She quoted proof:

> A skenning woman and a crowing hen
> Fetch the Devil out of his den!

'If you're goin' to work in a mornin',' she told Father

dramatically, 'and you meet one, or come across t'other, turn round, walk straight back home and do nowt all that day; then your luck will hold!'

'Except,' said the Old Man, 'I'll get sacked next morning for not turning in! Nay! You make your own luck, missis,' he told her, as indifferent to omen, good or ill, as his wife; 'but I will agree it's unlucky to sleep thirteen in a bed!'

For Mrs Bowlin hell existed in reality like, say, Ireland; indeed, the Ould Sod could have been an enclave of it. She loathed Catholics with that sort of faggot-lighting hatred which must have moved Elizabethan zealots. Idol-worshipping papists Aggie called them, and each single one would roast through eternity. When a 'Roman' family came to live next door to her she 'flitted' at once, only to find herself living in front of another lot. A priest paid his regular visits there. She waited, leaving her door ajar, until the moment he drew level, then slammed it hard. The landlady of a pub, Irish and new to the district, asked her once to do the weekly wash. Aggie was outraged. Her reply became a comedy catchphrase for us. 'Mrs Brannigan,' she told her, 'I'd beg bread in the gutter first!'

Catholic relics, bones, blood, bits of the true cross and such she found especially revolting. I loved to chat her up while the clothes were coming to the boil; Aggie had a sort of knowledge unobtainable elsewhere, especially on matters religious. 'Our Lord Jesus,' she told me once, 'left *one* sign of himself to the world, and one alone, and that lies upon the haddock!' This information amazed me. She stopped doing her woollens to tell me the parable of the 'loaves and fishes', which I knew well enough. 'But what they don't tell you at school,' she added, 'is that one of them fishes was a haddock! And when the Good Lord Jesus took it between his finger and thumb God Almighty in heaven cried, "Let the thumb mark be on the side of all haddocks in all the corners of the earth, now and for evermore! Amen!" So it came to pass. And to this day you'll see that mark on every single one you pick up!'

I listened, open-mouthed. 'Even on finnan haddock?'

'It comes plainer on that!' she said. 'You can't miss it!'

I hadn't then heard of Paley's *Evidences*, but it seemed to me that if what Mrs Bowlin had just expounded was fact, no further proofs at all were needed to establish the overwhelming truth of Christianity. I began to feel a kind of reconversion coming on to a faith already grown tenuous. She started to lift clothes out of the copper with a boiler stick and grew dim in billows of vapour. I wandered out of the scullery, then went back to the door. 'Why don't they show a haddock to Jews and heathens and pagans and such?'

'There's some folk,' she called, 'what just don't want to believe, no matter what you show 'em!'

I went and put the whole thing to my mother. She wasn't half as taken by it as I'd expected. 'Do you think,' I asked, 'we could have smoked haddock for tea?'

'We'll see,' she said. But later Ellie called in at the greengrocer's to bring back a whole yellow triangle of it. And there, for all to inspect, lay evidence beyond doubt – a clear dark mark on the skin, exactly the size and shape of a man's thumbprint. I took the fish to Aggie and pointed in silence. 'That's it!' she said reverently. 'The mark of our Good Lord Jesus Christ!'

I was anxious to discuss the theological implications of it all, but Mother showed no further interest, beyond telling me not to start arguing the toss about such things with Mrs Bowlin, because she was 'touchy enough' as it was. Soon after, however, I was shocked to discover that my mother had no faith in the Sign of the Haddock at all.

'But you didn't contradict her!' I complained. 'You never told *her* it was "nonsense"!'

'I'm not going to lose a good washerwoman,' she said, 'for the sake of superstition!' For once my mother disappointed me. She had been, I considered, quite shifty; surely wrestling with the great truths came before the Old Man's clean shirt! Feeling it useless to discuss the matter with my peers, whose concern for the verities was nil, I waited till the next scripture class at school and put the question to Mr Hales. As a communicant of good standing in the Church of England he answered without hesitation: the haddock mark was undoubtedly Christ's imprint, though this fact, he said, had not been mentioned in the Bible. Nevertheless we must remember that much was known about Our Lord that went unrecorded in the Good Book. In quiet triumph, I went home.

'Hales says it's right about the haddock!'

My mother looked unperturbed. 'As usual,' she said, 'in religion, Mr Hales tells you he knows things when in fact he only believes them.'

FEARS

My father's crony, Aloysius Murphy, was going on one evening, as he often did, about Ireland and her sorrows. This time he spoke of the 'Peep-o'-day Boys', a name new and strange to me. Mother laughed. 'We've one of those in the family!' she said, and ran a hand through my hair. 'Peep-o'-day Robert!' In childhood the dawn fascinated me. 'He's a bit touched, poor lad', my brother, Arthur, used to explain when the subject came up, '– a night walker!' We slept together at one end of a large bedroom, parents at the other; my rising used to disturb his slumbers. Around three o'clock on any summer morning I slipped from the covers. Mother, a light sleeper, usually heard this exit over creaking boards, but didn't object. 'It's a habit with no harm in it that I can see,' she said. Holding my clogs in one hand, I crept down into the kitchen, where the cat, its tail hoisted stiff as a flagpole, came to greet me. A little east window under the staircase stood flushed already. I trembled with pleasure and early morning chill, hair crinkling deliciously over the scalp. Yet in this delight both shame and fear lay mixed. *Was* I 'touched'? Had anyone ever, I wondered, experienced such queer feelings, or were they, as Iggy might have warned, a stage in the process of going 'batty'? I told no one of the joy or foreboding. Then through the shop, rank with the smell of pickles, soap, cheese, cat piss and creosoted firelighters, and away into the lifting dark. 3.20! Only Mrs Longworth abroad with a knocking-up pole, her clogs and mine clacking over the flags. 'Who do yer wake at this time?' I asked. 'On half past three,' she said, 'just four shunters for Manchester Victoria.' Through a couple of streets now, grey slits above, with the lamps growing wan, and over a wall into the brickhills to watch darkness die before morning.

Sitting alone as light grew over the waste, I was looking, though I didn't know it, upon the first passenger railway man had ever built and, as it happened, upon the very stretch where, one September day some eighty years before, the Duke of Wellington, rolling in state to the opening ceremony, had met his hottest reception since Waterloo. The duke, England's Prime Minister, had travelled in a sumptuous coach, 'thirty-two feet long and eight feet wide, covered with a crimson canopy set upon eight carved and gilded pillars; the whole surrounded by two ducal coronets'. Behind him in seven other luxurious trains came some 750 guests, an 'assemblage of wealth, rank, beauty and fashion'. In triumphant procession from Liverpool, the cavalcade had encountered nothing but 'cheering multitudes' until, west of the terminus, it reached our Salford hovels. 'The contrast between the departure from Liverpool,'* wrote Fanny Kemble, one of the guests, 'and our arrival in Manchester was one of the most striking things I have ever witnessed.' Thousands of the 'lowest orders' had poured from courts and alleys to meet His Grace in person. 'No corn laws!' they howled, and flung lumps of clay, brickbats and other missiles . . . 'Groans and hisses greeted the carriage,' Fanny wrote, 'full of influential personages, in which the Duke of Wellington sat . . .' 'High above the grim and grimy crowd of scowling faces a loom had been erected, at which sat a tattered, starved-looking weaver, evidently set there as a representative man to protest against the triumph of machinery and the gain and glory which the wealthy Liverpool and Manchester men were likely to derive from it.' Thus the new industrial proletariat gave sullen warning from the depths of the first industrial slums. Before me now stretched a desolation where starvelings once massed in 'living avenues' to curse a duke and send him scuttling back the way he had come. If the old ghosts ever walked there I saw none. But often on these summer mornings I stayed long enough to watch the sun break over the smoke of Manchester.† Grim, the city rose in the light of day, standing the first colossus born of a force that was changing the face of the world. Unaware, I surveyed a symbol of far deeper historical import than any of the small-time Runnymedes and Bosworth Fields they talked of at school. One of the prettier ways of describing the great cataclysm that is happening to humanity is to call it the industrial revolution.

* A vivid description of the event appears in Christopher Aspin's *Lancashire: the First Industrial Society*, Helmshore Local History Society, 1969.

† 'As great a human exploit,' Disraeli had called it, 'as the rise of Athens.'

In the middle of the eighteenth century a build-up of human knowledge exploded which ever since has been turning man into some sort of god, and the first clear evidence of it rose in the noisome streets of Manchester. A small human scrap out of those ways, I looked upon the city, waving its dark plumes over the morning, ready for another burst of gigantic toil. One day, perhaps, men, grown more conscious of a wider heritage, will gaze in awe at what is left of the old town, as they stare now at dolmens, Norman castles and other relics of cultures long dead.

Some mornings as I wandered about the spoil heaps Ignatius would appear from his wigwam, where at times he spent the night. He greeted me in our 'vernacular'. 'How! Four herd of buffalo [goods trains] passed; the last, seventy-eight head!' (He counted the wagons.)

I would stare impassively over the prairie, one hand horizontal across my eyebrows. 'And the paleface [shunters who drove us off]?'

'None movin', chief! Have yer brought the bread and jam?'

Ig, who 'worked' the cattle market and could get a restless cow to yield into a pop bottle, with expertise, always supplied our liquid refreshment.

One morning after breakfast Sydney appeared with Hollis, a fourteen-year-old about to embark on his paper round. I hardly knew him. 'Olly' polished off the last of our milk and settled by the fire. The conversation then went something like this.

'You live in a shop, Curly? That's all right, isn't it!' Ingratiatingly he then began to mention all the material advantages which accrued to anyone so fortunately placed. 'Toffees,' he said, 'loads of 'em! Biscuits! Cigs! Cake! Lemon squash! My! ...'

'. . . All spread out,' said Syd, helping him, '– in a morning, before it opens!'

'And the geld?' asked Hollis. 'I bet she keeps all that locked up, doesn't she?'

'It's all in piles,' I told him. 'On the dresser every night.'

He whistled. 'My! Nobody wouldn't miss a little bit off them, would they?'

'They wouldn't miss nothink,' I said.

'And you could blag some of the other stuff – just a bit, like, and she wouldn't never know, would she?'

'Wouldn't know nothink.'

Olly thought a little. 'Too late this mornin' now,' he said. 'I gotter go for *Dispatches*. Tomorrow, then, round five o'clock, I'll be on the step – me and Syd!'

'Run up a lamp!' I told him. Hollis looked surprised.

'He's yeller!' Sydney said. I pushed up my jersey sleeves. Syd withdrew the word. Ignatius tried to make the peace, as always, by explaining that I wasn't really 'yellow' but just scared of my mother – as he, he said, would be.

'I'm *not* scared!' I yelled. 'She – She just wouldn't want me to – that's all!'

The others looked unimpressed. Then Sydney indicted me. 'She didn't want you to blag iron from the yard, did she? But you done it! That's stealin'!' I stayed silent. 'She wouldn't want you to get ice creams off the vanmen, then skip it without payin'. But you done it! . . .'

'That,' I said, 'is just to learn 'em to take the money first, that's all.'

'Still,' wheedled Hollis, 'yer can't keep on doin' just what *she* wants all the time, can yer?'

'Just get us,' said Syd, feeling the matter settled, 'a couple o' bottles o' pop, some biscuits, say, an' a few bars of old "Nutty Nutty" – just between the four of us.'

'It's my birthday tomorrer,' Olly said pathetically. 'I'm fifteen!'

I suggested that he rose early and went and stuffed himself. He came towards me.

'I'll bloody flatten you, Curly!'

Iggy edged up to my shoulder. This surprised me, because he was never a lad who looked for trouble.

Hollis turned to Syd. 'Some mates you got!' Then he looked down, kicked a can near his foot and followed it.

'Go 'ome!' called Ig, coarsely, after he had gone a safe distance, 'an' tell yer mother there's a cow in the 'ouse!'

Syd got up and stared across at him. 'Listen who's talkin'!' he said, and followed his new friend, disconsolate.

When they had gone Ignatius stood around, saying nothing. I tried to explain again. 'Yer see, she wouldn't – we don't, none of us – we don't take things from the shop, see . . .'

'No, yer don't. You'd get a good beltin'!'

'It's *not* that!' I shouted, and gave up.

Sydney met me a day or two after in the street, anxious to heal the breach. 'It was Olly what put me up to it,' he apologized.

'Someone,' I said, with a sarcasm he remembered long after, 'is allus puttin' you up to somethink!'

The whole incident remained embedded in memory. I pushed it away, rather afraid, but it would return – the first clear confrontation, it seemed, with those twin incubi, good and evil; but through it all a rock-like assurance told me you didn't rob your mother. Such episodes of childhood often possessed one entirely. They flashed across reality, then, merging with experience, sank deep into consciousness, only to rise at a later date, the stuff of ill dreams. In print I had trodden sinister paths with Charles Dickens, trembled over Fagin and Bill Sykes, feared with the young Copperfield along the Dover road; but what was mere fancy compared with the real! Sixty years after those times I wake now and then with a cry at night, to remember I'm an old man. Dream has borne me back, a child once more, to walk not the dawn but the dark of Salford streets, and to go in dread. Fears long buried have stirred again, distorted, frantically absurd, horrifying. Old Mrs Cass I dreamed of. Derelict she had been in real life, and stinking in a hovel of a home – full of old clothes, they said. Saturday nights, late on, she would shuffle into the shop and my mother gave her, and others equally needy, the scraps of cheese, bacon or corned beef to make a Sunday meal. When she left the air hung with her odour. Grimly Mother sometimes got a bucket of water strongly disinfected and swilled it over the shop floor. 'That such things should be!' she said to Janie once.

On a midsummer day we saw smoke bellying from Mrs Cass's house. Men broke in, to be driven back by the heat. Somehow she had incinerated herself. Police arrived with a black van. The flames died as quickly as they had arisen. Two constables entered, but one soon came out again, his helmet off, white and sick. 'Get back!' he shouted to us. 'You must get back!' The ambulance men went in with a large grey sheet. Wisps of smoke drifted acrid through the broken windows. Then they returned, carrying with some difficulty, it seemed, something covered, and got into the van; the driver whipped up his horse and they left. Slowly the crowd melted, but I stayed with a few other youngsters in front of the gutted kitchen, gazing. A carter and his nipper from a railway lorry near by stood with us on the kerb. Then I saw the youth bend, pick up something small and charred and hand it to his mate. The man inspected it. 'It's a thumb,' he whispered. 'A thumb!'

There could be nights of real terror. On evenings in summer, close and brooding, many lounged outside their doorways until beyond the edge of darkness, loath to meet the rampant bed bug. One by one, apathetic, each family went in, gaslight illuminating paper blinds in turn. But during such times at weekend, when heat and drink had turned folk sullen or evil-tempered, the air felt sprung with tension. One stifling Sunday night a man in the back block, after staring for hours 'at nothing', slashed his throat with a razor and died, they said, 'running about'. An ambulance arrived and rushed his body away. Fearful but fascinated, we boys sidled to the small knots of adults who lingered, heads together, about the street, and edged in on their talk. A woman had come, one said, with bucket and brush and swilled gore off the pavement. 'He'd been going funny all day.' And then that 'sign' – that 'letter W' on the flagstones! They'd give him a Christian funeral, of course. Not like in the old days when anyone that did himself in was buried at the crossroads with a stake through his heart. 'That pinned the ghost down!' We listened; they sent us away and we gathered again, whispering under a gas lamp until Janie called me home.

'They reckon,' I informed my brother next day, 'that feller's blood made a kind of big W across the flags, and his name began with a W!'

'What the hell's that got to do with it?' asked my father, looking up from his dinner and glowering.

'Dunno. I was just telling him what they said.'

'Well, don't!' he ordered. 'Such damned nonsense!'

I had never seen the man who died, in his final act or before; but something, at times, runs crying through my troubled sleep still.

There was one Saturday night of intolerable heat, stench and gloom when, as it darkened, neighbours, over some trivial incident, seemed to go berserk *en masse* and fought, men and women together, in mindless hate. We, the boys, got to the scene late; a solid ring of spectators had already gathered. I climbed a lamp post at the back for a better view, half blocking the light. A woman turned. 'Get down off that bloody lamp!' she snarled. 'They can't see who the hell they're hitting!' Long after it was done, Father, putting up the shutters, saw two constables passing through. Peaceable men; who were they to have gone looking for trouble?

'Thirty-four black eyes,' Ed Franklin said in class the next schoolday, 'they reckon was dished out altogether!'

When Syd's mother came into the shop the Old Man served her jovially. 'What do you think of the bust-up last night, eh?'

Mrs Carey excused herself. 'Didn't hear a thing! Me an' Mick was havin' a set-to on our own.'

'Well, we've run out of stickin' plaster!' Father said.

Of course, there were benign nights too, when neighbours gathered in little groups to chat, often about the 'good old days', unhappily gone. Then, of course, law and order were 'respected', parents 'honoured' and children 'knew their place'. As lamplight grew stronger along the pavements one was called home to bed and drifted into sleep on the strains of some *ad hoc* choir fallen into harmony at the street end. It was in the warmer days, above all, that people felt a glow of 'community', a sense of belonging each to each that, for the time being, overrode class and family differences.

But on early Sunday evenings in winter loneliness along the streets seemed almost palpable. Odd cats abroad stared at the infrequent passers-by, for all men who had homes to go to now sat behind those dim squares of yellow window blind, snug by their own hearthstones – untold thousands of them in acre upon acre of lowly dwellings. This was the family hour before all others. A week's labour done, a wife in her best clothes, if she possessed any (though a symbolic white apron would do), had removed newspaper covers off certain articles, laid the rug and polished fire-irons and furniture, which shone now in the flames of a heaped coal fire. Fathers waited on the formality of Sunday tea, usually after a couple of hours in bed; their august selves, with any elders present, taking 'first sitting', the children eating afterwards.

I used to wander from the warm brightness of our own kitchen into the dark. Distant over the railway clanged a bell, gathering Christians. Iron upon iron, it sounded across a graveyard, the Bolton to Bury 'cut', standing green under lamps, the lines of our Lancashire & Yorkshire Railway and a marshalling yard, vast, and quiet now. I used to climb a gate in the wall and gaze far over to where the church stood, finger against the sky – a glim of light flickered here, a gleam there, and on the wind a whiff of malodorous waters, for the

Irwell slid close by. A furlong away, across the village, limiting our purlieu, a second wall rose. Beyond it lay the brickfield, raped and left in chaos, in the manner of the old exploiters; more railway – the Cheshire Lines – then a solid mile or more of little houses to the banks of the Manchester Canal. From there, softly, ships blew horns, sighing across the night, and always for me they were bidding adieu, leaving our squalor and dark vacancy behind and speeding away west to sunlit oceans and some fair Hesperides. I used to stand until the church bell ceased with three single knocks upon the evening – one for each of the Trinity? – then silence. At times, down a by-lane, some woman would go calling a boy home, with that high, forlorn cry they kept for the purpose – 'Jo-o-o-oh!' It came wailing down empty ways, all despair, like the sound of one lost in limbo. I crept back for human company.

Always, on evening errands in winter, one hurried quivering past certain entries where evil, we felt, lurked waiting to pounce – the Napoo gang, or 'garrotters' who specialized in strangling boys from behind. One night a 'thing' in a narrow ginnel turned my heart over with terror. Often when Father was bibulous his thoughts settled on tripe. Requirements were simple but precise; he wanted only the best and at once. 'Go,' he would command, 'and get me half a pound of double-thick fat "seam"! Understand? No "honeycomb". Now, what are you askin' for?' I would repeat it. 'And tell Mrs Jackson it's for me – for your father! Understand? Half a pound of double-thick . . .'

'Let him go!' my mother once said irritably, looking up from her sewing. 'They won't kill a special cow for you!'

I had on no account to get the stuff from a shop on our own doorstep; there, Father considered, the proprietrix looked a 'dirty bitch!' You had to plod to a place at the edge of the village. Once, on a night of drizzle, when our world of soot gleamed sleek, I was returning from such an errand, the meat, newspaper-wrapped, in a fold of my jersey. I glanced down a catwalk, and there it was – in a blur of light – a gigantic, spider-like object, three feet across, jammed in a back door, one tentacle-end glinting, and in the centre – eyes! And it roared! With a shriek I dropped the parcel and ran; but not far. The roar was hitting my ears with meaning. 'Help me! Christ! Will nobody help me?' I knocked at a door, trembling. A woman came. I told her.

'It's that boozy old Baron,' she said, 'down again with his peg leg!' And there we found him, crammed in a recess, arms and legs out stiff and a condensed milk tin crushed on the end of his wooden stump. 'I just turned in the entry,' he said, 'slipped on summat and couldn't get back on me feet!'

Picking up my tripe, naked now on the pavement, I shook it well, wiped it hygienically on a sleeve, and went anxiously home. But, growing drowsy, the Old Man had forgotten his supper and gone to bed. Mother looked at my offal with disgust and threw it on the fire, covering it with coals. Then, alert, she looked at me. 'It fell,' I told her. 'Something — frightened me.'

'Go and wash,' she said, without comment, 'then we'll try a new line from the shop — kind of beef tea, it is — Oxo cubes. Penny each.'

Acting as drudges of the drudges, children walked miles to satisfy the wants, whims and fancies of parents, and woe betide one who, having been ordered on a distant mission, made his purchase from a shop nearer home. Some people used to send a child across town, and he would come back, perhaps having spent too much, or with the incorrect article — Jeans' Emulsion, say, instead of Scott's (men had a child-like faith in advertisement). Here was a chance for a father to show before his family the authority he so often lacked in the world outside. 'Take that back at once!' he would bawl, and wearily the child would set out again, primed with some offensive remark which he was instructed to repeat when the article was handed over. Afraid to address a bourgeois shopkeeper in such terms, the youngster would offer euphemisms, only to be punished on reaching home again for not stating the precise message the father had been too cowardly to deliver himself. We at home were happily spared this; the Old Man went back and did his own insulting.

In a society where few could afford the services of a doctor — indeed, the mere visit to one conferred a certain status on a family — patent medicines and their efficiency were a standard topic for discussion. People swore by this and that, often drugging themselves into a stupor.* From time to time Father had a pain in his back which could only

---

* The taking of opiate drugs was far more widespread than it is today, and the problem in fact more serious, but very few people realized it.

be cured, he believed, by a belladonna plaster from a chemist his mother patronized in the wilds of Pendleton. She was with us one night in his troubles, sympathizing. On her appearance, we noted, Father's agonies always increased. Tough as hide, with his mother there he became a boy again, 'soft', his wife informed him, 'as a boiled turnip'. 'We can get a plaster locally,' my mother said. 'It's a proprietary brand.'

'Eeeeeeeh! My! A *what* brand?' asked Grandma.

'You can get the same damned thing down the street!' Mother snapped. But the Old Man thought he would be much happier with a plaster from Gill's, the usual place, in west Salford. I groaned.

The short way there lay along several streets, up two flights of wooden steps and across our bridge. This structure stood by the gasworks. Narrow, iron-trellised, it soared over cattle sidings and a deep gash through which trains rattled to the docks. At night a dark and lonely place, often shrouded in vapour from mountains of steaming coke, I travelled its considerable length in fear, trotting from lamp glow into shadow to see, sometimes, away under the next gleam, a hulk advancing towards the trough of night between us. And it would have to be passed within two feet, cased close by trelliswork. Heart pounding as the thing approached, I used to listen for the clink of irons on the concrete walk. Then one knew at least that the peril would be human, for no phantom wore clogs. Now that scalp-moving instant when the figure came abreast! Would it pounce? But no: some tired labourer went by without a glance; that 'bludgeon' by his side only empty dinner dishes borne in the usual red handkerchief. But the bridge, we knew, had other perils: was it not the haunt of one Spring-heel Jack? I had seen an artist's sketch of this menace on the back page of the *Police News*, hanging in a newsagent's window – terrifying! He had devices on his boots which allowed him to bound ten feet and sink fangs into his victims. We boys were convinced that Spring-heel was none other than Jack the Ripper himself – mechanized.

Desperately afraid to go to the chemist's that night, but rejecting the long way round (which would only have proved my cowardice), I appealed to Mother in the shop to let me get a plaster near by, pointing out the frightful hazards which her son must otherwise run. Only that week, I said, two mill girls going to work in the dark had been attacked – 'by a leaping man! Bill Eccles told me – right on the bridge!'

'And what did he steal?' Mother asked.

'Their – Their breakfast,' I said, 'and – their tea and sugar for a brew!'

'Right,' she said. 'If he holds you up, hand over your threepence, or the belladonna plaster!'

I went on my way, bitter at such cold indifference.

But on these night missions a boy often managed to get one comforter and friend to go with him cheerfully along the lonely ways – his winter warmer. Just as, on January days, Victorian ladies had carried hot roast potatoes in their muffs, we too bore heat, in an even more sustaining form. For our contrivance one needed first a container of the correct size, and happily we found this easy to come by. Few houses of the time, even the poorest, failed to hold in their medicine chest a stock of 'health salts'; indeed, a penny pack often constituted their total safeguard against illness. The salts, a mixture of bicarbonate of soda, purgative, sugar, cream of tartar and flavouring, came in tins large enough to fit snugly into a boy's hand. We punctured one of these receptacles with a few holes, top and bottom, stuffed it with cotton waste (always on hand in mill towns), ignited it, replaced the lid and blew through the holes until a small golden eye stared back at us. The slow fire, heating the metal, provided a pilgrim with enough warmth to see him through any errand – a boon in the night. It could be carried in a pocket, worn pressed upon the navel by a tight jersey, or borne in hand, needing only a breathing caress from time to time to keep the container pleasantly hot. But 'for best results', as the advertisers say, care in management was required. One evening my brother Arthur, believing his winter warmer extinct, went to bed with it in a trouser pocket. In the middle of the night my mother woke to an acrid smoke pervading the bedroom. 'The damned house is alight!' the Old Man roared, and rushed to our bed-rail, to find Arthur's heater busily burning out the seat of his pants!

VENTURES

ERRAND-going, night or day, children found a detested chore, but during holidays many tramped miles on their own account. Our small posse would set off, taking the usual rations of bread and Spanish licorice water. On the way one met other little bands, similarly equipped. We passed like caravans along the desert routes, each intent upon its own mission, for every group had an end in view. Now and then Iggy appeared from nowhere and attached himself to us. Certain members of our party objected to this practice; they felt his presence lowered tone. 'You can't get into museums nor nowhere with him!' Sydney protested. 'One look, an' it's "Out – the lot of yer!" He puts the block in everythink!' And this was sadly true. Still, however unwelcome, our pariah trailed on a few feet behind for a while, then joined up. And away we went, past the gasworks and along the 'Barbary Coast' with its twenty-two pubs, they said, over a measured quarter of a mile, haunt of men home from the sea. In passing we duly noted, among 'foreigners', the ever-present 'Lascars'. In single file they came, bareheaded, save for the odd fez, emaciated, all in blue denims, threading their way to the markets. Some looked shy, even innocent, I thought, smiling down with large, soft eyes. But Englishmen, we knew, called them 'treacherous', the 'scum of the ocean!' They'd knife you soon as look! But then, you couldn't trust foreigners of any sort. Taking our cue from adult canon, we lived by the belief that all 'niggers' were congenitally stupid and funny, all 'sheenies'* dirty and ridiculous. The Lascar, however, we considered a 'sort of nigger' but 'not comical'. In fact he

---

* My cousin Alf, whose family lived near the 'ghetto', used to light fires for pious Jews on 'sabbas' at a halfpenny per ignition. He reported that many of them seemed 'quite clean'. We were gratified to learn of this turn for the better among foreigners. Nearly every boy in our own group, it is true, had head lice himself; but they were English bred.

hardly rated as human at all. When a string of Indian seamen passed by, one didn't even bother to jeer. And these men, I discovered before leaving school, ranked with *us* as fellow patriots of Empire, being representatives of that sub-continent which gleamed the 'brightest jewel in the British Crown'. It rather, one felt, took the gloss off it all.

On our pilgrimages beyond the 'Barbary Coast' we surveyed, among other attractions, Eccles Cross and 'Ye Olde Original Cake Shoppe'; Barton aqueduct, where one canal passed over another; the rhubarb fields of Flixton; the Jews and gaol down Strangeways; the dead in Weaste cemetery; Trafford Park, on its way to becoming Europe's largest industrial estate, and the 'millionaires' mansions' along Eccles Old Road. Sometimes an outing took us over the Irwell. 'Keep away!' our elders admonished constantly. 'You'll get fever.' We heeded them not, for here tumbled a river on whose purling waters the very rainbows appeared, at times, to melt, though basically it ran the colour of plain chocolate. But catch the stream in happy mood and under one's eyes brown would dissolve into Mediterranean blue, azure slide into rich crimson, frothing like dragon's blood, and on again to buttermilk veined with green. Standing entranced upon a bridge, we threw quantities of rubbish over to mix the creeping palettes. Then, for a little while, glory departed as spews of effluent from the dyeworks drifted on to Manchester. By Irwell's bank more dyers* worked than anywhere else in Britain. And there laboured others, too, who made more solid contribution. Indeed, the viscosity of our Isis was such, some critics asserted, that near Victoria Station brickbats 'protruded' from the surface. This was a libel. 'All things flow,' said Heraclitus, and Irwell no less – like cold treacle. 'Undefiled for the undefiled!' the poet has cried, in love with some crystal stream. 'Bathe in her, bathe in her, mother and child!' Once they must have bathed in our river

---

* Even by 1854, on the Salford stretch of the river, there were twenty-seven dyeworks. In 1862 one statistician announced that 72,500 tons of cinders a year were being tipped into the Irwell and Mersey. In addition barges brought refuse from outlying districts, via the canal, to convenient spots, from where it was taken by cartload and dropped into 'flowing water'. The Irwell's bed rose; in 1866 Salford suffered its most disastrous flood. By 1907 the river and its small tributaries had '327 manufactories' along their banks.

too. As late as 1740 salmon had leaped there; by 2040 they may yet leap again; but in the early years of this century, unparticular though we were, we drew the line at a dip in the Irwell! *En route* to join with her two sisters, Irk and Medlock, she swung in a great loop past Royal Technical College and high 'Crescent' – befouling one of the most dramatic urban vistas in northern England. Then, together, the filthy trinity moved on, not to meet Neptune at last, and the 'white waves heaving high', but to drop their dark offerings into a dock called Pomona (goddess of fruits) and the Manchester Ship Canal.

One morning four of us set out to discover 'Cheshire', a venture of magnitude which meant the shedding, with some recrimination, of smaller group members like my young brother, too frail, we felt, to undertake such a journey. Among the baggage carried was a tent made, with Mother's help, from sugar sacks, which we hoped to erect somewhere on what our geography book called the 'rich Cheshire plains', eating and drinking our provisions within; a glorious prospect! Two bearers humped it importantly, one behind the other, like a rolled stretcher. The plain, we required, had to have a forest attached, because we intended to make a fire of branches (preferably 'beech or oak') on a principle laid down by Baden Powell, and then brew tea in a condensed milk can. The water for this, Bill Eccles recalled half a century later, hadn't to be taken out of the canal but drawn, on my insistence, from a stream, because 'running water was pure water', an observation which much impressed him. Starry-eyed, the expedition set off, moving southward, and after three hours lit upon a demarcation stone in a lane between Stretford and Sale. Stout Cortez himself, newly eyeing the Pacific, could have registered no more joy. In turn we straddled the post, 'one leg in Lancashire, one in Cheshire!', then crossed boldly into virgin lands. Each told the other how 'odd' he felt; a clear but indefinable sensation had now taken hold of him, similar to that which one got bestriding the mark on that bridge between Salford and Manchester, but very, very much stronger! Everything, somehow, we said, looked – different! Even the policemen, it turned out. Our party had penetrated no more than fifty yards into the unknown when two 'rozzers', 'disguised in postmen's hats', barred our passage.

'Where are *you* from?' one asked.

'Salford, Lancashire!' I told him.

'And where d'yer think yer goin'?'

'We have come,' I told him, 'to explore Cheshire!'

'Gerrout of it!' He swung his cape,* moving forward and knocking me into a hedge while the other snatched at the tent. In a panic our bearers dropped it. The whole expedition broke rank and fled back over the border. 'They can't follow us here!' Bill gasped, but we kept running for a while none the less, then went listless on to Salford. Life, I was beginning to discover, despite its rich promise, had such a habit of disappointing. Back home, I told my mother all about it and wept a little, for we had set out in high hope and the loss had been grievous. 'Never mind,' she said. 'When I get enough sacks we'll make another tent. But stay in Lancashire next time!'

Not all ventures took us far afield. One February evening after a day of torrential downpour I stood with Eddie on the bottom of our local clay-pit and looked upon what appeared to us an amazing phenomenon – some two acres of what had been dry plateau were now covered with water about six inches deep. We sat down and watched a while as it shimmered under the moon, then I rose and spoke like God: 'Let us build an island and inhabit it!' Inchoate matter lay about in the shape of a million broken brickbats. Drawing upon these, we set stepping blocks to mid-ocean and for the next two hours transported basic stuff until an eyot began to rise from the deeps. And never since having hands had they been used, we felt, in a task more fascinating. At the south-west corner of the domain Eddie reared a mountain, and we stepped now and then upon its peak to scan the main. Once, standing there, I named our land. 'Let this place be called the Island of Magadora!' We laboured on, till faintly, on an east wind, the Manchester town hall clock sounded nine. Eddie dropped his bricks. 'Gawd! I'll get murdered!' He shot along our causeway, up slopes, and vanished over the brickfield wall. I was alone! A Crusoe, lord of his own island! Supremely happy, oblivious of time, I passed to and fro, bearing sods ripped from loose earth to flesh the rock. Finally, out of a disused railway tunnel hard by, I fetched kindling and fuel to make a small fire in a hearth. And there I crouched while the waters rippled round and the moon

---

* A usage much recommended for children now by nostalgic supporters of 'law and order'.

sagged low, staring between two gasholders. Far off a clock struck once more. I didn't even bother to count. Who needs the hour on a desert island? Tomorrow we would build a hut *and* a raft . . .

'Robert!' I almost jumped from my skin. A tall figure was bestriding the waves towards me. 'Wait till I get you inside!' Then the Old Man slipped. I cannot record that 'full fathom five my father lay', but he certainly got his boots full. Yet on he came still, baying oaths to the moon. Sliding off bricks at the other side, I made for home by the shortest of cuts.

My mother with Janie hurried anxiously to let me in. 'Where on earth have you been? The whole street's up seeking you!' Wet and filthy, I explained. 'A quick wash in the bathroom,' she said, 'and bed at once!' Two minutes later my father arrived.

'Where's that lad? Where is he?'

'Upstairs,' Mother told him. 'He didn't know the time. He was making an island,' she added, as if this was the most natural thing in the world for any boy to be doing at nearly twelve on a February night.

Father hit the table with his fist. 'Making a bloody island! An island! Playing in a puddle o' water at close on midnight! Mad! I tell you – we've got a goddamned idiot for a son!'

'Well, we made him together,' she said peaceably. 'Just give me those wet socks, will you? I'll lock up.'

I heard him bang his boots into the hearth, then I skipped off the landing and dived into bed.

Next morning, even before breakfast, Eddie was peeping in at our shop door. We dashed away, over the brickfield wall, down the hillocks, then pulled up in utter dismay. The ocean had disappeared – drained off down runnels by early workmen, and our magic land lay, in the light of day, a mess of rubble on the clay-pit floor.

On one expedition, seeking a park on a day of August heat, we came upon some wax torsoes in a milliner's side window. Somehow the 'bubble' within a pane had acted upon one as a burning glass. The whole of an elegant female's head, from left hair line to chin, had crumpled into dripping amorphousness. One eye lolled on her cheek; a modiste's 'creation' in feathers had slid over the other. We laughed; the other boys staggered about the pavement in over-reaction, pointing helplessly, clinging to one another. For some reason, as I looked more, it began to sober and disturb me. Turning away, I went out of the passage and shouted in at the shop doorway to a woman sewing: 'Your bust is meltin' in that side window, missis!' Some nights later the elegant lady entered my dreams, but smiling now – alive! I cried out in terror, wakened, heard my mother's voice, comforting, then slept again. The next day she mentioned it. 'In your sleep you called out, "*I* didn't laugh! *I* didn't laugh!" Whatever were you dreaming of?'

'Dunno,' I said. 'Can't remember.'

At the rear of one of the great houses along Eccles Old Road on another holiday afternoon we fell in with a boy of about our own age, but much better dressed, dawdling lonely by a gate. 'How do!' I called in my matiest tones. 'Who owns this one, kiddo?' He stared at me. 'My father,' he said. This news stunned us. Like a bunch of tourists we entered the large cobbled yard *en bloc* to give the premises our awed inspection. Alarmed, the lad backed away, but finding us apparently harmless he soon became friendly. 'Call me Edgar,' he said. We mingled happily, casting an eye over things, trying doors and calling him Edgar. My brother discovered an iron pump by the stables, and we all had a drink. Then we pumped for pleasure, splashing until each was sodden to the knees. A back door stood ajar. 'No one at 'ome, then?' asked Syd carelessly. The boy shook his head. 'Not just now.' After inviting themselves into the kitchen it was not long before Edgar's visitors had filtered to an impressive hall. 'What's everythink covered up for?' asked Iggy, astonished. 'What's under all them cloths?' 'Keep the dust off,' said Edgar. But he was growing uneasy. 'Don't go any farther, please! My mother wouldn't . . . Oh, don't!'

Our new friend didn't know it, but the Goths had arrived! Ig, having already removed a dust sheet from a suit of armour, was testing this hardware for stability when it fell. Sydney had disappeared upstairs. This was too much for me. 'All out!' I shouted. 'Coppers!' We returned quickly to the kitchen, Edgar in obvious relief. Alert as to what could happen, I was very anxious to be off. Syd, having picked up a scent spray, dosed us all liberally. Looking worried, our host dished out a few nuts off a plate. 'You'll all have to go now. My father's coming.' But Iggy had helped himself to a bottle of what must have been cooking sherry off a dresser. After a swig he passed it to Sydney, who drank deep, then, taking a handful of nuts, threw them at the ceiling. 'Whoops!'

They were both settling in nicely when a woman's voice, perilously near, sent us scudding through the yard and out into the back lane. Twenty yards on I turned, to see Edgar having his neck slapped by a stout woman in a raincoat. Quite a 'happening' for one afternoon. Ig thought the boy must have been 'very rich!' But we sneered. 'That was the slavey's lad,' I said. 'His father wouldn't own nothink!' The safari moved on, rank with perfume – even Ignatius, which was a change. But the incident had rather alarmed me. 'We gotter be careful,' I said, 'where we go in.' On excursions of any sort I used the powers conferred upon me from 'living in a shop' to control general activity, being backed by Ed Franklin, son of an ironmoulder, a kindly, intelligent lad. Together, without really being conscious of it, we set the limits of conduct to be observed by any scions of the labouring classes fortunate enough to enjoy our company.

One excursion took us to Pendlebury pit, which, we believed erroneously, was the 'deepest and hottest' in England. 'All the men there work naked!' We arrived and gazed at the winding gear. I recall stopping our little group dramatically. 'Right under where I'm standing now is a collier' (we never used the word 'miner') 'stripped bare, digging coal, a mile down!' This caused a sensation. We saw the morning shift coming off, and my brother expressed disappointment. 'They've all got clothes on!' he said.

One Shrove Tuesday, a favourite rambling day, having exhausted local wonders, I appealed to my mother for ideas. First she suggested swilling the yard, then, 'Why not go and find the poisoned wood?' she said. Mr Murphy had recently lent her a book which spoke of a forest 'beyond Kersal, killed by vapours from Manchester and Salford'. 'More than a thousand trees, it seems,' Mother told us, ' – great beeches – had to be cut down. The stumps might still be there. You could see how many.' This was a quest indeed! The idea of finding a poisoned wood and counting the casualties struck me as the perfect way of spending a Pancake Tuesday afternoon. A small contingent of us roved out to search Kersal Moor and areas adjoining, but, alas, we sought in vain, though I did hit upon Kersal Cell, where, Mother said, a certain John Byrom had written 'Christians awake', a carol known to us all. The whole incident, so vivid then, had almost gone from my mind, but many years afterwards, in a book, *Essays and Sketches* by Abraham Stansfield, written at the turn of the century, I came across the very passage my mother had referred to. In a woodland near Kersal Moor on the edge of the borough 'noxious vapours from Manchester and Salford', wrote Stansfield, 'attacked the trees, mostly full-grown beech. 1,200 giants of the forest had to fall. Every year they are dying in great numbers.' He himself had the melancholy task of 'condemning the decaying trees to the axe – trees once beautiful and still sturdy-limbed enough, but surely and steadily sinking into a condition in which they would have been utterly worthless'. So there the last wood in Salford had indeed lived and died. These same 'noxious vapours' we ourselves breathed in concentrated form: our own streets stood immediately under the gasworks in the path of prevailing winds. Sometimes the air stank abominably for days on end. But very few questioned the right of industry to ruin our health and environment; in pursuit of profit the poor were expendable.

And so, wearing the irons off our clogs, we children, like countless others, wandered the twin cities and their suburbs, seeking places with names as entrancing to us as any that bejewelled the East. And we went just as men climbed mountains, 'because they were there' – Boggart Hole Clough, Tootal Woods, Daisy Nook, the Pepper Hills and – Brindle Heath! A name for me a poem in itself. Agog to be involved in the human comedy, we dodged and wove our way through the streets, looking in upon bakers, blacksmiths, coal yards, sniffing the warm, sensual reek of the cobbler's shop, to which place some boys, waiting to be 're-ironed', confessed a strange, erotic response! *En route*, hopefully, one tried the locks of all vacant premises, chased cats, called up lobbies, and, catching lads travelling illicitly on a lorry back, shrieked together, urging the driver to 'Whip behind!' We accepted the order chalked on walls to FOLLOW THIS LINE and at the end, silent, took in the message or insult appended. Then away again like foraging pups, avid for any incident, and into the first greengrocer's on the offchance of 'faded fruit'. Touching lucky here, perhaps, for a crushed apple or two, we came up against one of our standard taboos – care had to be taken at all costs not to eat any seeds; certain boys, according to the lore, had swallowed pips, with fatal consequences. One child we heard of, having foolishly ingested an over-ripe pomegranate, fell ill through the seeds germinating in his stomach. From these, plants developed so vigorously inside him that, to eradicate them, doctors would have had to kill the patient. But he died anyway, with foliage, it was said, sprouting from various of his apertures – a cautionary story that left its mark on all younger listeners. Beetles, and flies too, swallowed inadvertently, and 'breeding', could lead to similar tragedies. It behoved a lad both to pick at his fruit and never to rush around with his mouth open. Such tales we told one another, in all earnestness, as we straggled on towards our bourne. And these were certainly not the mere imaginings of contemporaries. In industrial slums a lore, much attenuated, still existed which had come down from the pre-literate society where folk had told or sung their tale instead of reading and writing it. Many elderly people, especially the illiterates, knew our sagas well enough and like Horatio, did in part believe them.

On one trail the party never failed to peep in at a barber's emporium where a school friend, Joe Orris, laboured as lather boy holidays and weekends. Joe, we knew, soaped under certain instructions. If an unknown man called, the barber had told him, late Saturday (the shop closed at 11 p.m.) and seemed curious about his age, Joe must reply, 'Fourteen, sir, going on for fifteen!' Should the assistant's low stature then be queried, Orris had to answer, 'Small, sir, yes! But all our family's on the small side!' 'That puts the inspector off, see?' he explained to us.

We always approached this hairdresser's (a dive where shaves cost two for three-halfpence) with a thrill of anticipation. Through its doors, Joe had assured us, a customer might, on occasion, be seen to emerge wiping his face madly and howling with fear: all this, we understood, on account of Billy Marks's, the barber's, ripe sense of humour. Most of us, on looking in at the shop, had seen a green parrot high in a corner, its cage usually half covered with a cloth; but no one had ever heard it say a word. Yet here hung the joke. At the very moment, it seemed, when a stranger to the shop sat back in the operating chair, his neck bare to the barber's razor, some old customer would rise quietly and whip the screen from Polly's cage. Upon which, according to Joe, the bird spoke in sepulchral tones. 'Cut his bloody throat, Billy!' None of us on jaunting afternoons had been lucky enough to witness the reaction; still, we gave the barber a call. At sight of us, Joe raised his head to stare 'wistfully at the day', but only to close in again on some scrubby chin

as he harkened to his master's command: 'Rub it in, boy!
Rub it in!' The wayfarers passed on, often jingling, till we
grew tired of it:

Tiddly Wink, the barber,
Went to shave his father.
Made a slip and cut his lip,
Tiddly Wink, the barber.

Reaching outer suburbia and longing as always for something to happen, we manufactured 'events', ringing the door-
bells of the bourgeoisie to beg, unthirsty, for drinks of water.
Some personages responded kindly, but on the whole the
affluent didn't take to us at all. Big-bosomed, overbearing
women followed maids to the door and, in tones and accents
which fascinated, severely reprimanded us for daring to
disturb their seclusion. One, I remember, had been dislodged
from the 'conservatory' and another incommoded at her
'correspondence'. 'On no account must my front door bell
be rung again! Understand?' We hung our heads, feeling a
satisfaction, secret and malicious. 'In future you must go to
the back and send a boy to ask Cook!' Now would we
promise . . . ? Solemnly we gave our word. Most now
despatched us; but now and again a servant would appear
with a jug and tray, and we drank from tumblers – a pleasing
experience. Myth had accreted round this juvenile custom,
too. One heard of boys whose humble request to the 'haves'
for water had got them bottles of lemonade, vanilla ices, and
one child a sailor suit. There were cases, unauthenticated, of
lads receiving handsome sums in specie, or even being
adopted! Hope ever springing, minutes after one class confrontation we would invest another residence and all trail
up the front door steps to bell the middle orders again,
sometimes each ringing in turn to give clear notice of our
arrival. And, disappointed but undismayed, on once more,
past hedgerows now, and in the 'country'. There we made
fires and marauded, filching a little of what there was, and,
when caught, wept and lied to authority, swearing that never
again . . . All day we ran wild through worn fields and
scraggy copses that held their arms to the smut of Manchester, then traipsed home weary with the evening, feeling
that life was pretty good and it would go on for ever.
One afternoon towards the end of a summer holiday several

of us, including Iggy, trekked to Prestwich Clough on the outskirts of northern Manchester. We were passing a large house, trim and hedge-bound, when Ig clutched his throat.

'I got a thirst coming on!'

'Not that one!' I said shortly. 'My auntie lives there.'

They laughed and teased me, disbelieving; but I hurried past, not wanting to be spotted in present company. My father's middle-class sisters all called on us from time to time, their fur coats and bourgeois air much impressing the neighbours, but they never put on 'side'. Our visits to them, however, seemed few and fitful. In spite of strong family ties common at the time, some of us children remained strangers to their homes. One day, however, I received an invitation from Aunt Marie to proceed with Father and pick up several items which her youngest son, Harold, wished to dispose of, he now leaving school for 'business', aged seventeen. Fitted out in new, post-Whitsun wear and a straw hat called a 'cady', I set out, full of apprehension, with the Old Man. 'This fine weather,' he said, as we went to board a tram, 'Uncle Basil' (who was high in grocery) 'will most likely be about the garden. When we go through the gate raise that boater. Understand?' My fears multiplied, and with reason. I'd never worn a hat before, much less raised one! In that day headgear of some sort was considered compulsory. Even the poorest tried to conform, but my mother, eccentric as ever, had looked early on my mass of frizzy hair and decided it didn't need a hat, though for a formal visit to the middle classes even she gave way. The cady, clamped hard on my skull now, was moored by strong elastic to a lapel to prevent its blowing away.

Our well-heeled relatives occupied a residence in a select part of suburbia. On top of the tram I rehearsed mentally the confrontation to come. 'Good afternoon, Uncle Basil!' Then lift it straight up – about six inches, say? Or kind of 'curve' it off? That might be better, perhaps. 'How do you do, sir! Uncle!' 'Sir Uncle!' Each try-out seemed more foolish than the last. Every second I grew more nervous. The house rose forbidding. And Uncle Basil was there! As we approached he got up from a deckchair and came along the drive. 'Hello-o, Robert!' he called to Father, and held out his hand. This was it! I stepped a pace ahead, tried to raise the hat, but couldn't: tight to start with, a band of sweat had glued it round my sconce. I tugged, levered, pulled. The

121

cady shot up; then the elastic, over-strong, jerked it back on again. Crimson, not having said a word, I slid it off and it fell, bouncing about my abdomen. Uncle Basil looked down on me, smiling.

'That hat's a bit small for him,' the Old Man said.

'Or perhaps his head's swelling!' suggested Uncle. At this shaft of wit they both laughed heartily.

Inside, Aunt Marie and the girls – two of them school-teachers, it seemed – welcomed us cordially, kindness itself. By now my ear lobes hung with sweat and clothes were sticking to the body. Shortly afterwards Cousin Harold appeared, in flannels, carrying a tennis racket, which impressed me profoundly – tennis, we all knew, being the pastime of the upper classes. He was tall, spotty, very pale and as thin as a pole. 'Take care of Robert, dear, will you?' Auntie said. Amiably he led me to his room, and there lay riches! Soon I was the possessor of a willow cricket bat, hardly used, four stumps, a ball and one bail, several table games, a pile of books gripped in a leather strap and the *Boys' Own Annual* for 1905. We grew chatty. Harold, it appeared, didn't like sport at all – except tennis: 'You meet the girls there.' He hated school, too, was happy to have left, and seemed amused that I should be 'mad on cricket' and enjoyed books. We went downstairs and mooned about in the back garden until joined by a fattish youth about Harold's age, with another racket. The newcomer looked somewhat put out by my presence. Without a word they made for a large shrubbery at the end of the garden. Uninvited, I followed, kicking a way through rotten rhododendron leaves, and watched them, a little ahead, volleying bits of vegetable matter at each other, though their thoughts, I felt, were not at all on tennis. At last I caught up. Harold began to whistle, and his friend joined in, singing under his breath. 'Down in Arizona, where nobody goes, Take a little girl and . . .' – a parody. I knew it well enough, and others like it, as all common boys* did,

---

* In 'Parody and impropriety', a chapter in *Lore and Language of Schoolchildren*, the authors, Iona and Peter Opie, write, 'Genuinely erotic verse, however, is unusual. That there are villains among children, as among adults, the *News of the World* offers frequent testimony; and from somewhere the ogre child acquires his strange salacious prescriptions, taking criminal pleasure in pressing them on juniors and inscribing them on the walls of the school lavatory. But we are not here discussing delinquents.'

but it surprised me that such a versicle should be current among young gentlemen. By a lean-to hut they made water, the fat youth 'flashing' his penis, a demonstration which left me totally unembarrassed. 'How's that?' he asked. 'Not bad,' I said, without interest. He started singing again, then, 'Are there plenty of girls down your way?' I didn't answer.

'They'll be wanting you at the house,' said Cousin Harold. He opened the hut door. I strolled off. And Harold was right: the maid stood calling from the back steps.

In something they called the 'morning-room' I played billiards with one of the young ladies on a 'home-size' table, walking across thick carpet to register my score on a marker. It seemed to me the most fascinating entertainment man had yet devised. Aunt Marie came in. 'Have tea before you go, dear,' she said. This astonished me: I hadn't thought of going!

Father sat in the dining-room already. An oval table in the middle, shaped like a great tablet of Pear's soap, lay polished

This strikes me as an astonishing observation to make on the child's world. After long experience of delinquency I cannot believe, despite attestations from the *News of the World*, that bastion of righteousness, that there are child 'villains' around, versed in sexual aberration, or little 'ogres' who, for 'criminal pleasure', go hissing, 'Now, Oscar was a cabin boy', and the like, down the ear of innocence. Of course, one meets sexually precocious children. As were the young in earlier generations, many, even now, have been deliberately kept in ignorance about a natural force which deeply disturbs them. They hear and see erotica, repeat it, try to understand and 'interpret' it – wondering all the time. Under strain, some will commit overt sexual acts; but not 'criminal' acts, even by legal definition (the age of criminal responsibility is fourteen years). Such conduct society considers anti-social. But always the young are seeking both meaning and the need to satisfy a basic natural urge. To call troubled children 'villains' and 'ogres' taking 'criminal pleasure' is, I feel, inept. The lore and language of children stand all of a piece: there is not, surely, a broad 'delinquents' section which lies, through its wickedness, beyond ordinary discussion. I recall one fourteen-year-old I taught in prison. Brought up 'strictly', an exemplar he had been in his village – 'clean', they said, 'in mind', 'tidy, respectful – playing the piano at Sunday school'; but he murdered an old woman horribly none the less. Some giggling, nudging and whispering among his peers in childhood might even have saved him.

and bare save for flowers in a vase of silver; but the maid flitted about, setting a much smaller board for two in the large bay window. Soon she had it crowded with dainties of all sorts – Uncle Basil wasn't in food for nothing! High tea now; knife and fork, in the northern fashion! Father took a chair across for me. We were to eat alone, then?

'They have dinner later on,' he explained. 'They do things different from us.'

Surprisingly, we now heard what sounded like an altercation, blurred but unmistakable, emanating from the back regions – voices in anger: Aunt Marie's, the maid's and, mingling with them, the shriller tones of a female who plainly belonged to one of the more populous parts of Salford. Father grinned. 'That'll be the slavey in trouble. Your Aunt Marie's not the sort to stand any impudence.' Then, just as suddenly, all fell quiet again. Soon the servant came in, looking tight-lipped, with a tray. In front of us she put plates of smoked haddock over which butter pats melted. It smelled delicious. Then Auntie herself entered, smiling but flustered, bearing a gilt teapot.

'Do enjoy yourselves, dears. I'm busy for the moment.'

She vanished again. The Old Man poured tea in silence. Down the garden Uncle stood, unbusy, clipping at a bush with a pair of secateurs. In the best party manner I lifted my cup: drank, and pulled a face.

'Dad, this tea tastes horrible!'

He frowned. 'Get it down you!'

I left it untouched, but stuffed myself comatose, noticing carefully that after the first gulp at his own cup Father didn't drink again.

Quite soon afterwards we departed, the family hovering about us in the hall. 'Come again, some time,' they said. I decided I would; high life had much to recommend it! Loaded with treasure, I went down the drive, Father following, after what seemed a few confidential words with his sister. We made our way back from the tram, taking short cuts through the gridiron of little streets. In more ways than one this had been a unique occasion; it was, for instance, the only time throughout childhood that I ever walked in public with my father. Along an alleyway near home most neighbours, men and women together, sat airing themselves in the westering sun, their children sprawling by the gutters. Father passed a pleasant word as we went on. 'It costs nothing,' he used to say, 'whoever they are, and it's good for trade.' In front of the corner house one of our customers, Mrs Kenny, a lump of a woman, sat on a stool. She looked up and smiled, swopping a joke with the Old Man, then, pointing at my hat, 'Good luck for a cady!' she said. People often 'wished' on the first straw hat seen in spring. I stared back, but not at her! Pressed to her side stood one Master Ernest Kenny, aged two, erect in his little clogs. Eyeballs tilted, he was taking suck after the manner born from a breast bare and big as a bladder of lard, the while his mother scanned the *Evening Chronicle*. We turned down a ginnel and crossed to the shop. With us 'titty' on the threshold was a common enough feast, but on that evening never had it, and the whole district, seemed to me so deplorably low!

The next morning Janie approached, smiling. She had sat up the night before to overhear Father's 'report'. 'Did you like it yesterday, then?'

'Fine!' I said. 'Lovely big house!'

'Should be. Uncle Basil gets twelve pounds a week!'

I gasped. It seemed an enormous sum. 'They gave me plenty of things!'

'Plenty to eat *and* drink?'

'Tea tasted rotten!'

Janie laughed outright. 'No wonder! The slavey got sacked for giving cheek, then, while their backs was turned, she brewed your tea with the haddock water!'

But the visit made a deep impression on me. That's how the rich lived, then! Fancy food, great rooms, cases full of books, carpets, massive furniture, paintings, silver teapots, and billiards in the morning-room! My eyes bounced around our kitchen. Paltry! I could see now. Yet how it had dazzled Ignatius. But I remembered with a mental sniff that Ig was really no class at all, as Syd so often said. And come to think of it, who was Sydney to talk! So did smug class-consciousness develop.

TRAVELLING MEN

No fewer than eight commercial travellers called regularly at the shop, grappling for a share in a trade which, before 1914, never exceeded fifteen pounds a week. Anxious, down-at-heel men, rather gentlemanly dressed, they came in, pushing their biscuits, smallwares, patent medicines, confectionery, all playing a role of some sort. We children, eavesdropping as usual, found their selling 'act' both entertaining and instructive. For us these men constituted a solid contact with the manners and outlook of the petty bourgeoisie.

Two 'commercials' competed, daggers drawn, to supply our establishment with groceries. For Mr Law, representative of one of the larger wholesalers in the city, Father had high respect. He felt flattered that such a firm should deign to solicit our trade at all. And to send a gentleman like Mr Law! In a cut-throat provision world travellers seeking orders haunted shops even as small as ours and usually got short shrift. Mr Law called one day just before Christmas on his initial visit and stood back courteously, waiting until the customers were served – a big, rubicund man in overcoat. 'I thought,' said Mother afterwards, 'he was some sort of police inspector.' Would they care, he asked urbanely, to open an account with him? He spoke expertly of the trade, quoted rock-bottom prices, gave assurance of top quality. Even their smallest commission, Mr Law said – fifteen shillings, ten shillings! – would be 'much appreciated'. Father, at home that day, was very impressed. They gave him an order for a pound's worth of goods, upon which the city man said he was 'most obliged' and would certainly 'look after' them.

'A real gentleman,' the Old Man used to say of him, especially after Mr Law left him a cigar. 'He's stood the Food Exchange, you know! A proper commercial traveller, you can see that! Not like that other jumped-up toffee-nosed warehouse lad they send from Bolder's!'

'True,' my mother agreed. 'But he often comes half kettled, all the same. What brought him our road on, I wonder?'

Mr May, the 'toffee-nosed' one, who called Tuesdays, soon realized he had a rival in the field, and took one week to find out who it was. Then, by hint and innuendo, he began to stab him in the back. I myself held Father's low view of Mr May, a lanky, small-eyed man in a belted raincoat and bowler. The shop order from Bolder's was delivered Wednesdays by horse and cart; but the day before, as Mother told the traveller her needs, he would lean confidentially over the counter and say, 'You could send the lad round to the warehouse *Thursday* for the bacon roll. It would save – you know!' What I carried home on Thursday didn't appear on the current week's invoice, so all the bacon, say, would be sold before it had to be paid for. But, unaware of this, I believed the traveller was deliberately using my muscle and free time to spare the grocery horse, and Mother merely finding something for 'idle hands'. I hated his guts!

On first coming to the shop years before, Mr May in his role-playing had tried patronage, a standard tactic of the lower middle class in dealing with their social inferiors, but Mother soon cut him and his order down to size. He was astonished to find, too, when it came to accounts, that the speed and accuracy of her calculation far surpassed his own. Then again, in discussion, naturally, she used words and phrases that one wouldn't expect a 'corner-shop person' to know. One afternoon when he had arrived on his weekly round I was sitting under the counter, sorting, messily, bundles of firewood to find a stick for a kite cross-piece. It was an ideal place, too, from which to listen in. Our traveller was holding forth about his boss's recent holiday 'along the Rhine', from which he had returned, it appeared, reflecting the prejudices of the time, to denigrate all things German. As a provision merchant Mr Bolder had come down specially hard on Teutonic jams. 'Little fruit in 'em at all!' May told my mother. 'A few plums, or blackcurrants, say, mixed with loads of a certain vegetable – something like a beetroot – funny foreign name, it is – er . . .'

'Mangold-wurzels!' I told him from under the counter.

'Well, I'll be jiggered!' said Mr May. 'Fancy a boy of ten knowing a thing like that! Incredible!'

'It's not all that strange,' Mother said. 'The children are very fond of words here. We all like to play about with them. But if he's not out of that mess soon I'll mangold-wurzel him!'

Mr May, having found he was dealing with an odd woman, trod carefully, but still pursued the class tack in an effort to impress. His line – 'life among the upper orders in Higher Broughton' – became a comical legend with us. Mother heard and in our presence duly reported to her husband on Mr May's sidesmanship at church, the whist drives he went to, the 'conversaziones', holidays at Llandudno and a fantasy, several times repeated, about 'dinner at the Midland Hotel!' 'At last, my dear, I picked up the chicken wing in my fingers and nibbled it. And believe me, the whole table followed suit! Alderman Smethurst! His lady! "That's a sensible idea, old man!"'

'Rather like Belle Vue at feeding time?' Mother had suggested.

'Oh no, dear! I knew what I was about. According to the best books of etiquette it is quite correct, perfectly good manners, to take the smaller, more awkward bones in the fingers and nibble them. It's done in the very best society!' Then he would draw out one of his 'Oval Egyptian' cigarettes from a gilt case and light it with a flourish. It smelt, my father said, who smoked 'thick twist', 'like a dustbin on fire!'

My mother remained undazzled, and the order stayed the same no matter how far Mr May soared up the social ladder. Smarmy to us children with our parents around, whenever I saw him at the warehouse he completely ignored me; and with good reason! In apron, at a counter behind hills of stock, our 'commercial' stood weighing out flour, sugar or peas into paper bags. If sweeping the floor, he would try to dodge out of sight into the shadows. From time to time Mr Bolder, a bully of fine order, would appear from his cubicle. At once all the staff quickened their rhythm, while the boss, a barrel of a man, stood glowering about him. 'Is anyone attendin' to this lad, 'ere?' 'Oh, yessir!' A counter hand came hurrying.

Mr Law knew Bolder & Co. well and expressed his complete contempt for the firm. 'A slop shop!' he used to say. 'No standing in the trade at all. They put warehouse Jacks on the road – a quid a week plus threepence in the pound "commish". – and call them travellers!'

Of course, neither man would come into the shop if the other had arrived first: each waited at the window, Law with a smile, whistling to himself, 'Warehouse Jack' scowling. 'I dunno!' Janie heard him say one afternoon. 'There must be something wrong when a big concern, size of Margisson's, sends a chap like him beggin' for orders in twopence-half-penny places such as – ' And he stopped.

'Why?' asked my mother. 'Isn't our twopence-halfpenny as good as anyone else's?'

'Oh, n-oo! I didn't mean . . .'

For all his airs Mr May had a kind of desperate courage. He would arrive every Tuesday, coat tight about him, bowler on the tilt, umbrella rolled, always with the same cocky superciliousness. One January day he came through frozen fog. Underneath the pince-nez, the thin nose, a smudge of moustache, his lips were blue. Mother had a large black pan boiling on a gas ring at the counter end. The whole atmosphere exuded hot pea soup. 'That smells rich!' he said. She gave him a pint potful with bread. He wolfed it down, sitting one knee over the other on a mineral-water box, and I noticed to my surprise that one of his shoes was almost without heel. When Father came through, Mr May rhapsodized over his wife's cooking. 'Soup – delicious!' 'I'd give that bugger nowt!' the Old Man hooted later. 'He'd have a six-course kipper dinner waitin' for 'im up in Broughton!'

'There's all sorts of poverty,' my mother told him, 'besides ours!' A remark which puzzled me.

One evening a middle-aged woman, frumpish but befurred, clearly middle-class, called at the shop and talked quietly for some time with Mother. Curious as always, I wanted to be in on it, but here lay mystery. The cryptic observations of our elders afterwards made no sense, and even Janie, a high-class ferreter if ever there was one, could tell us nothing, except that it had something to do with 'Margisson's man'. 'He still gets my order,' I heard Mother say. When Mr Law came he too fell into cahoots with her over the counter. We spied in turn from the small window that gave on to the shop from our kitchen, hearing nothing. Jane, I remember, then began to use her vivid imagination and whispered out a tale so unlikely that even I, the sucker, couldn't take it. This annoyed her, being, as she was, the eldest, and, usually our 'unimpeachable source', she had great standing among us. Mr Law, we noted, talked low and fast – explaining. No urbanity now! Three times perhaps, afterwards, our city man called again professionally, and on each occasion got his usual order, then he came no more. A snooty young clerk, my mother said later, sent by Margisson, arrived to collect the account outstanding, didn't even solicit an order and left 'without a "good day" '.

My sister Ada and I hung around on Mr May's next visit, and an early remark of his to Mother – 'Did you see it in the papers?' – sounded ripe with promise. We took up 'listening posts'. My mother turned to us. 'Go out of this shop!' she said, 'and stay out!'* Dutifully we obeyed – up the kitchen, left at the landing, and left again to a small enclave that jutted into the shop behind the cheese board. 'Sound' was poor here, but by concentration we could just get the drift. The lady in worn fur, we gathered, had been Mrs Law herself, doing the round of her husband's customers, destroying his reputation for her own good reasons. 'Of course,' we heard Mr May remark, 'Margisson's wouldn't put up with that again! Law was their Number One once – best round in wholesale grocery – made a tenner a week, they said.' Then voices fell and we heard little else.

All this mystification didn't do for Janie at all. She felt that her position as head fiddler-out of family secrets lay at stake. One Sunday evening some little time after, as a gathering of elders mulled over the affair in our kitchen, she listened on the stairs and came back word-perfect. Mr Law's downfall, it appeared, had been 'drink', of which the gentleman was so enamoured, they said, using a phrase of the times, 'he'd sup it out of a sweaty clog!' That, Father had explained, was how he got 'his cash mixed up with theirs. Then he takes up with this light o' love!' Jane gathered from the buzz of talk that Mr Law had been dishonest on two occasions. 'The first time,' she explained to us, all her old authority restored, 'after his stealin', the boss let him off, but they took his very good job away, see, and made him go down places like Salford and Ancoats getting orders in the very little shops. Then, what do you think!' We stood round her, gaping. 'He starts stealin' the money again and buyin' bottles of whisky and going with another lady that wasn't his wife! And they both ran away to New Brighton!'

I was aghast. That such a personage as Mr Law could do such things amazed me. 'And where is he now?' I asked.

'In Strangeways,' she said, 'doing twelve months!'

Mr May's weekly order was safe again!

* She told me once that she would keep a diary and let me read it each night: it would save me much trouble!

SUPERSTITION

FEW houses in our district stood vacant for longer than a fortnight before ghosts got in. Irish neighbours usually gave first warning of the new tenants, then children heard of it. 'I see,' said Mrs Connell one day in the shop, 'there's summat stirrin' in that empty No. 7! Raps and moanin', they reckon, at night – something terrible! That old Mother Tamworth's back, I'll bet!'

Father scowled. 'Well, she went owin' us thirty-five bob! It could be on her conscience!'

'Never!' said my mother. 'It didn't trouble her in life. It won't now!'

The Old Man always scowled when he heard this neighbour's name mentioned, and with good reason. Mrs Tamworth held the distinction of having 'blued' the shop substantially on two occasions, and this when she had had 'regular wages coming in'. The debt had left him bitter, and on the old lady's decease he expressed the pious hope that she would 'fry in hell!' This, his wife said while we giggled, was quite a possibility, since, in common with some other elderly folk in our area, Mrs Tamworth had gone to her Maker with a layer of fat bacon upon her chest – sewn to the inside of her bodice. Fatty rashers, so placed before winter came on, were thought to ward off bronchitis, though after Christmas they tended, too, to discourage finicky visitors. And now the ghost of our old defaulter had returned – a troubled spirit!

I wasn't long in letting the Zinc Street boys know, and we stood around the haunted premises that nightfall, waiting noisily on performance until driven off with abuse by a live tenant next door. When passing No. 7 Mrs Connell crossed herself, much troubled. I knew from gossip at the counter that she had only recently got 'shut' of a domestic phantom of her own. And not for the first time, either: Mrs Connell had ghosts as other people had mice. On this last occasion the apparition had been none other than 'Ma' Fagan, her

131

own mother. That old lady's deathbed wish was already very well known to the neighbourhood through her daughter's frequent repetition of it. 'Find your poor brother Mick a shake-down when he's nowhere to lay his head,' she adjured her, 'or I'll never rest in my grave!' Her daughter took this as a warning. Michael, massive, simple of mind and given, when not in prison, to tramping four northern counties, would vanish for months on end and then suddenly appear at his sister's house, after many nights in doorways and the like, begging to 'sleep warm' on her sofa, buried under old coats. Unfortunately Mrs Connell's husband, Joe, a fiery five-foot docker of whom Mick went in dread, forbade entrance at any time. Catching his brother-in-law in residence he promptly thumped him out into the street and clouted his spouse. The late Mrs Fagan, now watching beyond the veil, let this pass once or twice, then got down to business. Soon her daughter gave notice to all about that 'Ma' was 'on the walk'. Things happened after midnight when the house lay abed. What was more, the old lady, sour-faced in life, had turned skittish! She let cats 'in' or 'out', skewed pictures, took firewood drying in the oven and scattered it about the hearth, pushed Joe's breakfast, left overnight, on to the floor and emptied half a bottle of Guinness. In the shop Mother offered a natural explanation for all these phenomena, but Mrs Connell wouldn't have it. 'And who is it, then,' she asked, her nose in the air, 'what keeps goin' into the back, turnin' on the tap and pullin' the lavatory chain, then gets up on that squeaky rocking-chair?' Some customers, winking, advised her to call Father O'Shea in to do an exorcizing job, but others, knowing that gentleman, warned it could run expensive. Mrs Connell now pointed out to her husband the awesome consequences of his denying the old lady her last wish. Joe listened, and promised solemnly that should the wanderer ever call again he would thump him out of the house just as usual. One winter's morning, however, Mr Connell failed to rise for work, and within a month lay dead of 'miliary tuberculosis'. Much relieved at the news, Michael now came back and settled to slumber on the couch whenever he wished. More ghosts, it is true, infested Mrs Connell's later (Joe's included), but we heard no more of Ma; satisfied, no doubt, by how things had gone, she returned to her long sleep.

Ladies susceptible to night noises roused a cruel streak in us boys. Eddie Franklin and I would creep up to their homes in the dark, breathe heavily on a window, each misting over a large area, then, pressing our noses hard against the glass, we brought them in a long swift arc down the pane. This produced a noise something between a squeak and a squawk, followed, often enough, by a satisfying shriek from within. Then silently we fled. This window trick, known as the 'robbers' knock',* was used, children liked to believe, by thieves to warn a family that, do what they might, their home would soon be burgled.

My sister Janie delighted in telling us 'true' stories of the supernatural, but always seemed a deal less scared by them than we were. Once she mentioned a girl at school whose mother had lately died and the whole family went in fear of her spirit's returning. This dumbfounded us.

'Didn't they love her, then?' asked Ada.

'Of course. But they're scared to death of her ghost.'

'They couldn't have loved her!' I burst out.

My mother stood without a word, knocking mashed potatoes from a spoon on to plates. Perturbed, as we all were, by this family's attitude and its possible effect on our parents, Ellie decided she might need assurance of our undying affection and made her a proposition on the spot. When Mother passed away in the unthinkable future, Ellie asked, would she, without fail, come back and haunt us – at any time, just at her own convenience? Because there was nothing any of us would want more! We all agreed on this. 'And haunt me first,' said Janie, 'because I'm the eldest!' Mother said she would think about it – if there *was* any coming back, which she very much doubted.

Many houses were racked with superstition and fears which grandparents and near-illiterate elders did much to foster. Pictures fallen, and, of course, broken mirrors, cast a real gloom, presaging, as they did, 'death in the family'. At the approach of thunderstorms all knives and other metal objects were rushed out of sight. If two people happened to say the same word simultaneously, a desire could be realized by hooking little fingers and making silent wish.

Besides the poltergeists which came on their own we had a gentleman who fetched them up. Mr Carley, a gloomy man with a heavy moustache, ran seances as a sideline in one of

---

* This is listed erroneously in *Lore and Language of School-children* as a Salford 'door-knocking' game.

the parloured houses near by; but his main interest was medical and, in especial, the treatment of what he called 'female bad legs'. Many housewives, through being constantly on their feet, suffered from varicose veins. These and other 'women's ailments' he professed to cure by 'herbs' and the 'laying on of hands', a therapy which gave rise to salacious gossip. But Annie Carley, his wife, a woman prone to sniffing, remained indifferent. Clarence was a good provider, she said in the shop, and as long as, every Saturday, his wages lay on the kitchen table she didn't give a damn what rose in the parlour.

Though quizzing often enough, we children got to know very little of the doings behind Annie's red curtains beyond the fact that contact was made every Tuesday evening at 7.30 sharp with the 'Other World'. Edie Carley, however, then a teenage friend of my sister Jane, once confided that her father had recently been wakened during the small hours by a frightful crash in their front room, yet not a thing appeared to have been disturbed. But the next Tuesday, after some hymn-singing ('There are angels hovering round us' was favourite) and a holding of hands, Mr Carley's familiar, a Red Indian, turned up with a solution. The thing that went bump in the night, they learned, was the sound impact of 'spirit vibrations' emanating from a tree which had crashed 'hundreds of miles away!' And Clarence, it appeared, had cause for gloom, for this timber, Edie said, contained the very wood which was going to make her father's coffin!

The story, as related later by Janie, much amused the Old Man, who in sobriety often showed a roisterous sense of humour. It reminded him, not for the first time, of a local undertaker, Eli Bellows, who ran a branded line in caskets to suit every pocket. Eli's wares were named after certain English rivers: the smaller the stream the cheaper the receptacle – a sliding scale which clearly showed that, for us, 'class' reached to the tomb's brink and beyond. The 'Esk' casket, last on the price list, was just the job for paupers and those among our poor who had foolishly backslid on their burial club premiums. Fashioned in elm, it tended, like the cheap macintoshes of the time, to split and to let in water. Most folk, however, went to await Judgement Day in the 'Trent', a good, serviceable line in seasoned oak. But bookies, publicans and the like left us in a 'Severn' or a 'Thames' –

mahogany throughout, with bronze fixings. This was, one felt, appropriate; all might be equal before the Lord (and that, as yet, wanted proof) but there was nothing to be gained in going shabby.

The whole Carley family hurriedly 'dematerialized' one weekend to avoid, it was said, the head medium's getting a 'laying on of hands' from one or two local husbands, and we heard no more of them. But Clarence's coffin planks must have been long maturing, for, more than twenty years after, I saw him (without familiar) selling Batty's Cough Drops outside Old Trafford football ground.

Our neighbourhood was disturbed on occasion by two other 'manifestations' which people linked vaguely through a sexual connection – Mormons and 'white slavers'. Immediately after articles in the Sunday papers had 'exposed' their activities, in revenge they seemed to make a dead set at Salford. There was some confusion among us as to the methods used by these organizations, but none about their aims: each, we knew, came hell-bent on shipping females overseas for the vilest purposes. White slavers went in more for chloroformed handkerchiefs pressed over the faces of mill girls on their way home from the weaving sheds – though some villains, we were told, favoured a syringe jabbed through shawls into the passing buttock. Drugged bodies were then stuffed into packing cases, always available, and conveyed by horse and lorry to Salford docks. The poor girls knew no more until they woke up, bilious, in Rio or Hong Kong to a life of ill fame. Just what form this took I couldn't find out; the *News of the World*, for all its 'startling revelations', would never come clean (or dirty) on it. After one great spread in the Sunday press, much talked over, several sinister tales were rife, especially one from Alice Oman, a plain, ageing spinster who lived alone. Alice swore that on no fewer than three occasions, returning from the mill, she had been chased along the canal bank by a man with 'something white in his hand'. This led to various speculations. When she vanished altogether one night coming home, people feared the worst; but cynics at the counter wouldn't have it. Alice, they said, was a known 'romancer'; and anyway, as one lady put it unkindly, she just couldn't see the 'slavers', on removal of their 'knock-out' pad, hauling Alice off for export! And the cynics turned out too sadly correct: a day or two later she was 'found drowned' under Cock Robin

Bridge, a favourite place for suicides, having preferred, she said in a note, exit via the canal to one more day at the mill.

Of Mormons there still remained an echo from their massive invasion which took place some time in the later nineteenth century. Then whole families had left the town and emigrated to America, all females in the company to become, the elderly believed, concubines of Joseph Smith, Brigham Young, or both. In its missionary work the sect now seemed to rely mostly on handsome young men, working in couples, a deft handling of Bible content, and pictures of the wonderful life out west. They also, it was said, 'mesmerized' young women into leaving home and becoming putty in their hands. We once got a pair of Mormons when a Yankee company appeared at the local theatre in a show called 'Pride of the Prairie'. Father, with Al Mulphy, brought them in one Sunday afternoon – earnest fellows in their middle twenties, accompanied by a plump woman who laughed a lot and, I noticed, got through a surprising amount of stout. It turned out, however, that she wasn't a Latter-day Saint but merely 'interested'. The males eyed my sister, Janie, with appreciation and spoke of the Arcady they came from, holding the Good Book as they did so, and handing round most attractive photographs of their home setting. Within what seemed a narrow theological range our proselytizers talked well, too, soon foxing Father, as he later admitted, and clearly unsettling Mr Murphy, for all his Catholicism. Both the elder men agreed that the Mormon faith had much to recommend it – until they heard of its prohibition of alcohol! Our guests then turned to my mother, who had listened without uttering a word. The quiet debate which followed I didn't understand much of, but it held me fascinated. There was a deal, I remember, about the finding of holy tablets in a certain American field by Joseph Smith, about probability, gullibility, Joe's veracity and liking for liquor, and much else, all put over, on Mother's side, with a clarity which left the missionaries looking uneasy: they clearly weren't used to this sort of opposition. One offered to bring her a book the very next day which would sweal away all doubts. Politely she asked him not to bother, because there wouldn't be anybody there going to the 'City of God' – 'Unless,' she said, 'it's my husband!'

'Oh no!' the Old Man told her, smirking, 'not if they're teetotal!'

'LOVELY WAR'

IN our village, as in others like it, to have served in the army or navy added nothing to one's social status; quite the reverse, in fact. The veterans of Britain's African and Asian wars, *in toto*, we lauded as heroes, and decorated the streets for their mass return, but individually such men were branded privately as 'low class', especially since nearly all came back to civilian life as unskilled labourers. But our local veterans enjoyed one 'perk'. Whenever a military play came to the Prince of Wales* they rallied to the stage manager's call to arms and marched *en bataillon* across the scene, appearing and reappearing, for one shilling a night and some free beer. After 1907 and the passing of the Territorial Army Act 'Saturday-night soldiers' came among us, so called because the drills and parades of this new amateur army took place in the local barracks during Saturday evenings. People complained that the Territorials had attracted nothing but 'scruff', out for beer money and a free holiday camp, and certainly in late 'set-to's' on Saturday night it was no uncommon thing to see, among those rolling in the gutter, several who soiled His Majesty's uniform; but some of these men, victims of the holocaust, were soon to roll their last in the fields of Flanders.

Children dutifully took from their mentors the patriotic fervour of the time. In our mock-war singing game, traditional to the streets, 'English and Romans', elderly people noted with amusement how over two decades the 'Roman'

* Though efficient as soldiers, they once failed badly, acting as the motive power behind a railway train. In a drama marked by realism the heroine was bidding her lover farewell for ever at Victoria Station. Wordily she got into her compartment through a 'genuine' door, with the rest of the train mere canvas and paint. After an affecting scene the lady began to leave us, with appropriate 'chuffs' from the 'engine' and a hiss of steam. But the stage hands, hitching their 'flat' too high, instead of wheels revealed a line of clogs moving in rhythmic file across the stage. She was waving us all goodbye from a sort of sedan chair!

enemy had been successfully replaced by Russians, French, Boers and finally, after 1907 and 1908, by Germans, all following on national feeling and policy. Again, as 1914 approached, the cowboy-and-Indian 'wars' made popular by the wild-west shows of earlier years gave place to street battles between 'British' and 'Germans' in which a 'foreign spy' often figured. Rising anti-German feeling started to show itself openly. One poor mongrel in our area, part dachshund, suffered wretched cruelties at the hands of boys 'paying out the German sausage dog'. Well before August 1914 women bruited it among us that Mrs Pratz, wife of the local German pork butcher, had given a customer a shilling in change with the remark 'You'll soon have the Kaiser's head on that!' Mother, hearing this, called it rubbish. 'No woman in her situation,' she said, 'would say such a thing.' But customers went on repeating it.

The poor *en masse* greeted the outbreak of war with the same excited anticipation as their children. Here was a colossal event that would somehow sweep meaning and purpose into dingy existence. Many among the old, the chronic sick, the depressed, the suicide-prone determined now to live on – just to see how it would all end. Only too often, among such derelicts, communal misery or disaster, suffered by no matter whom, brought a private consolation, a satisfaction even. Soon, as international slaughter began, the suicide rate would plummet all over Europe. In our world the more thoughtful elders were gravely disturbed. They seemed to sense that this was the supreme crisis of their lives – a break-up of the old order. During the first few days fears of food shortage sent children scouring the town seeking to buy flour, butter, tea and, above all, sugar; but anxiety soon passed as the assurance went forth from certain high authorities that the war would soon be over and won. There were men who rushed to join up in order to get in while there was yet fun to be had.*

In the manner of children since wars began, down Zinc

* Those historians over-fond of stressing the many benefits accruing to urban workers from the industrial revolution might like to note that, according to army records, Manchester and Salford – the 'first industrial society' – produced during World War I the 'smallest soldiers in the British forces'. About 90 per cent of the Bantam regiments, it was said (minimum height for entry, five feet), came from the area.

Street we formed a 'battalion' and, wearing anything that gave the military touch, marched around with a stretcher and a girl dressed as a Red Cross nurse. Finding some punctured paraffin cans in a railway wagon, two of us organized an 'oil drum' band, so impressive in its decibel output that, headed by a flag and general uproar, the whole contingent set off gloriously for Manchester. There, marching along Deansgate, we collected no less than twenty-five shillings. 'It's for the wounded soldiers!' our nurse explained, rattling the box. But near City Hall on Liverpool Road—catastrophe! A horde of local savagery from the dens round Knott Mill bore down on us. After a short, sharp battle we fled, much battered, losing our colours and every single drum. Back at base again, in an informal post-mortem on the débâcle, it was decided that since we, as troops, had fought and been wounded on the field of honour, there was nothing ethically amiss with dividing the collection among ourselves.

One odd result of static warfare in France was to stimulate boys at home into sinking trenches on any spare piece of ground where one could dig with impunity. I remember watching three lads, tough nuts from our industrial school, delving in a slit of considerable depth by the brickfield. One had a broken spade; the others threw out wet earth on slats of wood. I went and sat by the wall a few feet away next to Jud Pimblott, whose mother was a long-standing tick customer of ours. Jud ignored me and everyone else. Dull and slow, already turned fifteen, he had never worked anywhere from leaving school in spite of continual search. Every morning before setting off for his own job at six o'clock, Jud's father turned him out on the street. 'Get out, idleback, and look for it!' he was told. 'No lyin' in bed 'ere!' In the evenings the old man wouldn't even allow him to sit in his presence; most nights he had to stay out until bedtime. Morosely he wandered about, dodging in for a meal from his mother when her husband was absent. He sat now, staring with no interest at all at the activity before us.

Soon a bright-faced little boy of about eight skipped up, a stranger to us. Clean, he was, very well clad, and showing bare knees. I put him down as some child visiting friends or relatives at one of the main street shops. 'Hello!' he said, smiling at big Monaghan, the lad with the spade. 'May I help you, please?' I cocked up my ears and at once feared for him. This wasn't our language at all!

Monaghan stared, hesitated, then, 'Aye!' he said. 'Gerrin 'ere an' fill that there box wi' muck!' The other two lads sniggered. All eagerness, the small boy climbed down and began to scrape soil together. Knowing too well the sort of company he had fallen in with, I watched in trepidation, and not without cause. All went well for a minute or so, but soon, as if by accident, one digger began to throw slush about his shoes. The child stopped and moved a little way up the slit. Then another cast it at his legs and body. Finally Monaghan shot a whole spadeful into his face. The boy cried out in pain and fear. 'Don't! Oh, don't, please! Oh! You've blinded me!'

I ran forward, bent, took his arm, dragged him sobbing from the trench, guided him to the wall and tried to wipe his face with my handkerchief. Dark now from the head downwards in slime, he moved away, weeping bitterly, crossed the croft and made for home. Jud Pimblott had watched it all with total indifference. Happily the three boys were digging again. I paged through my store of abuse, looked at Jud Pimblott and considered. The Irish lad in the trench was two years older than me.

'Monaghan,' I said, 'you're a dirty big gormless get!'*

He climbed out. 'Say that again, Curly!'

I said it again. He drew his foot back. Then Pimblott spoke. 'Touch 'im, Irish,' he mumbled, 'an' I'll bash yer.'

At once Monnie returned to the earthworks. I gave a sigh of relief. But I'd gauged it right! Down Zinc Street you didn't 'live in a shop' for nothing! Jud's mother owed mine for groceries; we both knew it, and Jud knew where his 'duty' lay!

By now one of the diggers had grown uneasy. 'Let's fuck off for a bit,' he said. 'That kid's ol' feller might come!' And they trotted away, laughing, Monnie trailing the spade behind him.

Pimblott went on sitting without another word. I climbed alone into the brickfield, sat down on a heap of rubble and burst into tears. Soon, feeling ashamed, I wiped my eyes, but

---

* Unless hard pressed the sons of artisans didn't 'swear'. Though acquainted with all the oaths, they confined themselves, like the boy in Joyce's *Ulysses*, to a constant repetition of the epithet 'blooming'. Generally, only labourers' offspring used 'obscenities'.

stayed there miserable. Suddenly it seemed a dirty, wretched world.

Later Syd came up and looked at me. 'You been cryin'?' he asked.

'I fell off the wall,' I told him.

SKOOL

THE church 'of the establishment' to which our school belonged had been built about 1830. It stood on the north flank of the parish, whilst on the south rose an infantry barracks – both buildings being erected, some thought, to keep the lower orders on their knees. Our seat of learning, attached to the church, had opened its doors in 1839, several years before Friedrich Engels, whose factory stood close by, wrote about the district. In all justice we pupils could have sung, with Ernest Jones,* 'We're low – we're low – we're very, very low.' And they provided us with education to match. Year after year inspectors came and condemned our great sooty edifice by the marshalling yards. They damned the unqualified staff, the stinking rooms, the appalling cultural results. In all, they reported, a place of educational ill repute, even by the low standards of the times. But I found it delightful. So did all my siblings, and we blubbered and complained if anything occurred to stop attendance. Then, whatever inspectors might say, we scholars had reason at least for spiritual pride. 'The religious tone of this school,' reported the Bishop's examiners, 'is excellent'!

One day, after I had spent some months in the infants' department, a lady inspector appeared in class with the head-mistress. Miss Wilkie, our teacher, told us to sit up straight, fold arms and listen.† The visitor addressed the fifty of us

* Ernest Charles Jones (1819-69), 'The Song of the Lower Classes'.

† At other times, to ensure complete silence in class, this lady clicked a small wooden instrument called a 'signal', upon which we all placed a forefinger across our lips, pointing up a nostril, and stayed that way until she signalled release.

very sweetly and ended by asking me to stand on the form and read aloud from a primer. This I did, after which the headmistress presented me with a book, the 'progress prize', she said, 'for the little boy who has learnt to read the quickest in the whole class'! The inspector smiled and smiled.

I rushed home. Mother was with a neighbour, but I babbled it all to my sisters. Their reaction staggered me. Even Ellie, the essence of good nature, seemed displeased. And Janie was scathing. 'You could read very well before you ever went near the Infants!' This was true; all we younger children had been pupils in a perpetual seminary which the girls ran in various corners of the kitchen. Even by the time I was three Ellie had cut letters out of shop showcards and got me building words with her mobile alphabet. In a huddle the girls now discussed the affair, while I stood apart, apprehensive. Then Janie came up. 'You're a cheat! That's what you are! That book's going back! Give it to me!' I pushed it tightly under my armpit, broke into tears, called them names and settled myself miserably on the stair bottom. When Mother came home they surrounded her at once. Her response was quite different. First she pointed out that on the very day of my introduction to school she had told the headmistress I could read, and write simple sentences. 'And others join the class who can read too,' she added lamely.

'That's nothing to do with it,' said Janie. 'That prize is for the infant that didn't know anything – no letters, even – then learned quickest in the class!' Against this logic Mother remained silent. 'We should take it back!' Jane said again.

I stood there, glowering, still clutching the prize. 'We can hardly do that,' Mother said. 'After all, it's not Robert's fault. They could have given it to him,' she went on doubtfully, 'for his progress since starting. After all, he is a fine little reader.' But she didn't convince my sisters. 'That teacher was just showing him off – that's all!' said Jane. So the book gave me no pleasure; I felt a fraud, but couldn't understand why.

Soon after the mass ascent of sixty of us children from primary to junior school, an event was announced that set us all gabbling in anticipation. The headmaster's friend, a missionary just back from Africa, had been persuaded, as a unique favour, we were told, to give a lecture with magic lantern, and display, besides, certain exotic creatures 'in glass jars'. Some older scholars had had in fact, as cannibals might say, a bellyful of missionaries. Pretty well all those gentlemen who had escaped uneaten appeared to have performed, at some time or other, in our bailiwick, boring us numb. 'They're even fetchin' 'em now,' Janie complained, 'to the Band of Hope!' But this was to be different – lantern slides of Africa *and* weird things in jars! Excitement swept me at the very thought of it. Here was living! Then came cruel disappointment. Teachers now informed us that we had far too many pupils for a general show. Selection would therefore be made from the 'very best-behaved boys and girls in the school' (about thirty) and preference given (except, we knew, for teachers' pets) to those in upper classes. All the chosen few would duly receive blue tickets of admittance to that holy of holies, the 'Teachers' Room'. As a new member of Standard II I had no chance of a card, but both Jane and Ellie got one. To crown their joy Mother went to Mrs Mallin's and bought each of them a 'rinking' hat, with crest attached – headwear so much of the vogue to be that not a single girl in the neighbourhood had yet sported one. They hopped about. What a chance to show off on the day!

As for me, I moped around the house, and soon, like a devil denied paradise, my foul heart began to plot evil. When the saints went marching in, I resolved, I would be among that number, come hell or high water! Ellie must be divested of her ticket! A girl generous almost to foolishness, and alert besides to one's moods, she soon noticed my glum looks. Getting her alone, I whined and wept. More than anything in the world, I told her, I longed to inspect Africa and the 'jars', even if I died right afterwards. She listened, growing more and more disturbed as the blackmail took effect.

'Lemme go and I'll tell you every single thing after. I will!' My handkerchief came out. 'You're mean if you don't!'

She looked upset, but didn't answer and hurried away. Day after day I trapped her, laying on the same line.

'But I *do* so want to go myself,' she said weakly, 'and see everything and show my new hat. Anyway, Mother just wouldn't let me give you the ticket.'

That was certain; but cunning had found a way. I pleaded again. 'Ellie, please! Please! And you can still show your hat. Come to school with me on the day. Don't tell anyone at home. There'll be lots of girls round the door watching the others go in. They'll see your hat. But, Ellie, do let me have the ticket now!'

She stood hesitant and, as always, twisting her handkerchief this way and that. 'I *would* really like to go. Don't keep asking me, please!'

Then I played my ace. 'Look! I'll give you my penny on Saturday for *four* weeks. There!'

She looked distressed at once. 'Oh, no! I couldn't *sell* it, really I couldn't! I'll – I'll give it to you!'

Triumphant, but suddenly feeling like a skunk, I took it.

'Better not mention anything to Janie,' she said, 'or Mother will get to know.'

On the great afternoon we departed early, leaving our elder sister to follow. Ellie looked so pretty in her crested 'rinker'. Boldly I went past the crowd round the school door, upstairs and produced my blue ticket.

Mr Hales looked down. 'Where's your sister?' (She was a prime favourite of his.)

'Ellie gave it to me, sir, so *I* could come.'

'Just like her!' He took another from his pocket. 'Here! Run home and give her this!' Overjoyed, I rushed down to the street. She was still standing there, and within two minutes we were both sliding our bottoms along the back row of desks in the sanctum. Rapidly the place filled to excess. Jane, hurrying in late, looked astonished to see me there. I smirked across at her. At last Mr Rowley himself entered, accompanied by the lecturer, a bald man with a beard, then Mr Hales, bearing accessories. First, after the Head's words of welcome, they displayed the jars, and these, for not a few of us, turned out a sad flop. In the mind's eye we had seen them as glass containers, about the size, say, of seven-pound pickle jars, holding a broad selection of the smaller African mammalia, all hopping lively. What we got was a series of specimen bottles that sped rapidly along the rows so that each of us caught a glimpse of something peculiar and very dead bobbing about in liquid. Then it was snatched away. So tightly had they packed us, an arm, once down, stayed jammed by neighbours' bodies. The heat increased. Our visitor talked in a 'London way', Ellie explained: difficult to follow. Messrs Rowley and Hales now placed blackout boards against windows, and a picture flashed on to a white screen. Glorious!

'Now what is that, children?' asked the gentleman.

'A lion, sir!' we chorused.

'Good! And what is another name for the lion?'

144

'The king of beasts, sir!' we told him.

'Very good.' Next we saw the lioness, then both of them together, followed by lions eating, drinking, yawning, lions with cubs, lions without cubs, cubs without lions. The whole continent seemed to be seething with them. Soon, with all window ventilation effectively stopped, the temperature soared. I began to sweat. Ears buzzed, head hung; I couldn't look another lion in the face. Now a sudden nausea rolled over my stomach.

'Lemme get out!'

Ellie bent towards me. 'You can't, silly! They'd have to put the lights on and move everybody!'

'Out!' I said.

'We're stuck, I tell you! Oh, do be a good boy!'

The missionary droned on and on. Then:

'I wanna be sick!'

'Quiet, there!' Rowley called over the gloom.

Ellie whispered, horrified, 'Oh, not here, love! *Not on the teachers' floor!* Whatever would they say?' Like many children of the time, Ellie looked upon our instructors as the Lord's anointed, guardians of total wisdom – the beautiful people!* Whenever any one of them chose her to go a small errand her face lit up: she went in humble pride, a dedicated acolyte. The thought of my heaving up over their floor simply appalled her.

Our immediate companions pressed away, giving us a few inches to spare and causing muttered protests along the dark. 'I'm gonna be sick!' I said.

Agonized, she looked down. There was no escape anywhere. Then gently she pushed my head to my knees and opened the rinking hat. 'Here,' she said, 'be sick in this.' And I vomited into her woolly sacklet. For the rest of it, face in her lap, retching a little, I knelt on the floor while she stroked my neck and murmured down, seeing little of the show.

After what seemed aeons of misery it was all over. Day-

* I remember standing in the school yard with a six-year-old friend as our teacher, the fair goddess Miss Wilkie, passed by, swinging keys *en route* to a lavatory. We watched in dismay. It came to us as a little shock that, like ordinary mortals, she too had to go 'on' the w.c. (The working classes always went 'on', never 'to'. In that connection the preposition is still a 'class' betrayer.)

light flashed in among us again and we shuffled off with the crush, her arm about my shoulder. Our eldest sister, hat perched on her plaits, stood in an admiring little group by the school door. 'Where's yours?' she asked sharply. Ellie explained everything. Jane looked furious. 'Things are always happening with *him*!' she said. 'Spoils everything, he does! A great big nuisance!'

'Leave him,' Ellie told her. 'He isn't well.' Full of remorse at ruining it all and moved by such kindness, I felt dumbly that greater love than hers had no sister.

In spite of abominable conditions in school some of us went on learning eagerly, at least a few of the staff showing themselves kindly, human and even gifted teachers. Though we had exceptions. Only a cursory interest was taken by any instructor in either music or art. A certain Miss Lampert, with twenty years' teaching behind her in the nineteenth century, enlightened us on both. 'Music' consisted of running up and down the tonic sol-fa modulator and singing the same three songs over and over again. Our chorus mistress didn't guide or conduct, but as we made a 'joyful' sound she stalked tall among us, suddenly ducking an ear to within an inch of a child's mouth and, if no note came forth, she brought the lad out and caned him. 'No silent birds in *our* little nest!' she said. We sniggered. Once 'Miss' bagged four 'mutes' in a single foray, unfortunates who even after hearing a melody a hundred times seemed incapable of producing it, in or out of tune. The quartet were lined up facing the class. 'Now,' said Miss Lampert, 'on my downbeat you four will sing together, "Sweet lass of Richmond Hill"! Right!' Her cane cut the air. Three mouths opened and closed in the manner of goldfish while she beat time; but no sound issued. She let them go on to the end, then punished each one in turn and sent them back whimpering.

Her art lessons to fifty of us in Standard II we found equally instructive. The subject made no appeal to me. From an early age, after drawing anything, in order to assist critics I always added the names of objects depicted. But Ignatius, who through frequent absence from school was labelled 'backward', could sketch, we thought, beautifully – a 'natural'. One afternoon Miss Lampert arranged a 'still life' competition, Ig by lucky chance being present. She placed an apple on a pile of books, giving each of us a piece of paper with two bits of chalk, red and yellow. 'Draw just the fruit!'

our mentor commanded. 'And I'm presenting it to the one who does best.' Good for Iggy. 'You'll win it!' we whispered. He looked happy and had laid foundations, all eagerness, before any of us had even started. Technically the pippin appeared to offer few difficulties: large, almost spherical; the left side glowed saffron, the right a bright red. After twenty minutes Miss Lampert began to knee her way between the rows, commenting here and there. Nothing seemed to please her much. I sat at the back, rolling chalk up a desk. My creation had a disastrous two-dimensional look; I'd given up. When the teacher reached Iggy, on a row immediately in front of us, she stopped, bent over and took up his drawing, showing it round for us all to see. It bulged splendidly off the paper. Then she put it down and began to slap his head. 'Here's a silly fool,' she said, 'who can't tell left from right! Yellow' (slap) 'where red' (slap) 'should be, red' (slap) 'where yellow!' Iggy put a forearm on the desk and laid his face upon it. Looking down, fearful, I saw I'd made the same 'error'. Like lightning the ball of my thumb went rubbing over all. Worse now! The apple had somehow transformed itself into an orange! Cursing art, I overlaid each half thickly with the needed colours, sat back and awaited Nemesis. Miss Lampert approached, picked up my paper and considered. 'Now here's a really beautiful drawing – almost like a photograph!' Publicly she awarded me the fruit. At playtime, feeling very uneasy, I bit into it, watched by two hangers-on, each hoping to get the core, the usual gesture of generosity among us. Iggy stood by the wall, staring; under each eye a smudge had dried like a little beard. With what could have been a qualm of conscience I went over, apple half eaten, and handed it to him.*

* I met Ignatius for the last time during the late 'fifties. He came and introduced himself again in my prison classroom and we chatted together of old, far-off things. A few days before, one of Her Majesty's judges, coining a phrase – 'You are a menace to society!' – had given him a savage sentence for still another in an endless series of paltry larcenies.

'Well!' said Iggy after our talk, rubbing his hands (he was still a childlike man). 'How are we fixed, then?' This, in lags' parlance, meant simply, 'What are you going to do for an old pal that is strictly illegal?'

'I can't get you the key,' I told him, 'nor the governor's daughter. But how about a handful of coloured chalks and a

From the middle years of Queen Victoria's reign thrift among the lowest working orders had been much encouraged as an alternative to starvation, and, later, we too were sold on the virtue by our Rector. He gave us little homilies on both frugality and ambition. 'One of the poorest boys who ever came, barefoot, to this school,' he said, 'is now a big man in the Manchester oil and tallow trade.' Opportunities were endless; but we must strive! Every Monday morning the affluent among us lined up to have family savings noted in a folder and placed in the school bank. These were later put into a leather bag and taken by our head monitor into the care of Messrs Williams Deacon. It was in the savings queue I learned that money 'talked'. If we were 'flush' at home and I handed in the occasional ten shillings the Head, taking it, smiled and made pleasant remarks; asked about my mother, perhaps, even made a little joke. The next lad's deposit got silence. What can you say for threepence? 'Class' received due recognition even at that level.

During my last two years at school I acted as 'number one' monitor, which meant release on most days from lessons, a freedom rather irksome, since learning drew me still. I lack-eyed for the headmaster, running his errands, seeking truants, checking lists and, of course, going off every Monday after-noon with the leather bag. Through a riveted reading each week of the *Magnet* magazine some of us boys were aware of the profound respect that the scholars of Greyfriars College registered for their headmaster, that revered sadist, Dr Locke; but I felt none for mine, or the school either. Without scruple I read all correspondence and confidential notes, picking up a deal of curious information, which was distributed for the interest and amusement of classmates. This way they got early warning of the visits of His Majesty's Inspectors. We noticed then how our teachers developed the jitters, how they suddenly became more anxious, patient, friendly, pumping us with answers to questions which, it was hoped, the dreaded HMI's would ask on 'Judgement Day'. And the great ones duly arrived, putting the fear of God into

sketchbook?' Gladly he took them and said there was 'nothing like "art" for passing the time'. And he had plenty to pass! Soon after leaving prison he died suddenly one night in a Manchester lodging house – a second release, if ever there was one. The pain of the world came too early to Ignatius.

everyone on the staff. But *we* loved them! Like Dutch uncles they went round the classes, treating us with a sort of old-world courtesy, always enquiring, and making us feel that, in school at least, girls and boys were the people who mattered. Among these men were some of the pioneers who dragged the elementary education system 'kicking and scream-ing' into the twentieth century. They came, and their questions ranged far and wide. 'Where, my boy,' asked one inspector, addressing Sydney Carey in Standard V, 'is the city of Rome?'

'On the Ganges!' Syd told him. (In geography Sydney put most places on that holy river, a weakness due to our possession of Empire.) The great man looked sad, and our teacher, Miss Bethel, bit her lips.

'Sir!' I shouted, shooting up an arm. 'Capital of Italy, sir! Called the Eternal City!' The old gentleman gobbled with pleasure and spoke to his colleague. I then proceeded to paint the lily! 'Also known as the "*Internal* City", sir, because it's chockful of underground passages and caves and cellars where all them early Christians lived!'

Now this was news to them. They smiled together, mur-mured a moment, then the elder turned. 'Well, hardly, my boy, hardly. But a very good answer indeed!' I fell back on my laurels and Miss Bethel shot me a lovely smile.

They moved among us like visiting royalty. All canes disappeared, and after several days of gentle but effective buzzing about our hive they summed it all up. Later the Head and some of his minions got their roasting, a cooled-off version of which appeared in the school log afterwards. Certain members of the staff were 'incompetent', 'unintelli-gent', 'unqualified'; 'unimaginative methods used; teaching conditions – appalling'.

Once a chief inspector came with an assistant who had visited us on an earlier occasion. In the aftermath old Rowley, the Head, looked, I thought, more shaken than usual. He stood by his desk after school closed and seemed to be in deep trouble. Putting books away, I busied about with both ears cocked. How pleasant it was to see the mighty humbled! The inspectors, I gathered, were deeply disturbed at his scholars' inability to express themselves. We appeared to lack something, mentioned several times, called 'oral facility'. I rolled the words over in my mind and, later, asked my mother about it all. 'They can't talk!' she said. The inspectors added that we had responded to their questions either not at all or in broken, ungrammatical sentences. 'Most disturbing!' Moreover we had been drilled, it seemed, into a sort of slavish passivity: the teacher addressed us pupils and we did nothing but sit and listen, and altogether there was no health in us. The chief inspector put his fist somewhere in the region of the master's chest, then brought it towards his own, spreading his fingers. 'Draw it *out*!' he said. 'Understand?' Rowley nodded dumbly. Expanded vocabulary, fluency, self-assurance, that's what they were after! Our Head defended himself weakly, pointing out the kind of children he had to deal with – 'the homes they come from . . .' But his critics now showed impatience; they had visited similar schools to ours and found the pupils far more articulate. Something had to be done, and that quickly. In among the ruck of words that followed I heard Rowley say emphatically that he too had boys who . . . and he called me over. This lad, for instance, from Standard VII . . .

The chief inspector gazed down on me kindly. 'I didn't see you, my boy, in the top class!'

'No, sir,' I said. 'I was washin' out Standard VI's inkwells all afternoon.' He then asked me about the family – how my father earned his living. Did my parents take a newspaper and read books?

'My mother reads all sorts,' I told him. 'History books, story books – everything. I'm in the liberry.'

'And do you talk at home?' the other inspector asked, 'in the family – conversation?'

'We've a shop, sir. It's talkin' all day!'

'Ah, well, now!' he said. 'That's understandable! Now can you tell me the meaning of the word "articulate" – ar-tic-u-late?'

'Able to speak well, I think, sir – express yerself, like?'

'Excellent! Thank you, my boy!'

Old Rowley was beaming. 'You can go now!'

The new regime to increase verbal flow and stimulate self-assurance began the very next week under the direction of a phthisic young Scotsman. In the hall Mr Mackie always made great show and taught us well, but behind a classroom door away from the Head's surveillance he fell at once into a coma of indifference, and precious little instruction any of us got. But now the heat was on. According to the log book, His Majesty's Inspectors required clear evidence, next time round, of an improvement in 'oral facility'. In any case, our school was to be the subject of a special report to the Board of Education. Fortunately, Mr Mackie had a brainwave: we would establish, he said, a 'moot', of which the old Anglo-Saxons had been very fond. We knew about the Anglo-Saxons! In our moot, problems of the day would be thrashed out. 'Everyone will be allowed,' he said, 'to stand up in front of the class and say just what they like. But no reading! Talk! Self-expression! That's what I want! The Anglo-Saxons didn't read!'

Mr Rowley, much enthused, came and set the first moot point, chalking it up on the board – 'Children should go to school until they are fifteen'. 'But write a composition on it beforehand,' he told us, 'then you'll have plenty of thoughts to go at when it comes to the public speaking. You can be *for* this, or against it, just as you wish.'

I turned out an essay of several pages wildly in favour of the proposal, and Mackie chose me at once as a protagonist. Unfortunately, in spite of threat or cajolery, he couldn't find a single other pupil willing to stand before the class and put the opposing, or indeed any, point of view, and this not for want of ideas but through fear alone. Free speech didn't come easily to children kept down at home and in the classroom. Just before the time for debate arrived, however, at which Mr Rowley himself would preside, the teacher dragooned a terrified girl off the back row. 'After Robert has finished his address,' Mackie told her, '*you* say a few words. Just a sentence or two, if that's all you can manage, but say *something*!' Having chatted the theme over with my mother the night before, I got on the box provided and did my three-minute stint without trouble. Rich people, I remember saying, sent their children to schools and colleges until they were twenty-one, so there must be something good in it. We would become doctors and teachers and chemists and explorers – things like that, if we went to school until we were fifteen. I was all for it.

Although Mackie had informed us that the audience was quite free to heckle or clap, they heard me out in dead silence. But both adult listeners seemed very pleased; the Head even patted my shoulder. 'Well, well!' said Mr Mackie. 'Very well spoken indeed! You almost convinced me! I've a story book at home for you – a little present. Now, Weeton!' (They dispensed with Christian names at school, even for girls.) My opponent, Lily Weeton, a pallid girl with plaits,

151

came out and stepped on the box. Her words were few but explosive. 'I think,' she said, 'we should gerrout to work at fourteen and fetch some money in for us parents.' Then she stepped off the box to a thunderclap of applause, cheering and clog-stamping that rocked the school. Bubbling excitement, our 'electorate' now went to the poll, and the headmaster, acting as returning officer, announced the result in professional style:

Roberts, Robert   2
Weeton, Lily   48

Storming cheers again for the victor. Eddie Franklin and a girl friend had given me a sympathy vote, but nevertheless admitted to being intellectually with the opposition. 'Even Mackie was against me!' I complained to my mother that evening.

'Humph!' she said. 'Shows how much sense *he's* got!'

Late the following week Ike Harbin, a lad in Standard VII, came across. 'Did Scotch Harry give you that book?'

I shook my head.

'You'll be lucky!' he said. 'I been runnin' bets for him to the bookie's for a long time on the quiet. He promised me threepence, but he never gave me nothink!'

Soon we heard through Weeton, Lily, that he still owed the caretaker's wife for half the wool in his pullover. After three weeks I boldly asked him one day after class for the promised gift. He stared a moment, then walked past as if I hadn't spoken.

Our last debate before the summer holidays, Mackie decided, would be 'political'. He ordered me to write a five-minute speech expounding the aims of socialism and the Labour Party. This had to be learned off by heart, he said, and only referred to if I broke down. Again failing to find anyone in the class ready to provide opposition, he proposed to speak against me himself. On Friday afternoon we appeared once more before our audience. I climbed on the dais as before, and stood mute.

'Go on, boy! Wazzermatter? "Ladies and gentlemen – " Go on!'

Tight-lipped, I continued staring in front of me. Dumb insolence! At last he came and snatched my script, gabbled his way through it, then spoke free on behalf of the Conservative Party, gaining a landslide victory at the poll which followed. Like their fathers, the children of the proletariat were, as yet, unripe for revolution. After that the moot collapsed. I never received my book.

Boys and girls about to leave school for work were anxious to get a written 'character' from the headmaster. Such 'testimonials' our Head turned out from stock with only minimal variation of phrase. 'James Jackson. Nine years in this school; average intelligence and ability.' 'Amy Brown. Below the mark generally, though clean and tidy. Signed J. Rowley.' Some parents set great store on receiving these dockets. Their offspring might well be backward, but they wanted written proof of it. And backwardness was no stigma. 'When it comes to schoolin',' one mother said complacently in the shop, 'our Lizzie is ninepence to t'shillin'; but she can earn her corn!' One girl we knew was so retarded they had to fetch her to and from work, but she made sixpence a day in between and that was what mattered.

As my fourteenth birthday approached I asked Mr Rowley for my own vital reference. He picked up what he called his 'meemo' pad, tore off a page and, clearly with his thoughts elsewhere, began to scribble. 'Average . . .' Then he stopped, looked at me, tore it up and wrote on a second sheet. This he rubber-stamped, slipped into an envelope and sealed. 'Give this to your mother!' I left with his note and, as it happened, the 'class prize', a heavy volume which I had had no hand in choosing, entitled *Heroes of the United Services*.

At home the Old Man sat smoking in the kitchen. He stared at my book, perused the contents of the envelope (which I too had read, carefully opening the flap before the Head's saliva dried) and gave a grunt of satisfaction. My mother came downstairs. 'How's that, then?' he asked, handing her the character. She scanned it, frowned, and read it again, slowly and aloud. ' "To Whom It May Concern. The above-named is a very smart, intelligent lad whom I can recommend. He will, I am sure, give complete satisfaction to any employer who might care to use his services." '

'Pooh!' She flicked it up the table and went into the shop.

Father reached and put my reference back into the envelope. 'Well, I dunno!' he said to the mantelpiece. 'If I live to be a hundred I won't understand that woman!' And for once I agreed with him. He was reading the novels of

Hall Caine at the time (an author he considered the 'world's greatest'), and he picked up his book. 'All the same,' he said, 'that's going to come in very handy when you have to start looking for a job.'

The prospect of another offspring launched on the sea of life and labour gave him much satisfaction. Two daughters already brought in weekly wages, whilst a third, working at home as servant-cum-shop assistant, more than earned her 'keep', as he liked to put it. Altogether Father felt now that he was beginning to be recompensed for all those years when, he believed, he alone had maintained the family.

His virtues, Mother used to assure him, were about to be rewarded! Sadly, though, his eldest son didn't wish to earn any keep. I wanted to stay on at school – any school.

'A pushin', nosy lot o' children you got, mostly,' Grandma had told her son on more than one occasion, 'wi' too much to say! That's what comes o' not keepin' 'em under!' My mother laughed. It was 'nosiness', perhaps, that pricked some of us on to learning early – not through any desire, though, for self-improvement. We just wanted to know. Scraps of lore, tags of history or geography – indeed, any idea at all – we sucked in from person or print with a sort of astonishment – 'Imagine that, now!' In this quirk of mind my elder sisters showed themselves even more 'pushing' than I. 'I've just been reading,' Ellie would tell us, 'Britain was once joined to Europe and there was no North Sea. Well!' Or Ada would announce, 'Listen, all of you! It says here Beethoven is pronounced "bate-oven". Get that!' Such nuggets would startle us into silence. One stared at another. 'Really, now!'

And we learned verse, any sort of verse – Ellie so much that, at times, she seemed 'high' on it. I used to go through the scullery, bearing a shovelful of fuel from the yard, with her seemingly occupied washing up at the slopstone. (We had no 'sinks' then.) ' "And ever against eating cares",' she would say dreamily . . .

'Eh?'

' "And ever against eating cares
Lap me in soft Lydian airs,
Married to immortal verse"!'

'Oh!'

I passed on with the coal. But many of the lines she threw out apropos nothing stuck on my mind like burrs. Once, after Ada had borrowed an anthology from the library called

154

Gems of Victorian Verse, they saved up and, for sevenpence, bought a writing book, deckle-edged, with a mock-leather cover. In this, labouring with love, they began to build a treasury of their own. I wanted badly to be in on it, and at last they allowed me to make a small contribution to financial outlay and be considered a partner. Within a short time, however, the thesaurus was almost full and I hadn't been asked to append one single gem. This made me furious. Apologetically Ellie offered me the last few pages. Sulking hard, I now proposed to grace these with pearls of my own composition. The girls objected, quietly but firmly: all the poets had to be dead, like contributors Shakespeare, Wordsworth, Tennyson. I got angrier still. They had not only got my money by false pretences, I felt, but were now imposing censorship besides. We took the whole thing to high court. 'How much has he invested in the scheme?' Mother asked. They told her. 'Very well. *I'll* give him his halfpenny back and buy him out!'

'We'll still let him put *proper* poetry in, if he wants,' Ada said.

'Don't want!' I snarled at this insult. 'I'm starting one of my own!'

Soon the family fell on hard times. In the years just prior to my leaving school Mother went into what people called a 'decline' and spent weeks together in bed. As children we never knew quite what was wrong. Relatives came, went upstairs, and left looking grave. We boys had our bed transferred to another room. Once, in a period of 'convalescence', I saw my mother standing in the back kitchen. She coughed, raised and lowered a handkerchief. 'There's blood on your fingers,' I said, ' – bright blood!' 'It's nothing,' she told me. Father often looked worried now. Trade fell off badly in the shop. He couldn't meet the bills. Every evening we saw him come home quite sober; at weekend he shortened his drinking bouts. We children grew more and more neglected, and looked it. Father's mother came to sympathize. Janie heard one of her asides and felt sick. 'You know well enough! Didn't her father go with it, and a brother and sister! Get a woman in to keep this lot in order!' But Jane stayed off from the mill. 'I can manage,' she said. 'We don't want any second-hand mothers!'

The doctor came, a tall, lean man whom both parents had known since before marriage. With him we were familiar;

whenever in the neighbourhood he had called – non-professionally, leaning his bicycle by the shop door. For half an hour together Mother and he used to sit and talk earnestly at the end of the kitchen. What was discussed intrigued us much, but we knew when to curb curiosity. Dr Delane visited us now. Once, before leaving, he stood in the shop with Father. Later the Old Man came in much disturbed. 'We'll have to get out of this place,' he said. 'It just doesn't do for your mother at all.' He stood before us, crumpled, like a boy in trouble.

'That's a discovery!' Janie said.

But she recovered. An older woman came down among us: more taciturn she seemed, and less interested in the world around her, even in us. Janie went back to work. Trade in the shop picked up quickly. At once all her children grew cleaner and better fed. Boisterous again, Father returned to his old habits. I won a special prize in a schools' essay competition. This pleased her. 'You should go on,' she said. 'Isn't there some examination you could take?' Excited, I asked at school. There was! But our Head didn't put pupils in. 'They have to know algebra and geometry,' he told me. ' – Well above anything we do.' Some homework, then? He shook his head; they didn't give homework. But I could enter, of course. No harm in that. But there was Father to face. And we had been here before!

Throughout her schooldays Ellie's intelligence was duly remarked on by teachers; she came home with high praise for her 'wonderful essays'. 'And a very sweet girl besides!' they said. This everyone found gratifying, especially Grandma. 'Ellie's not only the nicest child you got,' she had told Father, 'she's the cleverest! She'll pass that labour exam – no trouble at all! You'll get her off school for twelve an' into that mill. Not like them loobies so daft they got to stay till they're fourteen!'

My mother had other hopes, and we heard of them. Ellie sat one evening on the sofa, screwing a handkerchief nervously in her fingers. I hung around for the 'showdown'. Father had just fixed new heels on his boots and was putting the tools away.

'I wonder,' said his wife, 'if we could set by a shilling or two a week for a time till we've enough to send Ellie to one of those commercial colleges in Manchester?'

He looked up. Any saving at that time could come from

one source alone, and both knew it. He protested at once. 'Damn it, woman – pay for lessons when we owe the wholesaler every week and a man can't find enough to have his boots repaired!'

'You can always find plenty for beer!' she told him.

'Beer is my food!' he roared.* And that was it. Ellie sat lost in disappointment.

Father had no sort of business career in mind for the boys either. Quite early on he had let it be known that *he* wasn't bringing his lads up to be 'stool-arsed Jacks – sittin' all their days in some bloody office. They're goin' to do a man's job – engineerin'!' Finest work in the world! Father, like most of his generation, felt that all men who didn't work with their hands were in some way emasculated. Surprisingly, though, he offered no objection to my entering for a Technical School bursary. True, it meant the loss of twelve months' wages, but afterwards I might start 'up the ladder', with a job in some drawing office. Again, the girls were earning a little and shop trade had increased. He decided to make the sacrifice, only instructing me to 'get through'.

'Call at school,' the Head ordered me, 'the morning of your examination.' There he handed me a ruler, pen, pencil and set square. In a great hall of the Technical College, surrounded by neat, uniformed boys equipped with fountain pens and sets of drawing instruments, I attempted two papers. One, the English, gave me no trouble: the second lay well beyond my knowledge. I failed it hopelessly. One afternoon weeks later, just in from an errand, I saw the Old Man sitting at the table fingering a sheet of paper, a scowl on his face.

'So yer passed!' he shouted down the kitchen.

'Yes!' I said, bold with disappointment. 'I came top!'

He rose, threatening, from his chair. 'Get out!' he roared. 'Get out and find work!'

I went out and found work.

The young woman at the Juvenile Labour Exchange was pleasant about it. 'Just fill in this green card,' she said, 'and put what you want to be at the bottom.'

I completed the form and wrote on the last line, 'Journalist'.

---

* It was also his medicine. A jug of 'bitter', drunk smartly after the red-hot kitchen poker had 'mulled it up', did wonders, he said, for a cold on the chest.

Journalists weren't in demand, but they wanted a lad in a brass-finishing shop. I took that. Going home after getting the job, I stood on the iron bridge, took our headmaster's reference from my pocket, tore it to shreds and pushed it through the latticework. The flurry scattered far below on to a train of coal trucks roaring into the docks tunnel and vanished, 'Like the snowflake on the river, A moment white and gone for ever.' That was school done! I was entering the world of men.

SONG OF APPRENTICES

THE general engineering works which 'cared' to use my services employed about one hundred and fifty men in foundry, fitting, turning, pattern shop and smithy. Jammed in between a woodyard and the railway line, it blocked one end of a long, gloomy street. At an office window I had handed in my card from the labour bureau and minutes later a tall, shrivelled man appeared in billy-pot and apron. Behind him, like a page, stepped a small boy, perhaps a year my senior, with an eye askew. The man looked down and addressed me for about thirty seconds in a sort of clacking gibberish, then cocked his head, questioning, it seemed. Not having understood more than a few words, I stuttered in embarrassment. 'Tlitsch!' he snorted. 'See Tlitsch!' He pushed my card back at me, jerked a thumb to the lad and hurried away through a door into a rattle of wheels. Confused, I turned to go, but the boy stopped me. 'Tlitsch!' he said, mocking. 'Tich Tilson – that's me! You got the job, kid. He knows your old feller – been boozin' with him! Start on Monday!'

'Who – Who was that?' I asked.

He smiled. 'That's our Jack. Foreman – brass shop. Jack Oddie – all legs an' no body! He got no roof to his mouth. You 'ave to learn 'im, see – like a foreign language. You get used! Not a bad bloke, though. But Fred Fearney – charge-hand – watch 'im. That's a real bastard!'

'What do I fetch?' I asked.

'A brew can, that's all. And come 7.45 I'll be learnin' yer!'
he added importantly.

I hurried home and told my mother. 'Eighteen shillings a
week, it is, and they didn't ask for a character.'

The brass shop of youth lay a tunnel of a room, flanked
on the left by massive Lancashire boilers and lit, at the
opposite end from where one entered, by four windows
dimmed with a decade of grime. Two alleyways ran the
length of it. Along these stood hand lathes and capstans at
which journeymen and apprentices worked. A small region
to the right had been broken into alcoves. Here several elitist
craftsmen did tasks considered beyond the skill of common
mechanics on the alleys. At each machine an electric bulb
bloomed low, and above – twilight.

The next Monday morning, as a screeching hooter covered
the boilers with vapour, Tich led me to a small contraption
by a window, pulled a lever to put wheels in motion,
tightened a union nut on a pedestal, and ran both, by ratchet,
through a couple of whirring butterfly cutters. These flayed
and polished two parallel sides of the nut. He then arced the
pedestal through 120 degrees and again drove it through the
cutters to shave two more flanks.

'Now *you* do it!' I was about to begin when a scowling
man arrived.

'What you up to, Tilson?' he barked.

Tich stammered, 'I was just learnin' 'im, Mr Fearney.'

The chargehand, pincering his left ear, marched him round
in a semicircle. 'Fuck off,' he said, 'to yer own job! An'
listen! I'm watchin' *you*! Much more of it and you'll be
out! – arse over ears!'

Tich scurried from us, but only a few feet away to a
machine back-to-back with mine. Here he flicked a bar which
set pulleys turning and got to work with frantic speed while
Fearney stared.

In three minutes the chargehand had taught me all I
needed to know. 'Now gerron with it,' he ordered, 'and don't
let me catch you scowin'!'

Over the next two years, in between brushing the alleys
and brewing thirty cans of tea each morning, I performed
this simplest of tasks for eight and a half hours every working
day. This was called an 'engineering apprenticeship'. When
Fearney had gone, that first morning, Tich screamed at me
through the flying belts, 'See what I mean?' I nodded. 'A

159

proper —— he is! Know what he does at twelve o'clock? His lad sneaks in from the secondary school – dinner together! Bread and margarine and *one* bleedin' 'ard boiled egg between the two of 'em! He's that mean!' I registered disgust. Then Tich uttered the insult ultimate to any man in the trade. 'And he doesn't know his job, neither!'

We worked on. A sunbeam from the window slit the dusk and fell between our machines. Suddenly at one angle it turned into a cone of gleaming gold. I gazed in pleasure, not noticing the automatic grinder close by that spurted a stream of bronze motes through the air. With every breath we were taking in metal dust. By eleven o'clock, bored already, arm and leg muscles starting to ache, I lifted my head and looked up the shop. Twenty yards away a tinsmith's furnace on a bench glared, red-eyed, back. Mr Oddie, in a sort of pew, worked bent in light and blue smoke over an acetylene welder. The air stank. Rows of men and youths stood in line, heads down. Sullen they seemed, and concentrated, every one a stranger. Here, then, was the world of work. I felt alone, insignificant. A lifetime of this! Then at the nearest lathe, not six feet away, a white-haired old brass-finisher turned his face and smiled at me through steel-rimmed glasses. I started in recognition – Mr Dudley from the chapel! At once my loneliness eased.

In the local Sunday School this elderly gentleman (Abraham, our teachers called him) didn't take a class, but he dished out Bibles and little text cards, told newcomers where to sit, joked with us, took collection from the 'Primary' section, led hymns at Band of Hope sessions and acted generally as the minister's factotum. Withal he wore the air of a gentle saint. After reading *David Copperfield* I had often imagined him as some sort of attorney pushing the quill in a Dickensian city office. And here he was, a man clean of mouth and mind, in a rough brassworkers' warren among some who, I knew already, larded every other word with obscenity. This didn't trouble me at all; but what of Mr Dudley?

'I'll look after you, sonny!' he said the first dinner time, patting me on the head. I blushed; it made me glad to know him. We all sat upon lengths of planking reared on boxes under the windows, men and boys together, and ate lunch, drinking tea from cans and pint pots. Afterwards most of our seniors read the racing news, then scribbled their bets with pencil stubs on slips of paper, casually using every oath, indifferent to my tender years. One improver told a filthy joke. Several men laughed, but not Mr Dudley. He sat reading a book, glasses down his nose, a pilgrim untouched, I felt, by the vileness about him. 'Jockey' his colleagues called him in the shop, an epithet singularly ill chosen, it seemed to me, for such a Christian soul.

I was early the next day, first in the room except for an old labourer. We sat side by side on the raised planks at the end where the Lancashire boilers gave off warmth. Soon Mr Dudley appeared. In fifty-seven years working at only two firms in his life, Jockey, I learned later, had been absent only once, and never had he been late. He came down the aisle now, in bowler hat and frock coat – deacon-like, bearing an umbrella. The labourer greeted him respectfully. 'Eeh! An' it's a cold un, today, Mister Dudley!'

The old gentleman smiled and gazed down at me over his spectacles.

'It is really!'

'This morning, I'm afraid,' he said, 'there'll be more running noses than standing pricks!'

I gasped in dismay. A whited sepulchre indeed!

Very soon, like every other raw apprentice, no matter how cloistered from sex at home, I trod the primrose path to 'depravity' and 'corruption'. In the lavatories at the end of our fitting shop every cubicle partition, from skirting board to ceiling, carried a mass of graffiti which, in form and content, outfaced the walls of Pompeii. There, in sketch, rhyme and apothegm, man's sexual activities, normal and deviant, lay fully exposed; a true 'Open Sexame', as one wit had scrawled. Seated behind a bolted door, suspended, as they say, between 'time and eternity', we absorbed it all, wondering, and later, with many a snigger, asked questions of one another on this or that aspect, each one seeking self-adjustment to the new knowledge according to temperament and upbringing. One staid mechanic out of the alcoves, a social cut above the rest, it seemed, and a man who never used an oath, gave me early warning. 'Myself,' he said, 'I don't go into the works lavatories. You can catch crabs there,' a remark which baffled me.

But the younger men, some with war service behind them, had, for the most part, no qualms at all, either about vermin or the dangers of moral turpitude. Copulation, with the preliminaries leading to it, was a major topic of conversation. Gaily, in basic terms, they described their adventures, boasting of conquests, real or fancied, and we boys listened, the very comedy of it all often overlying any natural response. Yet, running with this new reality, the young apprentice retained an innocence, dreaming romantically still of some schoolteacher perhaps, a near-asexual goddess of childhood, 'mystic, pure, clothed in white samite', or worshipping a film star, remote and inexpressibly lovely. All this, however, in no wise prevented our having designs, unattainable but vile, lustful and guilt-riddled, on the plump young 'pusher'* at the greengrocer's, in which fantasy our graffiti could provide some peculiar data. One saw, for instance, that some boys reacted vividly to certain sexual variations which left others quite unmoved. Such 'tastes', it appeared, developed early indeed. Among the 'improvers', older apprentices, there was much serious talk about the dangers of taking 'damaged goods' into wedlock and the need to marry a virgin; but slowly it dawned on one, as the conversation grew more uninhibited, that this high principle often had its roots in sadistic desire. Out of the welter of talk the young male formulated a marriage ideal – his bride-to-be had to combine all the virgin purity of the school miss with the lubricity of that girl at the greengrocer's. He usually settled for less! And we younger boys pulled the levers, turned the handles and reveried, day after day, seeking respite from labour mindless and repetitious, and went on, thinking 'dirty', thinking 'clean', just as it came.

It was not long, then, before I understood that Mr Dudley's utterance on that second morning had been neither an item from a social survey nor, of itself, gratuitously obscene; he had merely offered, in cliché, a mild opinion on the weather. Nevertheless the old gentleman's halo soon grew even more tarnished. He was, I discovered, for all his chapel goings, a regular gambler, a devotee of the smutty story and the filthy postcard and, as Tilson confided, an all-round 'dirty old man', but none the worse, Tich obviously felt, for that. Rapidly refixing moral sights, I began to take his wagers to the bookmaker's in the foundry, and generous he was, too, when a 'nag' came up. For any winnings Jockey

---

* For eligible girls 'tart' (with no immoral connotation) and 'pusher' were the words in common use.

used to go himself, chuckling with glee. 'Caned thee that time,' he'd tell the bookie. 'Never mind,' said that great man, 'I'm only *lendin'* it to yer. It'll *all* come back home, like "one little piggy"!' And it did! For all his randiness, we boys liked the old man. Months after my starting in the shop, feeling perhaps that some apologia was needed, even to a fourteen-year-old, Dudley spoke out of the blue. 'That chapel – my missis is well in with 'em, y'know. That's why you seen me there – me bein' teetotal an' all!' The explanation seemed adequate. But whatever *we* felt about him, it grew clear that the men in the brass shop generally thought nothing at all of Jockey, and eventually, through hint, asides and plain abuse, we learned why. Their dislike had no connection with sex, but, as yet, we weren't 'old enough to know'.

For centuries until recently the new apprentice has been the subject of countless pranks played upon him by his masters, some harmless, others meanly cruel or humiliating. A boy needed to be aware. In the engineering trade this sort of espièglerie has a long history. Already, with other new-comers I had suffered several 'practical jokes', including the daubing of one's private parts with red paint. Now we were on our guard. Some old hands kept a special trick in reserve which, by long usage, only they practised. Jockey's was both inane and nasty. Doing a job which, over half a century, had strengthened his fingers abnormally, he used them now for what he called, smiling, 'my little nipper game!' 'Let's play,' he would say to some tender youngster just out of school, '"You pinch my bottom – I pinch yours!" Just in fun, o' course! You first!' He would then present a solid posterior, tight in greasy trousers, on which it was impossible for one to get any purchase at all. 'That *was* a poor do!' the old man would say. 'Now it's my turn!' Then he would nip the boy, squeezing flesh until his victim's eyes flooded with tears and he squealed in pain. This exercise seemed to give Mr Dudley much amusement. Once 'bitten', the lad limped away, 'honour bound' not to blab to some newer apprentice and so spoil the 'fun'. Now it came my turn! By chance, however, a day or two before, I had seen Dudley operating upon another innocent. Forewarned, I forearmed! He soon came shambling up, all smiles, whilst the others watched. 'Let's have a little game, eh?' He explained the 'rules', turned, bent and offered me a great hard globe, and I pinched – with a pair of pliers. He jumped a foot in the air, screeched, made a wild swipe

163

and missed. Afterwards everybody laughed, except Jockey! The nipper game was done for good.

One of our friends who left school to go into fitting, at a firm on the banks of the Irwell, suffered an experience which he thought at the time to be inexplicable, not to say uncanny. On only the second morning at work he went into one of a row of four wooden lavatories and settled on a pedestal. But a moment later he felt a flaming sensation, sprang into the air and looked down to see, of all things, a lighted candle shining upon the waters like a good deed in a dark world! Amazed, he rushed out and told the men, who registered shock or downright disbelief. Was such a thing possible? 'Tell it to the foreman in your own words!' They pondered, catechized him – a will-o'-the-wisp, maybe? Or had he fallen asleep, perhaps, and dreamt it? Was it weakened imagination brought on by self-abuse? Had he even, they asked gravely, by some trick of nature, 'passed' a lighted candle? All these possibilities our friend violently rejected. Much concerned, they wanted, they said, to get right to the bottom of it. But no; each shook his head at last. The whole thing remained beyond understanding. Meanwhile the stream that ran through the lavatories, undammed now, bore a candle on a little raft to join the waters of sweet Irwell.

As Christmas time approached Tilson let it be known that the journeymen on whose behalf we had brewed so much tea and gone on so many errands would soon show themselves most appreciative. A 'lump sum', Tich explained, 'is bein' collected and they divide it among all the first-year lads.' But beforehand, he warned, we would all have to perform at a concert to be given in front of our elders at dinner time on the last day before the holidays. This news filled us with alarm. What were we in for now?

In a free hour a week before Christmas a group of young apprentices gathered in the smithy, looking apprehensive. Two muscular men in leather aprons eyed us benevolently.

'You can't force us!' I said at once.

The smith flexed large biceps. 'Maybe not; but there's been a concert in this 'ere firm every Christmas since Adam were a policeman, and there'll be one this year, see!' We shuffled about and looked glum. 'All I say is – you do a bit of a turn and we'll show usselves most generous!' He looked across at his striker. 'How much was it last year, Jud?'

'Oh, pounds an' pounds apiece!' lied his assistant, producing a pencil and paper. 'Who's first, now?'

By threat and persuasion they finally managed to get the names of about ten boys who, though fearful of the prospect, promised to sing, play an instrument, recite or 'do a sort of step dance' before the assembled works company. Only one apprentice resisted, a tall, thin lad in ill-fitting spectacles, already a butt, whom they called 'Lamp post'. The very idea seemed to terrify him. 'Oh, no, mister! I just couldn't! Please!'

'Can you sing?' asked the striker.

'A – A little, b-but not before all them men!'

'I see,' said the smith. 'We'll have to coach this one a bit!'

And on Christmas Eve we entertained, standing on the bed of a great planing machine in the fitting shop, with a hundred or more men and youths crushed about the machinery before us. One by one the smith introduced his artistes. Any boy with the slightest claim to talent the assembly heard out and applauded. With a friend from our old school I had teamed up to harmonize in a sour rendition of 'Sweet and Low'. This scored a certain *succès d'estime*; but those performers who made little effort to please left under a rain of ribaldry, fruit skins and oily cotton waste. At five minutes to siren time only the palsied 'Lamp post' remained. Jud helped him, like an invalid, on to the planing machine bed. Unkindly the audience laughed; improvers felt for their missiles. 'Lo, Hear the Gentle Lark!' roared the smith. They laughed again. The boy began to sing, tremulous but true, gathering courage *en route*; no one jeered. By the time he had finished the first lines a whole machine shop lay in silence. Then his voice took on power and sweetness, and, as he trebled, belts and pulleys above slid swiftly into motion for the afternoon shift. His notes rang out now, high and pure, to mingle with that gentle lapping. He ended, red with relief, to thundering applause, a clash of spanners on steel, and the scream of the works hooter. The smith stood among us, smiling. With a showman's instinct he had saved his best turn for the finale. 'There's ten shillings for every one of you,' he bawled, 'and an extra ten for Lamp post!'

Every trade, of course, has its 'in' jokes, yet among engineers only the most gormless would allow himself to be sent around asking for buckets of cold steam and the like. Yet what to do when told to fetch the 'big dogs' or a two-and-a-half-inch female template? Female? One hesitated, only to be damned sharply for indolence. How to decide in a milieu where a rubber hammer was a foolish joke and a leather hammer a legitimate tool? Jargon and much else could confuse the tyro in this strange medium, where men at times seemed unpredictable: skylarking one minute, cursing, deadly serious, the next. One alley in the turning shop where floorboards shone with rancid grease we raw apprentices called the madhouse. It was our duty to visit it frequently to borrow micrometers and other small instruments. Men down the aisle, 'repetition workers', had done pretty much the same tasks day in, day out, since coming 'out of their time'. In an effort to escape boredom, and with their chargehand's connivance, several denizens had taken to acting out fantasy roles for the wonderment and perplexity of every new boy. Already 'Red' Bullen, an improver in the brass shop (and a real snake-in-the-grass, we discovered), had warned us that more than one of 'that lot down "A" aisle' had gone 'funny'. He put it down to their over-use of 'mystic water', an evil-smelling emulsion employed copiously to keep steel cool under the turning process. Like others before me, I was despatched one day to get a gauge from the 'bloke on the second lathe'. I entered uneasily and made my request to a sallow-looking turner bent over a headstock. He ignored me. I asked again louder. Suddenly his arms shot above his head; he turned, salaamed low to the east, rose again like a reed from the wind and went on with his work. I gaped, astonished. His mate came over and spoke kindly. 'Mr Ali Khan't isn't English, y'know. He comes from Bomcutta! Shall I translate for you?' I thanked him. Thereupon they began a discussion, quiet, abrupt at first, in what purported to be an oriental tongue. This they steadily increased in speed, volume and violence, oiling their discourse with gestures, mostly obscene, until, eyes glaring, fists raised, they would, one felt, soon do each other mayhem. But no. Ali, with another swift salaam, turned his back and returned to work. Whereupon his colleague smiled on me and handed over the gauge. 'Yes! He says you can have it!' Others, leaning over lathes, had watched the show, smiling gently too. I left in a daze.

A second inhabitant of the alley alarmed us even more. He ran a grinding machine at the far end, and, to judge by his postures when one caught his eye, seemed certifiable already. His, so the chargehand told us, was a pitiful case. 'Mister

Roger', a name at which he smirked, turned out astonishingly to be the 'owner's grandson'. Sacked, we learned, from 'Oxford College' for getting a girl into trouble, he had been put to trade by his family for five years as a punishment – an experience that was 'affecting his mind'. We could believe that! Red Bullen begged us to be specially careful in his presence. 'Good-natured, he is. He comes and paws yer, like. He won't do yer no harm – like a friendly monkey! But if you back away – Jesus! He hits the shaftin' – screamin' an' fightin' an' lashin' out!' One session with Roger we found more than enough! I discovered months afterwards that he in fact made wagers with workmates on whether his 'performance' would reach the last 'act'. Any new apprentice coming into the alley he greeted with chuckles, enquiries and endearments which, as a small audience gathered, the lad quietly accepted, giggling in embarrassment. Soon the boss's grandson grew more intimate, patting his guest here, there and everywhere and fumbling, at length, around the fly of his overalls. Only the stupid or fearful permitted Roger to proceed further. Once, on a failure, he staged a fit and the lad was rushed off to the manager with a brew can for a 'pint of brandy'. During the first few weeks at work one looked upon such men as half maniac, but soon their roles became so preposterous as to ruin all credulity. Then came relief and a feeling of being in on conspiracy as we saw later dupes fall victim to farce.

When the damp had dried behind my own ears, though detesting the job itself, I grew more aware of what workaday labour was all about and more skilful at sizing up those around. One lean-faced journeyman, Ernie Lester, at a lathe in the recesses, looked 'clever' – 'like Sherlock Holmes's younger brother'. I mentioned this to Tich. He agreed. 'Wonderful bloke, that Sherlock Holmes,' he said, ' – smartest sleuth in the whole world!'

'But he's not real,' I told him. 'It's just a made-up character.'

Tich expressed contempt at my ignorance. 'Bet you any money he's a live man!'

We each laid a penny on the result. But who, then, to arbitrate? Both feeling that there was no sage like an old sage, we put the question to Mr Dudley, and Jockey had the facts.

'Sherlock Holmes,' he said, 'doesn't exist.' I smiled. 'Not

now – he's been dead this many a year; but when I was a young man I used to see his name mentioned very often in the papers – them big criminal trials: "Mr Sherlock Holmes, the world-famous detective, now stepped into the witness box"!'

'Pay up!' said Tich. Unconvinced, I waited till the charge-hand's back was turned, then slipped over and put our quibble to Ernie Lester. He went on planishing, head down. 'Fiction,' he said, 'just fiction – Conan Doyle!'

'But Mr Dudley says . . .'

Lester looked up. 'If you're anxious to learn nothin' fast, go on askin' old Dudley!'

CLASS STRUGGLERS

SEVERAL men in the workshop had already gone out of their way to tell me what a fine reputation my father possessed in the trade, both as a craftsman and as a trade unionist, adding that they didn't think I'd turn out half as good. Father, for his part, asked kindly after them, all except one – Mr Dudley. 'I see,' he said one evening apropos nothing, 'you got that Jockey D. in your shop. I worked with him once at his old firm. He's *nowt* a pound!' Vaguely I wondered why. At last we apprentices learned the truth. Three times, it appeared, in his career Jockey had promised to join the 'Brassfounders and Finishers', begged workmates to sponsor him, and three times, on the night, he had failed to arrive at the branch meeting, having developed pangs of 'conscience' about 'Society' membership. Throughout the trade Dudley was known as a 'master's man'. Starting well over half a century before in a firm equally young, he had grown grey there with the boss himself. At odd times his master had still come through the premises, limping, slow, stick-helped, flanked by two director relatives. At Jockey's station he had always stopped and said a few gracious words. 'Dud' removed his cap to cover his heart with, and stood at attention. 'A touchin' sight!' my father used to say. 'That's the owd chap!' Jockey would tell them reverently when the retinue had passed. 'One o' the best! Allus speaks! Been very good to me!'

'Why didn't yer get down an' lick his bleedin' boots!' one of his workmates called across; but Mr Dudley turned the other cheek. Sincerely he believed that the boss, by hiring his body for a lifetime, had done him inestimable service. He felt nothing but gratitude. In spirit, as I too got to know him, Jockey reminded me of an old woman I heard of long afterwards in a Pennine village. For sixty years she had laboured for one 'master' at a cotton shed and, on passing, having no relatives, bequeathed her all, about one hundred pounds, to her old employer. 'He give it to me,' she said, making her will. 'It's his, really.' And duly he took it. 'Well done, thou good and faithful servant!'

Jockey, we heard, whilst at his old firm, now closed, had felt it his duty to work through two bitter strikes. One the workers lost, but 'Master' saw to it that his old hand's loyalty did not go unrewarded; he continued on a higher rate of pay than the rest. In a second tussle they returned victorious, and duly the 'scab' received an increase others had fought for. In any co-operative piece-work scheme where men combined with management to share the profits of accelerated labour (a practice good craftsmen abhorred) Jockey 'scowed', 'lay down on the job', they said, let other workers 'graft' for him. How different, though, in an individual system when each man competed against another. 'Dud' roared away at his lathe then, not looking up from morn to dewy eve. 'Tear-arsin'!' the other journeymen called it; a 'flier' he was then, compelling others to slave in like fashion. 'Jockey can turn out one hundred in ten hours,' the foreman told them. 'Why the hell can't you?' Drive! Drive! Drive! And soon the office would decide that hands were making too much bonus on the scheme and duly cut the rates. Then the fun began! When men damned their workmate and his practices he bore up courageously. 'You gotter look after Number One in this world,' he said mildly.

On the whole, however, our firm was by no means a 'sweat shop', the managers and foreman being easy-going and the chargehand's bark far worse than his bite. In piece-work schemes the 'right' price for the job was usually worked out amicably in the end. But some shops, often on the edge of the town, where 'gorby' labour came in docile, had a ferocious name for 'sweating'. One concern on the northern outskirts every mechanic in the city reviled; a man had to be hard up indeed to go seeking a job there. Yet after months of unemployment dire necessity might compel him. Many an iron-turner took work in the shop, a little rusty after a long lay-off, but competent and anxious to give his all. The foreman, a slave-driver in the Simon Legree class, stalked the aisles: every worker drove at it, not daring to lift an eye in his presence. Especially did 'Simon' watch the new hand. If he 'shaped' well the foreman did little beyond, perhaps, go to his machine and, with a flick of the hand, step the driving belt up the headstock. 'Gerrit faster!' But with others! Even before mid-day on the first morning he would come and throw two cards on a newcomer's lathe. 'Get yer coat on! Yer no use to me!' Publicly humiliated, the man was out on the street again – a brutal turning off he remembered for life.

Our own shop was so 'slack set up' that for years, during day-work periods, Mr Dudley had kept a little store under his bench, an activity the office winked at. Here one could buy tobacco, cigarettes, sweets and matches at prices over the odds. 'A proper little private enterpriser he was,' said Bill Bowers, the shop steward, 'till we put a stop to it!' Bill, like several others, had long since sent Dudley to Coventry, a mode of conduct which has so shocked some liberal minds since. But this in no way put him out. He went on singing at lathe and bench – a hymn or the latest dirty ditty, chatting to all who would respond, and picking losers, mostly, with the fancy. Never did we see him more triumphant than when our toolmaker, an ardent socialist, was picked up by the police suffering from 'exposure' down a back street and got nine months in prison. 'Some of 'em do well to talk!' he said smugly.

All trades had their quota of Dudleys, products of Victorian 'self-help', individualists, conditioned to subservience, almost feudalistic still in their docility. Such men felt they belonged by 'nature' to the working class; an employer 'gave' them their daily bread and to him they remained ever thankful. Yet, embalmed as they were in the old order, resisting all change, none seemed slow to take advantage of the better material conditions others had sacrificed themselves to bring about.

Again and again Bill Bowers, our shop steward, and his friend, Lester, stressed this point among us apprentices, but each from a different stance. One was a Marxist, the other a

'Christian' Socialist. 'Profit,' Bowers would tell us, 'is nothing else than the congealed labour power that a boss steals from the worker! Theory of Surplus Value!' He then gave us our first lesson in economics, with a sheet of tinplate serving as a blackboard. 'Example! Bloke has sixty quid and spends it on opening a little sewing shop. Rents rooms, sewing machines, buys cloth, etc; hires twenty women. Right!' He then chalked on the tinplate:

	Debit		Credit
	£ s d		£ s d
Cloth, etc	30 0 0		
Rent	10 0 0		
Machine hire	10 0 0		
Wages:			
Twenty women at 10s per week	10 0 0	Twenty women make 400 shirts to sell at	
	60 0 0	5s each	100 0 0

'Profit – forty quid! And where did *that* come from? Filched! Stolen! Robbed! The labour of the workers!'

We tried to follow.

Lester approached us on a different tack, spelling it out simply. 'All men are really brothers, see? We should work together and not against one another. The most obscene word in the English language is "profit"!' He pushed books into my hand. 'You're a reader! Get through that and keep it clean!' I devoured all he lent – *Merrie England*, the poems of Shelley, *News from Nowhere, Sesame and Lilies, Sartor Resartus* ('No good!' I told him), *The Golden Ass* of Apuleius, a book much in vogue among earnest working-class thinkers of the time, *The Ragged Trousered Philanthropists, The History of Trade Unionism*, and a volume in minuscule print of the works of William Shakespeare on which I joyfully ruined my eyes. On this last, however, Lester got a verbal dividend: pay-off from my good memory. 'What was that speech now, in *Macbeth*,' he would ask, as I passed by with a broom, brushing swarf from about his feet, 'that part where the bloke comes in and says, "The queen, my lord, is dead"?'

'Tomorrow and tomorrow and tomorrow . . . !' I would declaim and recite the whole soliloquy.

'Aye! That's it! What a pity! You should go and see it when Frank Benson comes to town.' From stock I gave him excerpts, en passant, out of several plays, much to his pleasure.

One hot September Saturday, an afternoon at the start of the football season, I went alone to see a third-rate company play *Julius Caesar* at a Manchester theatre. Seventeen of us, dotted about the gallery, peered down upon a distant stage. Every word, rising clear, held me spellbound. For a touch of variety, perhaps, the players had introduced song! As Brutus sat weary before his tent he ad libbed a little, asking for music to calm his 'troubled spirit', and a boy (masquerading as the 'wench' from *King Henry VIII*) appeared on stage and sang 'Orpheus with his lute' in an angelic treble that pierced my mind. When the lights went up I saw Ellie sitting by herself on the front row and yearned to talk to her about it all, but dodged away instead. In our teenage years, while friendly still, we had somehow ceased 'communicating' about such things.

Lester's special friend, Ike Ardle, a worker in the brass foundry and another devotee of Shakespeare, believed in socialism with passion but considered that no real progress would ever be made until religion, that 'opium of the people' as he too often told us, had been abolished. Ike devoted much of his free time to activities within the Secular Society, a certain national propagandist, Chapman Cohen, being his deity. He pressed old copies of the *Freethinker* on us. I got half-way through a volume of Haeckel's and completed Winwood Reade's *Martyrdom of Man*, this second book leaving a permanent impression. By now the last vestiges of my earlier belief were fading. Boned up on biblical absurdities, two or three of us went out, missionary-wise, seeking the conversion of benighted Christians. We would stop, en route to the foundry with a barrowload of brass dross, inveigle some younger Methodist or Roman Catholic into expressing received views on the 'Garden of Eden' or the 'Flood', then give him a verbal beating up. One elderly moulder reproved us for 'evil talk', on account of which, he said, we would in due course 'suffer the pains', a phrase which puzzled me. Did we know, he asked, what had happened to that arch-atheist, Charles Darwin? We didn't? Darwin, it appeared, 'when his time came', lay on his deathbed screaming to the Good Lord for forgiveness. But no! It was too late! In that last hour, the old chap told us, pointing upwards, 'God disfigured him! He died with the face of a monkey!' Ike poured ridicule on this story, then staged a trick common among militant atheists at the time. He pulled out his watch. 'Listen! If God exists, let him strike me dead in thirty seconds from NOW!' Tense, we waited. Ike's survival drove still another nail into the coffin of old faith.

One booklet in our armoury started a sort of revival movement among the journeymen: no tract found more avid readers in the shop than that entitled '101 Obscenities in the Bible'. After it had gone the rounds several men would gather at the grindstone – gossip corner in any machine shop – and there one or another would express horror and pious disgust. 'Have you read that one! Out of the old Puritans' Bible, an' all! Ezekiel, chapter 23, verse 20! "And she doted upon their Egyptian paramours, whose members are as big as donkeys' and who come with the abundance of stallions"!' There would be a howl of laughter to bring the chargehand hurrying across, calling nastily, 'Come on, fellers! Break it up!' Grinning, we apprentices soaked it all in. But how much these extracts from the Good Book, like our graffiti, 'depraved and corrupted' us I was never able to measure: the simple-minded seemed to stay as naïve as ever and the knowing no more debauched. We felt it all as a gay relief from the grim purpose of getting a living. These little breaks for laughter were no more than oases in the desert hours of monotonous toil.

The machine I ran in the brass shop broke down one day. Tich and I tinkered with its intestines and failed to find the fault. But probing through a small orifice in the heart of things, my long thin fingers felt what seemed to be a loose nut on the worm gear. 'That Luke Ramage,' said Tich, 'will come screamin' his bloody head off now!' I felt a twinge of fear; Ramage was indeed an authority to be dreaded. Several times before, it appeared, this machine had caused trouble between our bosses and Ramage, a great bully of a man but a fine mechanic. Luke was head of the fitting shop and next in line, they said, for the manager's job. Men stood in respect

both of his power and of his scarifying tongue. Bawling above
the roar of machinery, he feared nobody, boss or workman.
About my cutter, Ramage had sworn several times before
that it broke down only through the carelessness and ill
usage of the lads who worked it. On the last breakdown,
passing through the shop, he had caught Tilson *in flagrante
delicto* and there had been, Tich said, looking crestfallen
even then, 'real hell to pay!' I went over and told Fred
Fearney, the chargehand. He stamped back to the machine,
quite livid, accusing me of having done this, that and the
other. Truthfully I denied everything. After several minutes
attempting repair he gave up with a grunt of disgust. 'Go
and ask Mr Ramage to come!' Luke boomed in after me
almost at once, a great scowl on his face. 'What is it again?'
he bellowed, bursting into all sorts of abuse. 'Another bloody
imbecile apprentice you got, I suppose!' He too worked head
down at the mechanism for some time but couldn't manage
to get the two cutters synchronized again. 'I dunno!' he said
at last. 'We'll have to strip the bleedin' thing down.' He
looked black at me.

'I think,' I said timidly, 'it – it could be that . . .'

'When we want your fuckin' advice, James Watt,' Fearney
said, 'we'll ask for it!'

Jack Oddie, the foreman, came up. 'Has it gone wrong
again, Luke?' he asked mildly.

'Aye!' Ramage barked. 'Five bleedin' times in fifteen
months – and all because you can't train bloody idiots to run
it right!' And he roared away.

I had recently taken to wearing spectacles, one lens of
which had already cracked across, so that my right eye surveyed a world neatly divided into two hemispheres. In this
altercation, I remember, the glasses had steamed over with
sweat. I took them off, wiped the lenses on the bib of my
overalls, replaced them, and went after the fitting shop
foreman. 'Where *you* goin'?' shouted Fearney. I didn't even
bother to turn round. Luke Ramage stood, by now, in his
raised glass box at the end of the fitting shop. I knocked on
the half-open door, my knees trembling. His eyes fell on me.

'Well?'

'You mustn't call me a bloody idiot, mister,' I said. 'Because
I'm not one!'

'No?' He seemed astounded at the news.

'And I *didn't* break that machine, neither.' I put my hand

174

on the door jamb for support. My glasses were clouding up again. He loomed above in a warm mist.

'Who said you did? Me? Me?'

'N-No,' I told him, 'but – but you m-made the innuendo!'

'Eh? The what?'

'The innuendo!' I repeated, babbling. 'The – The insinuation!'

'Jesus Christ!' he whispered, then opened his mouth again, controlled himself, looking down at me curiously, and asked in a quiet voice, 'And what do *you* think was wrong with it, then?'

'I dunno,' I said, 'but there was a little nut loose on one o' them long screws when I felt inside. It was loose then, but not before.'

He stared, thinking; then, 'Come along with me,' he said, and we returned to the brass shop.

'Where *you* been?' called Fearney.

'Leave him alone,' Ramage ordered. He then took spanners, removed a casing and one or two bits of mechanism to get his fingers in, and felt for himself. 'That's it!' he said. 'Well! Out o' the mouths o' babes and sucklings!' And right in front of the gaping chargehand he apologized. 'I'm sorry, son, for what I said just now. You're *not* a bloody idiot!' Then Luke grinned down the shop. 'But "innuendo"! "Insinuation"! The size of him! That's made my bleedin' day!' And he rolled off. Later he told our foreman that I was a 'rum sort o' bloody lad, but he'll hold his corner!' I had never, in fact, been so afraid in my life.

TO THE EGRESS

FATHER was all in favour of education – if one could get it after work. 'That's the way!' he said. 'Earn and learn!' He liked the slogan and repeated it often. We then heard again about the chances *he* had missed through a lack of formal knowledge, and, in general terms, how far 'them Germans' had got ahead of us through sending their lads to technical schools and how we had to catch up. I felt no desire to catch up with the Germans, but at fourteen took an English course with some thirty others in an old Board School across the borough. Tuition by an elderly man was desultory in method and authoritarian in style. He asked no questions and we reciprocated. All Mr Kensit wanted was silence. Early lessons consisted of 'parts of speech', punctuation, the use of capital letters and something he called 'commercial English'. 'Take a letter! "Dear Sir, Yours of 25th ult. to hand; contents noted." '

One evening before class those of us who occupied the back row heard we were in for a special treat, but not one provided by our tutor. Furtively a sixteen-year-old called Chris, who sat at the end, showed us a pink envelope. It contained, he said, a letter – 'six sheets o' scented notepaper' – written by a newly married woman to her dearest girl friend, describing in unforgettable detail the first night in bed with her 'black' husband. When the lesson began he promised to pass it along, sheet by sheet, for our pleasure, the last boy to retain the whole until nine o'clock. But while the old man was, we had decided, a dodderer, Chris urged on us all the greatest circumspection. Our tutor had been some ten minutes under way, telling us about past participles, when I caught a whiff of the perfume Janie used – 'Parma Violets'! – and a sheet slid under my nose. The missive, written copperplate in green ink and in a firm male hand, began in standard form. 'My own darling Minnie, I always promised I would tell you of my wedding night with Alphonse.' Not only black, then, but French! The preliminaries, however, aiming to titillate, turned out to be many and tedious, Minnie's friend not getting down to the real 'pornography' until page 4. For myself, after nine months in a workshop, and 'wised up', I thought, already on the intimacies of life, I passed the contents on with no pulsating interest. But after class Chris complained angrily that he had passed six sheets, yet only five had been returned. All readers emphatically denied filching page 4. A 'real dirty trick'! Christopher said, when he had gone out of his way so much to entertain. Certainly one among us had held back the hard core for further perusal. I suspected a fat lad; he protested too much and worked himself purple damning the 'meanness' of others. But the fourth sheet stayed lost, and the value of the letter as a human document, Chris felt, had been seriously damaged.

Towards December Mr Kensit gave us our first homework, an essay to write on an 'Old-fashioned Christmas'. Having by then swallowed much of Dickens whole, I felt I knew just what he was after and gave him a script three times the length of any other sent in, written and re-written with loving care. He pushed it at me the following week in silence, but with his assessment of its worth in the top right-hand corner – 0/20! The lad in the next desk, who had confessed to being 'no good at all at essays', received 16. Quite shattered, for earlier efforts at school had got me prizes, I tried again, writing screeds on 'The Sea', 'Our Empire' and 'My Favourite Book' with like result. On the last occasion, however, our teacher, after dishing out the homework, went to the blackboard and in block capitals wrote a word thereon whose meaning none knew, then he turned to us. 'We have in this class,' he told us, ' – "no names, no pack drill", as they say in the army! – a smart Alec – ' We stiffened. ' – a lad who thinks he can take *me* in after forty years of teaching!' He turned to the board, pointed – 'See that?' – and spelled out the word: 'P.L.A.G.I.A.R.I.S.T.! What is a plagiarist?' He paused dramatically. 'One who steals other people's writings and passes them off as his own. This is an offence – a literary *and* criminal offence! Let the boy in this room, I say, beware! Let him not try it again!' He erased the word. 'Now, to continue . . .'

I sat angry, yet crimson with shame! As it happened, no one in the group knew who was indicted, since I had kept my humiliating results to myself. Our lesson ended at nine o'clock; the desks emptied. Mr Kensit put on raincoat, trilby, slipped a couple of books into his attaché case and turned to go.

'They were my own compositions, sir,' I called to him from my seat. 'What books would I take them from?'

'I'm not searching a public library to find out!' he said.

'I wrote them myself!'

'You *copied* them yourself – from books, or from some grown-up's work. Don't make it worse by lying about it!'

I got up and went forward. He swung past me out of the room.

Outraged, I gave the class up. After some weeks my mother noticed it. 'What's happening Tuesday nights?' she asked, and heard my story. 'But this is foolish! Whatever got into the man? He could have tested you easily enough. Take him my note next week.' I demurred, but there was no gainsaying her. Later she gave me a sealed envelope. What it contained plainly disturbed him. He seated me at once in a desk at the side of the classroom with an exercise book and several essay titles on a slip of paper. I chose one, wrote for two hours – poor, turgid stuff – and passed him the result. He read it slowly, turning over, and, from time to time, turning back, then, 'I'm sorry,' he said. No more. Unmollified, I went home. Only a few weeks of the session remained now. 'That class won't see *me* again,' I told my mother. She tut-tutted impatiently. 'Don't you realize? He really paid you a great compliment.'

'Some lads at work,' I said, 'go learning to dance on Tuesday nights!'

She looked across. 'Well, you disappoint me!' That hurt.

A few weeks later, however, by a freak of chance, I returned to language again. One Saturday afternoon a group of us made for Shudehill market, not to view chickens or hear spielers but to witness assault, we hoped, and battery. Billy Warlock, an old prize-fighter whose family dealt at the shop, had threatened to go that day, his wife said, and 'knock hell' out of a certain huckster. Billy had in fact suffered grievously in an earlier visit to the same market, and was still smouldering from it. On that first occasion, hoping to break into the greengrocery trade, he had bought a smart donkey and cart from a gypsy, the beast being highly recommended as a 'goer'. Returning home, Billy had pulled up at the Number Four public house and gone in, both for refreshment and to brag loudly of his purchase. After a time, however, the animal grew tired of waiting and dropped dead. On receiving this news in the Vault, Bill rushed forth and, the 'kiss of life' not then being known, applied other methods of artificial respiration, like kicking it in the stomach; but Neddy had passed beyond human aid. Sympathetic customers left their drink and, smirking at one another, helped the bereaved, now blaspheming, to load the deceased on to his vehicle, saying that it was a lucky thing, really, that he had transport to hand. Then Billy, attended by quite a cortège, placed himself between the shafts and pulled the cadaver home. The perfect case, my mother said later, of keeping a dead dog and barking yourself. Before the knacker's truck arrived many neighbours called at the Warlocks' backyard and asked to view the body, for few, except elderly folk, had ever seen a dead donkey. Now Bill was roaring mad again.

The Saturday before our visit he had gone to Shudehill and, always one for a bargain, bought a carton of twelve 'reinforced' Dreadnought gas mantles from Harry Brum, itinerant trader. Aloft on his podium above the crowd, Harry had extracted a mantle from a box and demonstrated its toughness compared with the frail specimens one got in corner shops at four times the price. But Brum was selling 'straight from the manufacturer' – a whole dozen for one shilling and sixpence! In a few minutes he'd disposed of the lot. On the afternoon of our trip we remarked with pleasure on the presence of Mr Warlock, and several other gentlemen besides, stalking about the thronged stalls. And each carried a carton under his arm which, we knew, had contained one reinforced Dreadnought gas mantle, and eleven boxes of wood shavings! But where was Harry Brum? Disappointed in our hopes of a fracas, we left for Tib Street, with its windows full of small living creatures, but not before I'd turned over books at a barrow and, on impulse, spent two-pence on a backless copy of Chardenal's French Grammar. The English tongue having been written off, I would, I decided, try another.

About this time the Old Man showed his displeasure with me. Hearing of my intention of learning the art of dancing, he promptly forbade it. One 'hopper' (Janie) in the family, he said, was more than enough. 'Coming in at all hours! – eleven o'clock! This is a respectable household!' No decent person could be found in the streets after the beerhouses closed. Dancing rooms, anyhow, held the scum of the nation. 'Look at that den' (our local hell) 'at the top of the street – lowest of the low! And don't you know there's nothing worse than these gig shops for giving consumption?' He mentioned by name two girls who had recently died in their teens – 'both dancers! Saturday nights you go to pictures or theatre and nowhere else, understand?' Nevertheless, choosing a 'den' well away from home, I joined the dancing millions of the time.

Our 'Latin Quarter' ran across the end of Zinc Street. Much of its hinterland, containing a dozen pubs, was given over to stables, some of them very large. Passers-by in the dark heard a constant clink of chains as if a gang of phantoms was preparing to go on night shift, but this didn't disturb loving couples whispering in the recesses. Along one side of the fronting road stood a flank of our theatre, with its stage door (what sights we saw there!) and farther on, up in the wall, a gate which took in scenery and animal performers. This came into spectacular use when cowboy shows arrived, bringing splendid horses which had to be blindfolded and manhandled up a street ramp. But with some of the actors in these western dramas over-close inspection could breed disillusionment. 'Running Bull', for instance, one of four 'Cherokees' appearing at the Prince of Wales, once aroused Sydney's gravest doubts, though the 'chief', like his braves, seemed bronzed enough. 'They're real redskins,' I told Syd, 'with squaws – straight from the American west! It says so on the placards!' He merely sniffed. That was Sydney!

Attached to the theatre we had, for the comfort of patrons, a massive iron urinal, open to the sky, which occupied the whole width of pavement so that one had to walk along the roadway to round it. One evening when Running Bull and his compatriots stepped together into our 'vespasienne' we pushed Syd up the front and he peered down at its occupants over the ornate façade. Then gently we brought him to the ground. 'What did I tell you!' He took breath indignantly. 'Not one of them is redskins!'

Days after the show had left, still hoping he was wrong, I asked Mrs Daley, who'd done for them in their digs, if we had really seen honest 'injuns'. She smiled. 'Sure, an' every single one of 'em was born and bred on the prairies round Bradford Road gasworks!'

Beyond the stage door lay a yard full of old scenery flats, then 'Digger's', our 'haunted ballroom' – 'Admittance – 4d'. Windowless, and built, to judge from its colour, in breeze blocks, it had the look of a vast spoil heap; but at night, past a lamp, up a passage, beyond paybox and frosted-glass door, the teenage offspring of labouring men found heaven, and a few, later, a bliss enhanced, or even realized, in some stable gateway. Our neighbourhood knew, of course, of this iniquity, and the matrons talked, quite scandalized. 'They should put the police on!' I never danced at 'Digger's' – the Old Man would have been shocked beyond all conscience – but we peeped in at times, three or four of us – tradesmen's sons, superior, ready for a laugh. Under lights dimmed often to give that romantic touch, the amber and green decor turned mouldy. Several mirrors, ledged – the sort one saw in barbers' shops – hung on recessed walls. Deep within, reflections moved like ghosts. To a three-piece band couples swung across the floor. Many were known to us. We edged in, I remember, one Saturday night and watched as they glided past. 'Jesus Mary!' said Eddie Franklin, 'look what the tide's fetching up now!' 'K-leg' Rowlands, a lad marred by rickets, came shuffling towards us bearing Ciss Craven in his arms. They were dancing cheek to cheek. We grinned. Cissie had been the butt of our schooldays: a gabby girl, endlessly confiding, with bad teeth and two short, stiff plaits. At school inspection once 'Nurse' had sent her home, damned as 'verminous'. She returned with her hair shorn to the scalp, tongue-tied with humiliation. Given house room by a bachelor uncle, a collier by trade, who didn't care whether she lived or died, Cissie, being of a literary turn, took early to the riper women's weeklies, escaping into a world of unreality where love is ever sweet, and Rodney marries Cynthia from The Gables, with Sir Rupert done down. Surfacing from her dreams one day, she asked foolishly if we would call her Daphne! Cruelly we did, and so did everyone else, to the end of her days.

As a child Cissie, in the class rating, stood pretty well next to nobody. Now, after twelve months' work at a spinning mill, not having anyone to sponsor her entry into society, she had brought herself 'out'. This Saturday evening she wore her 'pink lace' (a market throw-out, a catty girl friend told us) that 'dipped', or rather dived, at the hem and which so gripped her thin frame, above corsets, that two small breasts stood out like drawer knobs on a dresser. 'Daphne' had frizzed her plaits out now, raddled lips and high cheekbones, using 'red John', and matted her features with powder over Icilma Cream. K-leg, his face glowing, wore blue serge and hair so larded it curved dark over his domed, rachitic skull like treacle toffee. They skirted us now through an air-puff of 'Californian Poppy' and sweat, rounding in waltz time, her face pressed against his. Eyes shining, lost, neither even saw our grins. And to the music they were crooning:

> Play that dreamy melody, that soothing refrain,
> Play it sweet and tenderly.
> I don't know why it haunts me so-o,
> I seem to hear it everywhere I go-o! . . .

Daphne had found her 'Roddy'. Before they passed ungainly into the shadows it had stopped being funny.

'Let them have it now!' my mother used to say. 'Let girls go dancing, all dolled up. It's the only happiness a lot of 'em will ever get! Before long they'll be stuck down some warren with two kids and expecting again. That'll be "romance" for the rest of it!' Many girls knew this well enough. 'All dressed up in glad rags,' they sang, 'Tomorrow they'll turn to sad rags'—a few happy heydays of freedom now before the clamps of marriage. Our *mores* required them to get a man, romantically, if possible, but get one—a tradesman's son at best, though, in the end, almost any youth would do who had a job and could work. But don't be left on the shelf! And, true enough, one saw so many of them, a few years on, aged, blowsy, unkempt, hair back to plaits, scrubbing a step, or in clogs and twisted stockings, shoving a loaded bassinet. Yet they'd had their dream.

Still, my mother erred, I think, in believing that the 'married and done for' were finished for good and all with 'romance'. Many had a lifetime's affaire to come with the 'silver screen'. Early films were nearly all 'clean and moral'. Except for those long, passionate kisses, we didn't get much for '2*d* and 4*d*'. But the 'pictures' caused some of the weaker clay among us to sin grievously in our hearts. Many women, married or not, didn't buy photographs of stars like Valentino for nothing: they purchased fantasy too. The wife, we heard, of one of our middle-aged labourers was 'barmy about that Owen Nares—pictures all over the bedroom! After a "knock-off" the other night,' he told us, 'she says to me, "Well, you know who *I* went with! Tell me who you done!" "Theda Bara," I says. It was really the missis next door, but why make trouble?' We yelled with laughter. Copulation might have been, as the dowager said, 'far too good for the working classes', but they went on doing the 'act of darkness' (some couldn't perform with the light on), well aware of its enter-tainment value and price advantage over the pictures. From cinema (we knew of parents who went there four times a week, regularly, for years) they drew their reveries, and those among us who 'transgressed in thought' could have felt that marital coition without fantasy, however much a Christian virtue, came to little more in its mindlessness than the coupling of beasts. Variety, despite what marriage vows might demand, was the spice of sexual desire.

In early teens I drifted away from the family, to spend leisure in evening classes, swimming baths, dancing rooms and political meetings and, on Sundays, the Derbyshire hills, seeking at times the desolate places that imaged my growing loneliness. Then, of course, we went in droves to patronize both the cinema and those mock-Moorish edifices erected specially to keep workers from drink – the Temperance Billiard Halls.* At home, though, we children remained friendly and affectionate. In spite of much noisy argument and tiffs, there was laughter, singing, piano-playing. Ada studied the instrument seriously, passed examinations, but nervous disability prevented her becoming a good executant. Ellie, in what little spare time she had, learned to play the violin. Together they bought two dashingly romantic cameos of Mozart and Beethoven set in six-inch plush squares and placed them on the piano. These our eldest sister, who showed no respect for the illustrious dead, referred to as 'Burke and Hare'. Janie herself played jazz, or any music, with an assured natural touch which no teaching can induce and, privately, put the money given to her for music lessons to what she at least thought was better use.

By now Jane had grown into a very attractive girl indeed; she had looks, wit, intelligence and a dress sense which was exploited, with Mother, to turn her out what the locals called a 'fashion plate'. All these attributes she co-ordinated to twist any number of love-lorn young men coolly round her little finger. I remember parties at home where two or three of those in current favour would stand around the piano, gazing with sheep's eyes, while she sang and rattled off the latest ragtime. Some evenings Jane would call me aside confidentially. 'I seem to have got some dates mixed. Just slip to the hospital corner, will you – 7.30. There'll be an officer waiting in one of those army cars. Just tell him I'm awfully sorry but I can't make it tonight. Then walk on to Cross Lane – a tall gentleman in a grey overcoat and trilby. Ever so disappointed, say; but I'll see him again. Very sorry, of course! And here's sixpence!' A few minutes later she would be off, all dressed up, to meet some more acceptable beau, or away to a ball that had suddenly appealed. Like most girls of the day she was, as Father continually complained, 'dancing mad'. When my mother got wind of my missions she put a

* Such was the fascination of the game, billiards and snooker addicts existed just like alcoholics. Playing and gambling night after night, they came home penniless but at least sober.

stop to them at once. 'Don't you dare send that boy out again telling lies for you! I won't have it!'

Naturally the neighbours noted each of Janie's long succession of boyfriends, especially when one came with his motor char-à-banc and left it parked outside the shop. 'A terrible flirt!' they said. 'Off with the old love, on with the new!' One lady with an ill-favoured daughter of her own, feeling it 'wasn't fair to the men', couldn't forbear censuring my mother. 'Your eldest,' she said, looking down her nose, '*does* have a lot o' fellers! I'd be *very* surprised if our Winnie had so many!'

'You'd be *very* surprised,' my mother told her nastily, 'if your Winnie had one!'

In these later war years, having long left the weaving shed, Jane was doing very well for herself turning out shell cases on a capstan lathe at a large new engineering shop. One evening she brought home two jolly country lasses for a sing-song with soldier friends round the piano. Both girls, previously servants in a great Cheshire house, had been directed into 'munitions'. Green from the backwoods, they were lodging now down a Salford side street. 'What a life!' they said. 'Money to burn!* Lovely girls to work with, *and* fellers!' All the fun of the factory! 'You should see our foreman do a "Charlie Chaplin",' one told Mother. 'Talk about laugh!' Here was escape – straight out of a Victorian kitchen into twentieth-century democracy. Domestic service – 'All that kow-towin'! Yes, mum! No, m'lord!' – it wasn't going to see *them* no more! They 'bunny-hugged' up and down the kitchen with the fusiliers, singing,

> How yer gonna keep 'em down on a farm,
> After they've seen Paree?
> How yer gonna keep 'em from Piccadilly,
> Jazzin' around, paintin' the town . . .

Erstwhile servant girls like these, and serving men too, went 'jazzing around' all over Britain. The old order was wilting.

From 1917 on the shop started to prosper as never before. War had brought better economic times for the poor everywhere, and my mother began to wonder again whether a get-away might yet be possible. Her husband, after serious

* They never in fact drew more than £3 a week, but when 'living in' at the 'Hall' their wages had been £8 a year.

illness, was drinking less (the beer, he complained, 'had lost "body" '), attending to his work more, and 'reforming' generally. He now presided over the family not so much a king, as in the old days, but more as the loud-mouthed chairman. When the war ended, for the first time in a quarter of a century, they spent a holiday together, and one of a brand new kind.

It had the strange effect of changing Father's political allegiance for good. Wealthier members of the proletariat, in their week's unpaid annual holidays, took *en masse* to motor char-à-banc tours round Britain. Middle- and upper-class people, resident in posh hotels at spas and along the south coast, were startled, then amazed to see horny-handed sons of toil and their spouses sitting, diffidently it is true, but sitting, in the lounges and dining-rooms of places they had previously considered their own preserve. 'How in the world do they *do* it, my dear?' 'Well, some of them did very nicely out of the war, you know – munitions!' Fortunately the intruders usually disappeared again after a day or two. Still, it was quite disconcerting, really! But, *noblesse oblige*; there were those who felt it their duty to put the lower orders at their ease. At a Cheltenham hotel, where, with a 'chara' party, Mother and Father put up for a couple of nights, a colonel's lady fell into conversation with Bob Owen, the Old Man's friend and a mechanic like himself. She was kind but curious, mainly about the 'economics' of their holiday. 'And however did you manage,' she asked sweetly, 'to stay at a place like this?' Bob generously explained. Every week, he said, he always put away a little bit of overtime money in the Post Office, 'And the missis does a cleanin' job, see – Fridays, at a chip shop. That helps a lot!' The lady smiled happily, Mother (who overlooked the proceedings) told us afterwards. 'You an' your boss on holiday, an' all?' asked Bob. She looked slightly shocked. 'Oh dear, no! We *live* here!' Then she raised her eyebrows, ever so surprised. 'And you mean to say that, week after week – you and your wife, you both put that little something by, throughout the *whole* year, so that you can spend a few days together in a place like this?' Bob nodded, pleased. 'Well! Well! Really, I must tell my husband! How very *industrious*!'

Father had been listening, getting redder with rage. The lady now looked over and cooed at him. 'And you too?' The Old Man turned on his heel. 'Nah! I got mine robbin' a bloody bank!' He had voted Liberal for the last time.* 'It was enough,' he said later, 'to turn you Bolshie!'

A holiday glimpse of the paradisal south had strengthened my mother's longing to be off anywhere out of the slums of Salford. Five of us went out to work now, and she was really saving money at last – £150 in the bank: unheard-of wealth! But I loathed my job. Going to work, I used to wonder about possible ways of breaking a leg, or an arm – some sort of accident that would put off still another day of monotonous labour. There, in late afternoon, Tich and I, weary of standing for hours in one position, would each of us lift one leg for a minute, put it down, then raise the other, in an effort to ease aching muscles. I grew thinner. In two years three of our journeymen had died of tuberculosis. Every morning for months on end I had cleaned the brass shop floor, sweeping up metal dust and the spittle of consumptives, then, after my full 'promotion' to a machine, other fourteen-year-olds followed, doing the same task.

I went to night schools, and not only to please my mother, but all the reading and discussion done elsewhere had brought me visions! A girl came along and fell in love with me, a love 'returned' on my part only because it was expected. Then, our dance steps fitted beautifully (a major cause of matrimony, at that time, among the young proletariat). A sober, physically attractive girl two years older than me, Edie wanted to marry, too, and made her intentions implicitly clear. To her, in long walks through the dark, I poured out my discontents. She listened in real sympathy. I wanted out! Out of the job first, before everything, then out of the dirty, ignorant, hopeless sort of world we were both trapped in. Books! I said, I wanted books and music, theatre, art, ideas, travel: Italy, Germany, France – France above all! See things! Learn things! Live! 'This isn't living!' I told her.

And how Edie understood, she said, just what I meant. Wasn't *she* yearning for freedom! What a lesson in her own

* This was the spirit in the postwar years, multiplied a million-fold, that gave politics a new direction. Men began to vote Labour, not at all, as some writers appear to claim, through the miscalculations of Lloyd George and Liberal Party leaders: economic and social change had forced the development of political class-consciousness.

mother – slaving away in that hovel with umpteen kids; a lifetime spent wiping little noses and little bottoms! After marriage, no possible doubt about it, *she* was looking for someone who'd take her off from down our way for ever – and into one of those houses by the new bus depot, with bay windows and hot water. I groaned in silence.

'If you're really serious,' she said the next Sunday night, perhaps sensing change, 'I'll wait as long as you like. We're young. But even now – one has to know! Just whether you're serious, that's all. I can't go on, can I, wasting my time?' We parted company. There were other girls afterwards; they wanted a bay window and hot water, too, and who could blame them?

With two other apprentices I went one night and joined the trade union, standing for a while in a passage, on Fred Abbott's, the door-keeper's, instructions. We knew Fred; he worked in our fitting shop, a rollicking, untidy man, and a boozer besides. But in his best suit and stiff collar he looked neat and solemn enough now. 'Wait there,' he said. 'You will be called upon.' And duly a door swung ajar and he beckoned us in. In a chapel-like calm about fifty men sat in rows, fronting office-holders on a dais. Many of our own journeymen were present, giving us nods of recognition and welcome; no ribaldry now! Mr Lester occupied the chair. At once he and other officials initiated us, with a simple ceremony which informed each boy of the reasons for and the aims of the Great Amalgamated Engineering Union, and of his rights, duties and obligations within it. One felt proud to be a member. And men, we heard there, called each other 'Brother' and meant it. In those days this was no witless comedian's joke. With any imagination at all one could sense the suffering many had undergone in their efforts to get a living wage. Sitting, after induction, on the back row, I saw my father rise and speak on a minor issue of the time. He gave his views cogently and with a force and wit that delighted the audience. Once some injustice was 'damned' – a word he withdrew immediately, with apologies to the chair.

(Ten minutes before, I had sworn not to disclose anything heard in meetings, but my mother, I decided, was going to hear about that!) Soon we all learned that not even the mildest oath was permitted. One saw eventually in that, and other small 'rites', the branch's far genesis in the weekly Methodist 'meeting'.

We apprentices crept out early. At the door Fred Abbott held me back a moment to push a small brown-paper package under my arm. 'A little present,' he whispered, 'from Brothers Lester and Bowers.' It was the Webbs' *History of Trade Unionism*.

I reached home to find the house empty except for my mother – unusual, this – and the shop shut; we closed much earlier after the war. I told of the Old Man's oratory. She looked before her, then beyond, staring into the past. 'Yes,' she said at last, 'he had talents. He missed his way.' We sat for a time silent. I gazed at her with love – the same firmed chin and stern air; but she was ageing. I noticed the hair, iron-grey now, and the clear skin losing texture. She turned to me anxious. 'I hear you coughing in a morning?'

'It's nothing,' I told her; 'the brass shop emery wheel – we work close in – spurts dust half the day. Gets on the chest.'

She rose, and went and got me a glass of milk. 'You don't like the job, I know that very well.'

'I hate it!' I broke out. 'Every single minute of it. It's a rotten, stupid thing! I'd rather be dead than go on doing it. And living here,' I went on, 'in this filthy, miserable dump all our lives!'

She looked at me a while, then, 'I know,' she said quietly. 'I've tried to get out, I've tried. It isn't easy . . . Have next week off work, will you. Go round – look for something else. Or give the other up now. We'll manage all right.'

I shook my head. 'And Father finishing up again any time now! You know that. Two of us off. I won't give up! We'll never get out of here, anyway, while that old toper goes on swilling it down him!'

She sighed. 'Well, all right, all right. But I'd rather,' she said gently, 'that you didn't refer to your father in that way.'

For an hour that night we talked quietly together. I had often heard from her stories of the past, but never like this. Without self-pity she spoke of the early days and early hopes and of the slow acceptance of reality – the toil, the grind, the struggle, the poverty of it all, and of the even more barren lives of those about her; of how, in time, it stifled human qualities – kindliness, sensitivity, intelligence, and left no way out – the 'too much sacrifice' that 'turns the heart to stone'. I was moved, finding few words of response. 'But go on!' she said. 'Whatever you do, go on learning, and some time, somewhere, the chance will surely come. Then it will be a better life for you and your children. And when *you* know the way you can help others.'

'And what about you?' I asked.

'Time's passing,' she said. 'But maybe for me, too – some day.' But I could see she didn't believe it.

'I'll begin again with the English,' I told her, 'and I'm half-way through that French grammar.'

So we talked together till the family started coming home, tapping on our kitchen window to be let in through the shop. She had given me the assurance of her love, as always, and renewed hope, confidence, and the will to go on again – to where, I hardly knew. We got up at the first tapping. 'Have something to eat,' she said. 'You're as thin as a rake!' and we broke it up. That night I felt my boyhood had ended.

What Mother told me then, at some time or other she probably told the rest. Never a Mrs Lawrence, 'cringing' for her sons' love, she loved us all, but didn't try to keep any. 'Find the right sort of mate and make your own lives,' she used to say. 'That'll please me best.'

She herself never really came through. I have told elsewhere how, years later, desperate for some sort of respite, she left her husband, who, denying promises, refused in the end to move. She had a few months of peace in a quiet, clean district near a park and a library. But it wasn't for long. A hard road it had been, yet not so hard, as she herself would have said, as that of numberless other women who had lived out their lives in the dark slums of the industrial north.

When all was done, she lay in death with a faint sardonic smile; effect, maybe, of strychnine in the terminal drugs, or a final comment, perhaps, on the world as she had known it.

WILD WALES

ITS PEOPLE, LANGUAGE AND SCENERY

George Borrow

Wild Wales is a classic travel book, one that ranks with the work of Defoe or Cobbett. George Borrow immortalized the 'land of old renown and wonder, the land of Arthur and Merlin', the wild mountains, the green valleys, the tiny villages, the kindly, hospitable but mysterious people. Compiled by a great artist who understood and respected his subject, it describes landscapes and industrial works, mansions and cottages. Welsh heroes and poets have their high places, and even the people to be met with on the highway are rendered with astonishing vigour, for Borrow knew how to elevate a commonplace conversation and how to give it pathos and a new significance.

All Borrow's art, his insight, keenness of observation and feeling for human destiny, were used to give his readers an affectionate interpretation of the Welsh and their history. His own character and interests gave shape, as well as humour and directness, to a wholly delightful book. More than a hundred years after its first publication, *Wild Wales* remains the best book about Wales ever written.

THE LIFE AND DEATH OF ST KILDA

Tom Steel

On 29 August 1930, the remaining 36 inhabitants of this bleak but spectacular island group off the western coast of Scotland took ship for the mainland. Until the evacuation St Kilda was the most remote inhabited part of the United Kingdom, and indeed one of the most isolated points of the British Empire; its inhabitants had more in common with the people of Tristan da Cunha than they ever had with their fellow Scots in Glasgow or Edinburgh. The St Kildans had preserved a unique and unchanging way of life for centuries; untroubled by the fluctuations of events on the mainland, their tightly knit community had become a virtual republic in its own right. But increasing contact with – and later reliance on – the mainland in the nineteenth and twentieth centuries gradually eroded their independence until evacuation became inevitable.

What their lives had been like for century after century, why they left, and what happened to them afterwards is the subject of Tom Steel's fascinating book. It is the story of a way of life unlike any other, told here in words and pictures, and of how the impact of 'civilization' finally led to its death.

'. . . first-rate recreation of a vanished way of life'
The Scotsman

'. . . compulsive reading'
The Guardian

INTO UNKNOWN ENGLAND 1866-1913

SELECTIONS FROM THE SOCIAL EXPLORERS

Edited by Peter Keating

How did the poor live in late Victorian and Edwardian England? In the slums of London and Birmingham? In the iron-town of Middlesbrough? In a Devon fishing village? In rural Essex?

This is a fascinating sequence of extracts from the writings of those individuals, journalists and wealthy businessmen, a minister's wife, and a popular novelist, who temporarily left the comfort of their middle-class homes to find out how the other half lived. Peter Keating includes material from Charles Booth, Jack London, B. S. Rowntree and C. F. G. Masterman as well as by such lesser-known figures as George Sims, Andrew Mearns and Stephen Reynolds.

'. . . a brilliant and compelling anthology . . . *Into Unknown England* is not only an education in itself, throwing into three-dimensional chiaroscuro the flat statistics of "scientific" history, but a splendid example of prose which is always immediate and alive.'
Alan Brien, *Spectator*

'The writers collected here used all the techniques they could to solicit sympathy. Their descendants are a thousand television documentaries.'
Paul Barker, *The Times*

'. . . a rich collection of passages, intelligently presented.'
The Guardian